COMPANY OF STONE

A MEMOIR

JOHN RIXEY MOORE

BETTIE YOUNGS BOOKS

Cover design by Tatomir Pitariu
Author Photo of John Rixey Moore by Nicholas Paulos

BETTIE YOUNGS BOOK PUBLISHERS
www.BettieYoungsBooks.com
info@BettieYoungsBooks.com

Bettie Youngs Books are distributed worldwide. If you are unable to order this book from your local bookseller, Espresso, or online, you may order directly from the publisher.

ISBN: 978-1-936332-44-1
ePub: 978-1-936332-45-8

Library of Congress Control Number: 2012944149
1. Moore, John Rixey. 2. War. 3. Bettie Youngs Books. 4. Monks. 5. Coal Mine. 6. Men's Life. 7. Spirituality. 8. Healing. 9. SE Asia. 10. Scottish Highlands. 11. Rock Drill Operator. 12. Monastary. 13. Canada.

Printed in the United States of America

DEDICATION

This book is but an inadequate tribute to the memory of those remarkable people who appear in it, most of whom, by chance or by choice, would probably have passed completely unremarked from the world's chronicle–fleeting shadows, perhaps in some cases even by their own families un-missed–and but for the indelible resonance in which they linger in the chambers of my own life, unremembered.

There may be two exceptions to this common untraceable anonymity: Claudine, the painted Paymistress at the mine (whose last name I never learned), could be living on in a kind of dusty half-life on the pages of some now-forgotten company ledger; and the mysterious Beresina (whose first name I came to suspect was a pseudonym of convenience) might yet be found, smudged and fading on some crew list among the stacks of yellowing Nazi U-boat records.

I don't know about the guys in the monastery. There are probably records somewhere, though accessibility would surely be restricted and difficult in other ways, too.

Except for such tenuous traces the very existence of these unusual individuals would surely have passed unrecorded–and with them, the larger experience of their lost personalities evaporated like steam. I am often reminded of them, for time has not withered, or custom staled, their rich improbability.

CONTENTS

Part I: Aspirant

Part II: Troglodyte

FOREWORD

Most people live in character, that is, within a certain normative range of experience, where their early years provide an impetus to a reasonably expectable middle and end. Yet there are also other kinds of lives which, nudged by some unexpected transverse force, are diverted out of their inertial plane and remain somewhat crosswise, angled for the rest of one's time, even through outwardly conventional forms.

Dramatic events, such as warfare, sudden fortune or loss, have served to deflect the lives of millions, either by direct action or by leaving in the wake of their passing a flotsam of altered perceptions. I am one of these, whose views were profoundly changed by the experience of close combat, whose values were forcefully reshuffled. Enforced re-evaluations, though, need not be all bad, for my astonishment at surviving it left me with an enlarged receptivity to life's rich festoon, and a nourishing appreciation for unlikely encounters within its infinitely improbable presentments.

My parents are both from old families of the American Southeast, whose roots stretch back to the very early days of colonialism when a colorful combination of imaginative adventurers, second sons of English nobles, and entrepreneurs were settling the country. When I was born, they were living in Venezuela, where my father, an oil production engineer, was working his way rapidly up through the Creole Petroleum Corporation, an important subsidiary of Esso (now Exxon).

Life in the oil drilling camps was fun. We had transitory but uncomplicated friendships, heavy industrial equipment to play on, coconut palms and mango trees to climb, where the fruit of both, when ripe, could be eaten from the tree, and when over-ripe, could be launched at the girls (always from a distance inconsistently calculated to be outside their range of retaliation). We made pea-shooters from the hollow stems of papaya leaves and blew coconut berries through them. We climbed and fell out of trees. We rode and fell off our bikes, skinned our knees, and kept going. It was an essentially innocent, self-sufficient and manageable universe, congenial to boyhood; a sort of powerful Emersonian center from which Tom Sawyer might have gone forth into a greater world.

There are only two seasons that close to the equator: the dry, when the temperature stays consistently near either side of 100, and the rainy, when impenetrable downpours carried on the hot breath of sudden black clouds would sweep in from the jungle, roaring like poured gravel. Rain or shine, we lived in blue jeans and t-shirts, and we went to school, three grades to a room, twice a day, with a break at the onset of the greatest heat to go home for lunch and the national siesta time, then back to class in mid-afternoon. Our teachers were young women recruited by the company and lured by the prospect of living in a tropical outpost where a lot of single men were working the rigs. My father often expressed surprise that we learned anything at all.

The conditions of life worked equally on us all, boys and girls alike, and we shared an easy companionship that I have never known with women since. The girls wore full skirts with white bobby socks in brown-and-white lace-up shoes, and we boys lived in the jeans and t-shirts brought from the States every two years. The life expectancy of this uniform was always just shy of two years. We put Brylcreme in our hair so that we could plaster it up in front like Elvis Presley's, then pretended we didn't really care what the girls thought.

In a country where the multiplication of insects had gone unchecked since the beginning of time, the camps were made habitable in part by periodic spraying with insecticides. Trucks equipped with large foggers would move slowly along the streets, putting out clouds of DDT, and we all found it great fun to run in and out of the mist and to watch each other disappear in the opaque white billows of poison.

There were long stretches of exposed oil pipeline that snaked into and out of the drilling camps. They were always hot to the touch, and their curvature presented a challenge to anyone who dared walk on them. At night we listened to the creak and groan of pump jacks and the strange cries from the surrounding jungle. Sometimes we pushed bananas into the perimeter fence wire to lure the Red Howler monkeys out of the impenetrable hardwood forest beyond. To this day, the smells of wet vegetation, the sight of an oil derrick, or the sharp redolence of hot industrial grease, will unfailingly bring upon me a wave of nostalgia.

It was an ingenuous time of simple homey virtues and corny humor. Adults wore hats. People believed that the United States had won World War II virtually single-handedly, while the country emerged unquestionably as the world's preeminent industrial power. America had saved the world in the name of democracy. Venezuela's abundant supply of oil was in great demand, and my father had returned from the Pacific to work the rigs with a kind of missionary zeal. I still re-member the smell of perspiration and crude oil in his clothes when he came home at night. Americans were welcomed in those days–before the Yankee was told to go home by a restless population whose gov-ernment had short-changed them on the benefits of emerging indus-trialization.

In later years I came to believe that because of my father's over-seas assignment, my parents had felt that they missed out on America's victory celebration, that they were unable to be at home during the country's swell of nationalism following the war, and so they saw that the soil of my childhood was nourished by the myth of America's gen-erosity, blamelessness, and general immunity from the world's evils. Theodore Roosevelt had fired these assumptions at the world like can-non balls; Woodrow Wilson had turned them into a sort of manifest theology; FDR had used them to inspire American war production; and my parents handed them down to me with a vision that seems now less the recollection of something real than a kind of waking dream, which I see today with a grateful but childlike and wistful objectivity.

By the time I became old enough to be drawn into humanity's favorite folly, America's ideals had so eroded that our government was willing to spend thousands of its citizens' lives to prop up a dic-tatorship it knew to be corrupt, in a fetid and distant jungle of no discernible importance to our interests. I was ideologically unsuited for the stupidity and barbarism, the ignobility, poltroonery and filth of Vietnam, and I came back from its medieval perils and discomforts profoundly changed.

The Green Beret Sergeant who kissed his parents good-bye the year before was much the same boy who played in the oil fields of Venezuela, layered over somewhat by military training, yet clinging naively still to the sad belief that adults in positions of authority knew what they were doing; but by the time I returned as part of the genera-tion's human salvage, that little boy was gone, as completely gone as though he had walked into the woods one day and never come back. In his place was a man whose patriotism had been chiseled down to a mere sense of belonging to a particular cultural order and whose confidence in government lay dead. A man who has been shoved into harm's way and shot at is a new realist, and what do you say to a new realist when you're trying to push a war onto the populace as a struggle over ideals, using the rhetoric of theoretical freedoms?

My parents were living in England by then, and after stopping in Virginia to fulfill a family tradition by having a formal portrait taken in uniform, I flew on to London. After I'd spent some weeks luxuriating in the voluptuous peacefulness of Britain, the photo arrived, and I was shocked to discover in my own eyes mirrored there the disturbed and empty reaches I'd seen in the eyes of other men I had known. They did not seem so much to stare through things, as is commonly said, as to be looking past the present state of the world into a realm that was permanently in the distance, yet somehow more immediate than the present. My family displays this portrait still, and even now the eyes follow me across the room, insisting that the price paid for their gaze be remembered. It's odd to be spooked by your own likeness.

This book is a memoir, an account of some singular events that befell me that first year back from Vietnam, starting soon after returning home to England in 1969. Had it not been for the emotional vacuum in which I felt adrift after the furious adventure of the war, I may not have been receptive enough of these experiences to be able now to record them. They constituted a journey of unintended discovery, an ambush of enlightenment, whose lessons, sometimes painful but often touched with bathos and irony, awaited me first in the isolated conventions of a remote monastery far in the north of Scotland, and then later the same year, in the periculant confines of a large commercial gold mine in central Canada, where at 2000 feet beneath the surface, life is not altogether different from that of deep sea divers, and the community, a foreign legion of misfits and assorted desperadoes with a cruel sort of monasticism all their own.

Yet the exogenous elitism of both places cloaked an ironic communal attachment to the "normal" world, for they both held populations of deliberate drop-outs, individuals who, for reasons seldom explained, had sought the sheltering obscurity of the cloister–or the tunnels–after long or fearful experience of life on the outside. At least two of the monks were ex-Royal Navy, and I have always suspected that at least one of the miners was wanted for war crimes.

The air hoses, though, worked only one way, for no one returned. I know of none other than myself who left either place walking. Today it both cheers and saddens me to think that, but for this writing, these men who so touched my life would all pass in the end into the great quiet dark, becoming as though they had never been.

Friends of mine who have a flair for the dramatic have suggested that an extended sojourn in the monastery followed by a mining job signified an attempt to explore both the heights and the deeper terrain of the spirit, in a kind of subliminal celebration of humanity following the corruptions of war. That is a subject for those more familiar with the psychology of survival than I am. If it is true, then the effort was certainly subconscious, for in my own view, these things simply happened in that unexpected, serendipitous way that life seems to throw the scenery up around some bend in the road when we think we're headed somewhere else.

Time is full of patterns. It is a fluid matrix which holds all things and events within its embrace until they are recalled. Perhaps my recollection of these experiences has come bubbling back to the surface at this time because, like paleontologists excavating bones from petrified mud, we exhume our memories when certain events in the present dictate our need to make sense of the pattern. Perhaps, but there happily, within the layers of sediment, I have found an amalgam of well-preserved detail awaiting resurrection.

Stories, with their "beginning, middle, and end"-ness can distort the truth and the texture of life, giving it a shape and a determination, a sense of destiny, which lived events seldom share. So, other than simply straining out the inedible from the soup of memory, and the problem at this remove of sorting through the jumble of feelings that attend our daily lives, these recollections are faithful to all that transpired from one of those chance turnings in the road. It is my hope that they will allow the pulse of discovery, fear, humor, and pain that I felt to pass through their sentences with the same haunting vivacity that events themselves bestow on all our experiences.

John Rixey Moore
Pine Mountain, CA

PREFACE

In early 1969, I returned from the war in Vietnam to my home of record, my parent's comfortable flat located just by Hyde Park Corner in Knightsbridge, London. At that time, my father was a Director of the Iraq Petroleum Company with offices on Cavendish Square, and England proved to be the ideal place for me to begin the process of coming down from the emotional strain of combat, to escape the marshaled forces of fate that had haunted every day of my tour of duty in that distant sodomy of hazards on the back side of the world.

The apartment went the full width of the building, thus facing both Knightsbridge to the front, and overlooking Hyde Park at the back. It was a beautiful building with sculpted stone filigree around the windows and entryways and with a handsomely carved frieze between the stories. It even had a name–Park Side–which completed the image it holds in my mind of quintessential Edwardian elegance, while the pastoral serenity that resided in the name provided a homey ballast of contrast with the fetid and apocalyptic jungle from which I had come. Being reunited with my parents in that special place served as a hospice for jangled nerves and a respite from the need to move about very much while a fairly fresh bullet wound in my right hip could heal.

My room was at the front of the building and overlooked the famous street of Knightsbridge, which was cobbled in those days. I still vividly remember waking up with a start to the sound of rain on the window glass my first morning home and the unfamiliar thrumming noise of traffic on the wet stones. Momentary confusion gave way to that first thrill of gratitude to realize where I was. To this day I maintain a pleasant, heartfelt connection to the sound of tires on cobbles, an increasingly rare noise, as we continue the world over to bury the history of our thoroughfares beneath more practical and cheaper layers of macadam.

I relished everything about that place: The release from danger, the embrace of my family, and the English indifference to America's little Southeast Asian folly, about which I was seldom questioned and, except for the pain in my hip, rarely reminded. It was a great place in which to undertake early efforts to grope for the illusive nature of normalcy.

I spent a happy month or so indulging myself in the company of the family, lounging like a slug on the living room sofa with its view of the park, where the seagulls wheeled above the Serpentine, and the Royal Household Guards would practice formation riding along "Rotten Row" in the fog. I went to the theater every week, and nosed about the antique book shops with my mother. It was a truly carefree interim.

Then one day, my mother showed me an ad in *The London Times* requesting volunteers for a small archaeological project in northern Scotland.

"Why don't you apply?" she asked. "It sounds like fun."

I did, and was soon rocking gently toward Scotland in a paneled railway compartment on a fast train called The Grand Scot.

The dig was fun for a short while. We were looking for examples of Roman ruins along the northernmost of Hadrian's two walls (most people don't realize that the standing one today is a second effort). We were uncovering stone floors, examples of which I had seen before, but other than the initial thrill of watching a conjectural plan of the vanished buildings congeal in the air above the excavation, we were not finding anything especially revealing of much that was not already known of Roman occupation in the region. Besides, it was soon apparent to me that I had undertaken the job before I was sufficiently healed to spend long periods on my knees in the mud and intermittent rain.

Reluctantly, therefore, after some two weeks of effort, I decided to abandon the dig before any of the others might misinterpret my diminishing contribution for slack effort or incompetence. As I thought it would be fun to take a short walking tour to see a bit of the countryside before getting the train back down to London, I was given a hand-drawn map to a different town than the one at which I had arrived. The unexpected adventures described in the book that follows resulted from that simple decision.

As an incidental footnote, I learned years later that shortly after I left the dig, they made a fascinating discovery: they uncovered the floor of what had been the tanner's shop. Among the ingredients the Romans used in tanning was the urine of goats, which has a strong and unpleasant smell. Partly for this reason, the sump in the floor of the tanner's work space had served for a while as the communal dump. Because of the preservative nature of the tanner's run-off, a number of interesting discards had been held in the oxygen-deprived muck for almost 20 centuries, to be recovered in pretty good shape.

They found a pair of leather sandals that had been thrown away because of a broken ankle strap. Published photographs showed that the heels were worn on the outside, not unlike the way my own shoes wear. In addition, among fragments of writings, they recovered a portion of a Roman field manual that prescribed the proper way to crucify. It indicated that the "cross" was actually a T, the cross member from which the victim was hung being a wooden timber that archaeologists estimated must have weighed some 200 pounds. Mortised in the center, it was hoisted into place to receive a tenon at the top of the standing portion.

Very interesting, and exactly the sort of find for which I had hoped to be on hand while working the dig, but by the time they made these discoveries, I was otherwise occupied in a way I would never have imagined.

JRM

ACKNOWLEDGEMENTS

I am deeply indebted to the members of the Wednesday night Writer's Group of Studio City, California for their long support and kind critique of this project during the sometimes distressing effort to chip from my memory the images that are now contained in the accounts of *Hostage of Paradox* and this second book, *Company of Stone*. It was the safe support found in the group's membership that encouraged me to write after I had joined them as a reader, and it was they, with consistent guidance, who continued alongside, greasing the training wheels through wobbly tentative drafts of the manuscripts.

In particular I have been greatly helped by James and Dallas Mathers, founders of the group and the ones who established its culture; the unusually talented Clif Potts, close friend and one who believed in the worth of my story months before I did, and the versatile Debra Rogers, actor, writer, and insightful critic; to Brennan Byers for sneaking it to a wider audience before I'd had a chance to suppress the effort with false modesty, Dave Hadley with his personal enthusiasm and ferret-like nose for type-os and cumbrous wording; to Sean Akers, Film Producer and publisher; and especially to the profluent Roy Samuelson, computer prodigy and publication Sherpa, voiceover star, and great friend, whose macroscian influence lives in quiet anonymity throughout the formatting of this effort. The reader may recognize some of these names for their many performance credits in film and television. Their literary talents are, for the present, less well known. Whatever adventures may come from the circulation of these books will be a shared legacy of theirs.

Lastly, I must acknowledge my publisher, Bettie Youngs Books. Bettie's personal insight and delightful friendship are singularly responsible for bringing this memoir to print. Her sharp eye for detail has guided the necessary refinements in presenting a work worthy of wider audience attention, and for that I am extremely grateful.

My gratitude for and to all these extraordinary people surpasses the limitations of language. Thank you all.

Part I
Aspirant

1
Chance Encounter

Say what you will, but spirit of place takes a more important role in the affairs of humans than most people seem willing to acknowledge. Whether in an old house, an empty theater, a cemetery, or upon the ground of some past conflict, a tangible energy haunts such places, and it can attach itself to a visitor from the present in varying degrees of persistence, depending perhaps upon the magnitude of the events that gave rise to it, leaving a restless energy trapped like a silent echo in the place where things happened. I came first to accept the reality of this in the winter of 1969, while walking a lonely road in the rugged northern reaches of the Highland mountains in Scotland, shortly after my return from the Vietnam war.

The persistent bullet wound that had ended my tour in Vietnam had also driven my reluctant decision the day before this hike to abandon my participation in an interesting archaeological dig among Roman-era deposits in the bleak and sterile heath lands north of Hadrian's second wall. Nursing a secret fear that the pain in my hip was ending further efforts at digging in the wet earth on my knees, I chose to stop before being labeled a malingerer. Upon learning that I wanted to make a walking tour through this part of Roman Britain to the nearest town from which I could find transportation down to London, one of the artifact analysts on the dig had kindly drawn a map for me on a sheet of classification paper which I now carried folded in a jacket pocket.

From their description, I thought the distance to the town as indicated on the paper wasn't especially far to the south, perhaps just a bracing afternoon jaunt through open country. However, in their efforts to steer me in the right direction, nobody said anything about how far it was or how long it might take, and I neglected to ask. I was soon to learn that, though understandably crude, the map was, at least to my interim regret, exhaustively out of scale.

Well, I say "regret" only because had I known in advance the long and painful anabasis of trudging that lay ahead through an interminable wet night and all the next day, I would probably not have undertaken the walk. Yet with the advantages that hindsight delivers to a fuller understanding of our lives, "regret" was to become subverted by such extraordinary events that the very decision to go seems upon reflection to have somehow summoned them, to have conjured them forth from the ordinary and set still others into motion. They were to prove so significant that they have inhabited me ever since, remaining down through the years, and sometimes still, in moments of quiet reminiscence, lodging in my throat to claim their indelible place among life's defining experiences. That hike and the places to which it transported me became one of those rare points of convergence between unwitting chance and hidden opportunity that emerge from life's accrued inertia long afterwards to stand in review, that we may point and say here, at this place and time, my journey changed—from this moment on I have thought differently of myself and of others, and here took my place in the world with a humbling new regard. It served to break the seal on my mind with respect to the true nature of coincidence, of synchronicity, and it caused me even to re-evaluate my conception of reality. Ever since then the ghostly character of ancient places has often risen to writhe about me, demanding recognition for things gone, but are yet still here and living just out of reach under a kind of spell—a charm that has the power to confuse our understanding of presence and absence.

I set out in the late morning with hopeful expectation along a well-paved rural road and carrying a small leather suitcase. The day was propitious of adventure, the weather clear, and I was in a rosy mood as I crested the first rise and turned to look back across the way I had come. In the distance I could still make out the dig—a tiny wound in the ground near an angle of broken wall, the miniature figures supplying the only movement in a vast panorama of land and sky.

Ahead, the road wound its way through a storybook landscape of tumbled boulders and rolling green hills worn soft and feminine by eons of weather and upholstered with a carpet of grass through which light breezes swam in gentle waves. The road itself appeared to be well-maintained for so vacant a region of the country. Though supposedly designed for motor traffic, like many roads in the back country of Britain it was only about 10 feet wide, which would have allowed no room for two modern vehicles to pass, assuming any ever came this way. I wondered at the absence of any pull-offs and if indeed it served

only as a one-way course scratched into the ankles of the mountain and engineered for views known but to the locals.

From the high places that provided an expanded view across the countryside I could see no evidence of a village or even a break in the hills that appeared large enough to suggest the location of the sort of place I thought I might be going. I saw no valley of sea mist, no tell-tale church spire, not a single cottage. In fact the land gave no indication, other than the presence of an incongruously maintained road surface, of any human presence at all. If the space aliens were to come down here, I thought, judging this place to be remote enough to safely land for repairs, I would be *it* for humanity. It would be entirely up to me to represent the whole population of the earth. It was amusing to imagine myself trying to help by handing them their tools while they bent to the mysteries of an inspection hatch.

Even though it was becoming clear that I had a longer journey ahead than expected, I enjoyed the scenery, though my mood was tinged with niggling regret at abandoning the dig and leaving some of the people I had met there, but I had come to realize that the many times each hour the job required kneeling, leveraging the earth—often in steady rain—and standing back up again, had all been undertaken before I was actually healed enough to do my part free of enough pain to off-set the enjoyment. So, still anticipating a mostly downhill tour of a few additional hours, I looked forward to setting an easy pace through the ancient undulant countryside that marked the farthest point of northward penetration that the Romans had made before being stopped in their tracks by the wild and painted Picts.

However, as the hours of walking passed, and the day began to fade, the empty road ahead lost its promise of revealing any shelter for the approaching night, and my shoulders had begun to ache from repeatedly transferring the weight of the bag. Months before and on the other side of the world, a military surgeon had warned that the pain from damage to the hip is often felt in the groin, which can affect the comfort of walking, and I was beginning to feel again the confirmation of his words with each step. In addition, the arches of my feet were becoming sore in their thin-soled boating shoes, and the knuckles of my toes were rubbing against the inside of the leather uppers. Despite calluses created by months in jungle boots, I was coming to the painful realization that yachting shoes are not designed for distance, no matter how large the boat.

From the high ground I could see across the broken stone-ruptured land below that at least as much wilderness stretched before me into the gathering gloom as I had already traveled. When I stopped to rest at the foot of an enormous overhang of rock, I was surprised to see that a great mass of steely clouds had risen behind me. A damp and mournful breeze came up as I stood there watching the changes. It pressed against the side of my face and tugged at my clothes. It grew in gusts and carried the scent of rain.

Overhead, dark stains ran down the shadowed precipice, lending a melancholy note to the immense and silent stone walls that leaned into my view of the heights. A bit farther down the road a processional of huge fallen blocks lay tumbled on the sloping ground, where above, in its inevitable destruction, the excruciatingly slow violence of geology was gradually dividing the serrated curtain of stone in horizontal cracks, and far below, trapped among the green hills, centuries of grit-laden wind and freezing rains were gradually reducing the fallen giants to sloping foothills of weathered scree and gravel, ground so small a man could hold a piece in the palm of his hand.

With the weather turning restless, I continued on with failing hope that any shelter might present itself. Then, at some point toward dusk when I had about resolved myself to the likelihood that I might have to spend the night outside, the nature of the trip began to change.

I don't know quite how to describe it, but I think to this day that I was joined on the road out there by someone or something. It began as a slight drop in the receptive mood I had been enjoying all afternoon, a faint wound of silence on my consciousness. For some reason I began rather suddenly to develop a peculiar unease with the surroundings. I spent some time trying to determine what might be causing it. At first I thought that it might have something to do with the somber light and gradual changes in the inhospitable terrain, or maybe it came from the very desolation of the landscape. The feeling was as though I had become an object of singular attention by some unseen presence. Yet it was more general than the similar sense of being observed when walking alone in a populated place. It felt as though the land itself were watching, as though it held a conscious awareness of my presence.

I told myself that I was simply imagining it, probably due to the solitary nature of the place or the awesome stone eminences the road was entering, for their very mass grew as the day faded, and it lent them a kind of life energy, a magnified geomorphology. After all, I was a stranger in a strange land, and as the day was fast waning my visual references were diminishing. The world was closing in. It was only natural to feel a certain outsider's discomfort. Yet an odd sense of low-level dread came on without any clear provocation, and my efforts to rationalize it failed to provide an escape. It raised my hackles, and it grew with a quick and conscious insistence. It took on shades of expression in a vaguely reminiscent congruence with captured memory. But there was something else, too, something present but invisible, as though a willful spirit of perdition dwelt within it like a malevolent soul.

It was all too familiar. I had experienced such instinctive awareness enough the year before—indeed had developed it—while deep in the fastness of Southeast Asian jungles on long-range reconnaissance and interdiction patrols, to have a heightened (perhaps excessive) sensitivity to being watched. There the danger had been physical and, though unseen, known to be near. Yet here, I had glimpsed no other person since leaving the dig. I had been, as far as I could tell, entirely alone on the road.

I tried a while longer to shake it off by telling myself I was just being silly, that I was only growing tired on a hike that was proving to be a greater undertaking than expected and with every step advancing farther into an unknown place, barren and cold, with closing weather and no shelter in sight. However, whatever the cause of the initial feeling, and despite my little tricks at self-deception, it continued to work its crooked fingers inside me, to clutch at my entrails, until I just had to stop and look behind me. I stood there for a long minute watching the way I had come for any sign of movement. I used an old recon trick of opening my mouth and throat to equalize the pressure on my eardrums in order to hear better and strained for the slightest sound. Nothing. I had to admit the thing was giving me a full-blown case of the willies.

Where the morning light had fallen opalescent and pale over the rumpled landscape, now hours later an evening chill was rising, and thin feathery mists were reaching their way downward from between the shouldered deans, out of the weathered intrusions and fantastic igneous ravines. Overhead, a layer of heavy, moisture-laden clouds had begun assembling and were being driven on freshening westerlies, joining forces to form a dark ceiling whose ragged undersides trailed like orange sea grass in the pale dusk.

Unable to shake the strange restlessness, I kept checking over my shoulder and searched the road ahead for any movement whenever breaks in the surrounding hills or the crests of high ground allowed a view of the narrow pavement's empty progress through the remote and disquieting landscape. Yet on every hand I was alone. Alone and feeling smaller in the rising emptiness of the tilting, vacant hills. I began to feel a childish dread of the coming dark.

Ahead in the fading light of east-flung shadows lay a skeletal starkness populated by enormous remnants of volcanic rock that rose spectacularly out of the sloping ground, as though bursting through the pavement of the earth, and off to my right, where the land fell sharply away into open air, the debris field continued below. There the glacial till had eroded over uncountable centuries into grassy slopes that struggled feebly to contain now the slow, inexorable advance of fallen boulders broken from the weathered sills of stone, and layered out toward bare green meadows far to the south. Wild grain along the selvedge of the road heeled and clashed in the rising wind, while behind me, the late afternoon sun, misshapen in the risen moisture, began to break slowly and dissolve into a thick orange pulp at the far edge of the world.

The place bore a tangible spirit that embraced the lay of the land, the fold of the hills, the fading sun, the mist, the grasses, and the smell of bare earth carried upon the wind. Perhaps I was unreasonably spooked by the movement of the air itself, which tended to impart a restless presence to the emptiness, but ancient places have sometimes since given me an odd and somber awareness of how present, yet irretrievable, the past really is, especially in those sudden "hot spots" that can impart a sense of old forces of convergence, where some event in the gone world, like a battle, or the site of a long-vanished house, still resonates in silent valediction. These experiences can heighten one's acceptance of the way eternity rises to haunt quotidian inconsequence, but the feeling can be unnerving. It can frighten.

As the dimming fallow sun at last sloughed out its form in a broad gap of the mountains, and was slowly sucked away to tinge the misty hills before me with a dim uncertain afterglow, the lingering day faded like a guttering lamp. Ahead, the slender road climbed toward ominous uplands, standing wreathed in a nimbus of gale-borne condensation, where impending evening and the lowering sky had conspired to swallow the land. Just before true dark, a tiny white cloud appeared in the high distance against the rising gloom, doomed to be devoured, yet serving in its infant sacrifice as a touch of hope on the gown of approaching night and its vague promise of uncertainty.

With nightfall came the first of many long curtains of cold rain that soaked the land, the road, and me, sweeping down from the hidden gorges of the mountain in regular procession, obscuring the heights and hissing softly upon the wild meadow grass in its approach. It started quickly with large drops that plopped loudly on the brim of my hat and slapped against the leather of my jacket, accompanied by a sound like a distant train, made hollow by its progress through the steep ravines. The temperature dropped with the arrival of the softer rain, and my hand soon grew numb and cold with the heft of my valise. I shifted the bag to the other side and felt once again the slow spasm of blood recoil in my arm.

Continuing alone through the dark, the niggling feeling that something was aware of my presence intensified. It was exceedingly disconcerting, sometimes seeming very near, and at others, as though farther away, observing from a distance. I knew with a conviction born of instinct that something was out there that could see in the dark. Once again I stopped and peered into the night, straining to hear any sound through the rain, but then I felt that by standing still, I was giving whatever it was a chance to come nearer, a chance to fix my position, to fasten its gaze upon me. I turned and hurried on.

Gradually, through the repetitive tread of my shoes on the roadway, I came to realize that in my effort to escape the presence I had begun counting cadence by repeating old emergency radio frequencies and rendezvous co-ordinates I would thankfully never again have to know. How hard they had been to memorize in the first place, I thought, when so much had been at stake in the knowledge, and now that I was mercifully free of the war, now that I would probably never again see any of the men whose lives had been gambled on my ability to retain the numbers—now that it no longer mattered—I could not suppress their recollection. Hard-won survival skills die slowly when at last they are relieved of duty, and they deserve the quiet dignity of retirement to those shade-dappled glades of the subconscious where so much of our anxiety and remorse find refuge.

I turned my collar up to the weather and tried to concentrate on keeping in the center of the road, while memories of hot Southeast Asian rains surged in upon my inner silence. There, the equatorial monsoon had descended with an instantaneous violence that a westerner can not imagine for sheer volume and noise. The very weight of rainfall pounded down upon you with alarming force. It was all encompassing, like everything else in that land of dreadful extremes. It took away the air. It made the world black then split the blackness with swords of light. It caused the jungle to shift, as the great trees creaked, rocking back and forth, and the bamboos clattered. Sometimes the unremitting sound of it frightened you because you thought you could hear intelligent patterns in it. Unseen animals scurried for cover in the undergrowth, while terrified parrots darted in green and scarlet arcs through the roaring forest aisles.

It had been both friend and foe, reducing visibilities to the point where contact with the enemy was made mercifully unlikely, yet it rendered our weapons unserviceable and air support, including rescue in case of trouble, impossible. It dissolved the earth, washed out the trails, and made of the ground an impenetrable slough. I had watched as my skin went white and pinched in its ceaseless downpour. I remembered lying down to sleep in 6 inches or so of warm rainwater and finding that, with all the other things to worry about on a deep-penetration reconnaissance patrol, there was something soothing about sodden clothing, an accumulation of earthy filth beyond caring, and a poncho liner that is 9 parts water, so long as I didn't roll face down.

Here, though, far north in a cold climate, there was no brooding jungle with swaying boles, where both leaves and snakes grew larger than a man. Here, an arctic chill carried upon the wind, telling of those silent eternities where the meridians of longitude are gathered, and the realms of magnetism lie icy and still. Here, the few trees were stunted and drawn back upon themselves in attitudes of confusion, or fear. The harsh climate provided them an abundance of rainfall, but by their agonized looks in the grainy dark, the bounty was hard to enjoy. And here there were other presences.

The pavement narrowed and doubled back on itself as it climbed through steep shelves of stone, until at last it rounded a fold in the earth, and from there, leveed by wind-tossed hedges, it plunged downward again into silence. The wind, blocked then by the ridge, chuffed gently at my ears, and in the abrupt stillness between its gusts, the air felt almost warm.

My coat lay heavily across my shoulders, slack with rainfall, and where the water had seeped through, a musty tarpaulin smell of lanolin and long confinement in a drawer rose from my sweater. From high on the hillside above came the faint sibilance of grasses, like the ghostly tread of other men who had crossed these ridges long ago wearing coats of chain mail.

Indeed, it was then that I first heard, then turned and saw them. The air went suddenly colder as figures as real as any in the day-lit world came from behind me and moved obliquely past, treading audibly on sodden ground, their spear points making a bobbing picket in the air, accompanied by the faint clink of harness and the squeak of leather, to fade in the rain, drawing the unintelligible mutter of their voices with them. The air warmed slightly again with their passing.

I was stunned. Displaced and terrified, I almost fell down. I had read of such things, such what, visions? I stopped, not to march among them, then stood transfixed as the last of the men passed and evaporated before my eyes. As they faded, I saw that they were not walking on the ground as I had thought, but just above it.

I did not realize as I stared after them that my mouth had fallen open until I tasted rain water in it. I was severely shaken, and for a long while I was afraid to move and just stood there staring and heaving with heavy gasps. Though marching at an angle to the road, the figures had gone roughly in the direction the road was leading me. I was not at all certain that I wanted to follow.

How are such things possible? Did it really happen? The experience was as real as any daylight event and has remained with me ever since. The question crowded everything else from my mind, and has lingered in wonder through everything afterwards. No amount of hard "reality" has erased it. Perhaps there is a certain level of mind that can generate a sufficiently powerful residuum of energy as to persist in the psychic ether, free of time yet somehow attached to place. Perhaps when atmospheric conditions are right this resonance is powerful enough to manifest telepathically when another mind of compatible receptivity is present. Maybe such events recur in remote or abandoned places all the time but go unobserved. The effort to explain it did nothing to calm my fright or to dispel the misty reality their passing pressed upon me.

At last I gathered the courage to move ahead with tentative steps, hoping that I would not be subjected to another display of spectral traffic. I soon discovered that there were other apparitions, too. Startling black shapes loomed out of the night when the rain slacked away.

Enormous lifts of bedrock canted forth in the dark to watch my passing with the brooding immutability of all things whose ancient sovereignty of time and place have always made me feel small. The soft smack of my shoes on the wet pavement sounded distant and childlike in the new stillness. Before me the mountain rose against the hurrying night sky. The bag pulled rhythmically at my shoulder, and my hip socket ached with the changing grade.

After winding through a garden of massive boulders, the road dipped sharply downward again, where in an instant, a heavy dampness fell into my clothes. The air itself went utterly black, as the chill of it moved against my face and hands like the breath of things long dead. With alarming suddenness, all the dim objects nearby winked into a profound and impenetrable darkness. I slowed my steps, then stopped. With eyes wide, I turned slowly about, completely blind in the absolute dark. It was deathly quiet, another dimension, devoid of sound or movement, which had absorbed even the tenebrious ambience of night. I stood there in the road for a long minute, listening to the haunting silence while the blood pounded in my ears. It was profoundly eerie; as though something was about that even the crickets and night birds held in dread.

Stepping then cautiously forth with one arm outstretched, I felt my way along, sliding one foot tenuously before the other where I thought I might feel the edge of the tarmac, and thus advanced timidly through a clutter of imaginary obstacles—frightening, unknown beasts that come nightly to drink. Still, I stumbled several times and once collided painfully with a wall of rock. I left the road twice, once falling heavily into a drainage ditch, where I had to take a moment to recover my breath and to feel for the suitcase. The grass smelled somehow faintly of watered whisky.

Later, dogged with fatigue, I found suddenly that I was standing in a meadow, ankle deep in wet, motionless grass. My heart caught in an instant as I realized that my sense of direction had fled. A hot rush pumped into my neck. How did it happen? Did the road curve out from under me? At what angle did I leave it? It was frightening to be so reduced amid the free forces of nature, lost within the smallness of my own reach. The pavement was my only path, the only hope of finding my way through this haunted terrain and the strangely impenetrable darkness. I knew nothing of the country, and in a split sec-

ond of time, the entire world had been reduced to a colorle
wrapped around me at an unknown distance.

With no idea of which way to turn, I felt powerless to take another
step. At last, with mounting anxiety and a mad trust in chance, I began
gingerly to grope my way across the slope in a rising perpendicu-
lar track to its fall, breathing heavily and desperate that I might have
turned in the wrong direction.

When at length I stumbled back onto the pavement, a wave of relief swept through me so profound that it carried away for a moment
the strength in my knees. With my heart pounding against the bones
of my chest, I dropped the suitcase in the road and sat on it to catch
my breath, my brain crowded with solitude and this latest dimension
of dread. Then, in the vibrant silence that followed, it began to rain
again, pattering all about and beating on my hat with tiny fists.

Vietnam had done much to inure me to outrage, but it had given
me a deep and lasting fear of situations I could not control, of being
powerless before the inscrutable will of larger forces, before the immutable face of paradox. Now, as I sat there on that lonely Scottish
road, I knew not how far from any shelter, an all-too-familiar feeling
of sickening vulnerability settled upon me. A cold salivation rose to its
paroxysm and caught in my throat. I swallowed hard and sucked at the
air in an effort to keep it down, but it came on. I lurched and retched
once, painfully, the sound of it hollow in the rocks above. It echoed
back eerily in the night like the frightened cry of some provisional species loosed upon the world by mistake. My mood plummeted
as I felt once again the nature of myself reduced in an instant to the
faintest outline. I sat in the chilling mountain downdraft attended by
thoughts of the war, whose images, needing little provocation, crowded forth anew, articulated wet and black in my brain, nurtured by fear,
the darkness, and the spreading oceanic din of rainfall.

The war had pulled the pin from the axis of my universe and in
many ways had left me entirely alone among the shambles of an ob-
solescent paradigm. In combat you lose your sense of the definite, of
what might be reasonably expectable, hence your sense of truth itself.
I had looked upon the metal face of the age and been so stunned by it
that now, when I tried to look into the immediate future, I could see
only a place where all I had once counted important had been ban-
ished, or willingly fled. Much of what I once thought I knew about
the world had been revealed in the kill zones of Southeast Asia to be

grossly limited. Those obsolete notions had to be abandoned all at once, and without warning, before the mandates of its ultimate imperative—survival. All of life thereafter, though, even without known prospects, is touched with a strange importance.

My own passage through that sodomy of hazards had come upon me so unexpectedly that I was still, after a month and a half had passed, unable to completely reconcile my own survival. My claims to the common store of life seemed somehow undeserved and therefore tenuous and insubstantial. I felt severed from both antecedents and posterity alike, trapped in a private purgatory between the quaint conventions of a sheltered past and the imponderable mechanisms of a future to which my costly survival skills were not likely to apply — yet a future freighted with the need to achieve something noble enough to justify my breathtaking good fortune.

I stood up after a while in numb preoccupation and continued downhill, guessing at the roadway. When the mist at last gave way again to the night, I could see that the road was rising again toward a sharp ridge. There a fall of stones lay spilled among stunted trees which rocked in the wind, their leaves turned up to the sky like hands. At the crest, with the mist flying sideways, a strong gust took me by the sleeve and turned the suitcase in my hand. It broke my reverie, and I shuffled to recover my footing on the shoulder. A remembered image of businessmen in a city being pulled downwind by their briefcases flashed, and I had to smile at nature's blind consistency.

Being selected out of the ashes, called forth from the dust and rubble, is to be condemned to bear forever afterwards the most terrifying of questions: "Why?" "For what?" Perhaps, as they say, it is not for us to reason why after all; yet of what real value, as Aristotle asked, is the unexamined life? The metaphysics of the question held a niggling significance for me now that I would not have understood a year earlier. Yet it served as a dark background to set off the richer colors of every moment.

The more I thought about purpose and cause, the more I came to recognize my own hand in the question itself. There remained deep within the heart of my need to quarry for meaning in the shifting pentimento a secret and improbable spark of something essential to my own nature. There flickered beneath these thoughts some quintessential residue of my younger self that worked to find some conciliating balance with the present, with the ordinariness of daily events — like breathing, feeling the presence of the rain, and the very act of placing one foot in front of the other. I began to take each step with a growing awareness of the many small sensations of balance and swing that accompany walking.

Despite the dull wound in my right leg, and toes numb from long downhill pressure in wet shoes, it was cheering to think of each footstep as the first of innumerable journeys, bearing countless permutations. My mood stirred, shook itself, and rose. I began to play with the idea that by the simple act of hesitating on a single step, or by stretching my gait ever so slightly, I was altering the chain of all future events in some tiny but inexorable way, actually manipulating the time of my arrival at all destinations for the rest of my life. It was amusing, a little scary—and empowering. With each step, I teetered on the brink of new possibilities. With each decision not to alter a step I could discard, willy-nilly, an unimaginable complex of alternative futures.

I continued on with this game, trying every variation on pacing that I could think of—hopping, pausing, skipping, and baby steps—while gradually rising to a state of pure and exalted solitude. After all, before me lay a world alive with more or less incoherent possibilities, yet which held me to no formal call or destination. Was this not a potentiality rich with freedom?

The ground began to slope broadly away. I remembered from the map that in the darkness ahead spread a wide and undulating valley, once the bottom of an Ice Age bay, and intercut today with a tracery of little streams. Behind me rose the black pinnacle of an equatorial core which had formed some 300 million years ago, when even the dinosaurs were inconceivably far in the future. It had cooled and hardened and for eons had drifted slowly northward with the continent until it grew heather and scotch broom and was slathered with ice. I had spent the first half of the night tramping over its western slopes, and even now my legs trembled with the effort to balance my uneven weight against its southern declining.

In ancient times it had become the northern reach of tribe after tribe of invaders. Beyond it, the forbidding Highlands offered advantages to the individual defensive warrior, to the guerrilla who could move lightly among the tiers of stone, making use of terrain which constricted the movement of armies. Therefore successive generations of armed explorers had settled for occupation of the lowlands that lay ahead of me to the east and south, while in the mountains wild marauders passed on their heritage of revenge. I had enough personal experience with that kind of warfare to last several lifetimes, and though it had given me an eye for the terrain, it gave me the creeps to feel the long shadow of their eyes upon me.

I had read that Rome found one limit to its empire in this very place. With their paved roads and catapults, the Romans came into the Forth Valley, and on a day which must have been much like this one promised to be, looked up into the clouded Highlands and decided that enough was enough and left them alone. Gibbon wrote that the legions turned with contempt from the gloomy hills and cold heaths where naked barbarians chased the deer. Some miles to the south, the shivering legions erected a turf rampart on foundations of dressed stone to keep out the wild Caledonians, and ultimately withdrew from the country altogether, leaving a people so technologically benighted that for centuries afterward the Roman feats of engineering would be thought the work of giants.

The same arctic wind which had lashed the armies of old, now chased the rain, driving the water sideways from the brim of my hat. It had long since made its way into my clothing, and in the last hours before dawn its icy fingers felt around my ribs in a chilling, unwelcome caress. The tops of my ears began to hurt.

I could see no lights anywhere, not a single pinpoint of window light penetrated the weather from any direction to leave even a dim implication that somewhere in this wilderness someone was sheltered. I was wet, cold and deeply fatigued with the slog and with doubts of finding any kind of dry cover. If there was any to be had it lay somewhere ahead. There was no practical alternative to moving on.

Twice though, over the next few hours, I encountered rough-sawn feed sheds not far from the road and took grateful shelter in them, collapsing into the crisp piles of straw and using the respite to rub the stiffness from my leg. The record bullet fragment lay heavy against the bone, and the overland walk had stirred once again the hyena pain from its uneasy slumber. I rested contentedly for a while, feeling in my temples the pulse of the wound, while enjoying the tactile smell of wet earth and listening to the liquid random sound of rainfall stretching out to fill the surrounding spaces of the night. I began to feel myself a sodden wraith askulk in the gloom, passing unbidden and unseen through an enchanted land—some gnome or under-bridge troll of shadow—yet substantial enough to grow cold after a time, and so rose to set out again.

In low-lying land at last, the road crossed the braided flats of a small stream that gurgled with a chilled but pleasant sound in the earth-scented dark. I could barely see the thin trail it made as it decanted noisily from the ground and into a narrow culvert beneath the road. It held such a frail gleam borrowed from the sky that it seemed more like a moving memory of light.

Eventually, there appeared beside the road a bald, black sill of rock, waiting out the ages with its back to the wind, and I sheltered gratefully in the stillness that it made. There I remained, cloaked in stone, listening to the water dribbling steadily from the drip line beneath the overhang. In my fatigue, I soon became dreamy again, thinking about the misty narrative of the place, and trying to imagine the long timeline of the region, with its slow evolution of human events. How recently it had all come to pass.

Viewed in the long, long twilight of prehistory, it was really only yesterday that primates like ourselves emerged from the gene pool, a classic case of quantum evolution. Indeed, I thought, we are practically their contemporaries, recent descendants of Neolithic people, still striving to devise strategies for survival. Here I am, in the last year of the 6th decade of the 20th century, hiding under a rock. I wondered how many other poor clods down through the ages had sheltered beneath this same stone, trembling in their hairless vulnerability. Had there ever been another being like me, stymied by doubt and leached by wonder, who had huddled here, aching to know the fate of us all, wallflowers in the waltz of events?

As the rain slanted past, the living press of history emerged from the fields and moved all about me in the thinning dark. I thought about the years of fighting that had taken place on these very slopes in ancient times, wastes then hardly more reckonable than those blank regions on old maps where monsters were said to live ("Heer bee monstyrs"), and where there was nothing other of the known world but conjectural winds. How many men had fallen for the last time near this rock, cut down in some long-forgotten conflict and abandoned here in the whispering grass by comrades who fled southward, leaving the dead beyond caring and the dying to their pain, to the winds and to the wide, liquescent silence? It would have been pointless to return—except to rob the dark lumps of their weapons.

My mind filled with mournful images. Why was I so conscious of them? What connection did I have to them? I was haunted by people far removed in time, yet so tenacious of place that, centuries later, their lingering energy might touch a passing stranger. The place seemed held in suspension, the passage of days played out in quiet desolation at a pace so slow that everything was retained in the memory of the land itself. My vision, or whatever it was, of the marching figures hours before (If it was just a vision, why had I heard them so clearly?) probably served to impact the night with these ghostly ruminations.

From behind me came the rush of renewed downpour, bringing to the ear the same magnified and unreal sensation that light in high mountains sometimes brings to the eye. In a few moments the cascade filled the surrounding air with wet sound, and fleeting shapes seemed to dance about in the darkness. As I listened, there settled upon me a mood of languorous and contented melancholy, an aesthetic sense of alienation, which left me comfortably unencumbered by cares. Were my thoughts about history an attempt to locate myself in time? For what reason? With my own immediate past rendered somehow unreal, I felt happily extraneous, now and forever some shadow being, with exquisitely fragile claims upon the world. I was one of Fate's oversights, defaulted from distant peril to the present. Any loud noise or abrupt move might shatter the spell, and I would be recalled, but as all things from which I took my eyes or thoughts threatened to flee away forever, their flight would leave me hovering in an amniotic miasma of contented irrelevance.

Yet at the same time, the fearful concentration on each detail of my behavior which this feeling engendered released the tethered subconscious, freeing me to a fuller experience of every moment. By paring my attention down to the immediacy of the present, I became empowered to ascribe shape and form to every sensation. No injustices within the past awaited my remedy, and no foreseeable event would attend my petty remonstrations and needless solicitude—as long as I was careful not to disrupt the delicate balance of things. With a quick thrill, I experienced a moment of seraphic equanimity with all things that might depend for their existence upon my singular attention.

Gradually, almost imperceptibly, the darkness began to leak away as a reluctant, vaporous grey light seeped into the showers, insinuating the presence of objects nearby. Soon the rain tapered off and the sound of it diminished into a chorus of faint applause. By the time it ceased altogether, the deeper shadows had fled, leaving me shivering but with a resonant legacy of quiet well-being.

When at last I stepped forth from the dripping rocks, it was in a renewed state of raw awareness. The ground gave off smells so rich, and the sky such movement, I had to select the senses. I was stiff and cold, but I looked around unfettered by judgment or expectation, and breathed deeply the fresh breeze, which carried now the sweet, fecund smell of the bare earth, moist sheep manure, and fermenting hay.

High in the haunted uplands from which I had come, the rain hung like ragged lines of grey laundry among the dark and invidious cataracts of stone and glittering falls of scree. A cinereous canopy of bruise-colored cloud, impenetrable as actions past, clung to the distant rocks with fingers of mist, as though hoarding things claimed in the night. I was surprised to find that I stood now in the meadowlands I had been able to see so far to the south just before nightfall had engulfed the lower terrain and to realize how much ground I had covered in the long wet dark since leaving the higher elevations, where those crumbling towers of stone and restless grasses rose among the morning clouds, alive still with spectral winds and the tatters of bad feeling. Staring back up at them from this remove, I felt again a fleeting sense of sourceless relief that I had been permitted to escape something I could not name. I turned away then and wondered how much further the way might lead through drifting mists that curled now like restless grey phantoms in their silent patrol of the lonely glens that lay ahead.

The black road unraveled out of that high, mysterious ground and descended like flung ribbon through somber rock-strewn fields toward a desolate grassy moor where it became lost in captive mist yet before me. As the sky grew pale, and the waking world of shapes accrued around me, the wind died suddenly away, and in the silence that it left, the uneven tread of my footsteps on the wet macadam slapped intrusively at the sanctity of the dawn. I lightened my step.

At last a group of farm buildings, huddled in a narrow gorge, congealed from out of a thin strata of ground fog and took vague shape around tiny points of yellow lamp light, their narrow spires of smoke standing vertically in the windless dawn, so still the place seemed to hang by threads from the dark sky. This was the time of year when people huddle themselves inwards, hoarding the slowed pulse of their subsided powers, reluctant to wake, and even so, the little lights seemed early.

I could see that the road ahead actually passed between the low cottages. It seemed a good place for an ambush. It was countryside designed for brigandage and foray alright, with the advantage here being to the lower ground, and instinctively I took in the surrounding fields and the lie of stone walls with an eye to evading the settlement. Then I stopped, catching myself at the old game. I pulled myself from the brink of such obsolete imperatives, and heart-struck by the exquisite absence of danger, just stood there in the empty road feeling the manifold sensations of freedom in the open and indulging myself in an ecstatic release of care.

All around me the scene lay in misty repose, revealing itself by degree, a living composition by J.M.W. Turner, where dark grays gradually disappeared through a peaceful, layered landscape which filled the depths of the canvas with paling layers of green. The stillness was broken only by the distant warble of a bird whose cry I didn't recognize but which let fall its silver notes in diminishing prodigal enchantments, pure and serene. As it wheeled away, a smoke-scented silence healed over its passing.

I started again and walked carefully, reluctant to make any sound as I approached the cottages, while my sodden shoes slurped on the road. Flooded ditches on each side reflected the faint pewter light of the sky.

All of a sudden the serenity was shattered! A pair of great dripping hogs rose out of the water snorting like oafish demons routed from a fen! Startled witless, I stumbled back and fell over the suitcase, as the pigs trotted away. They passed through a yellow rectangle of window light and, grunting indignantly, disappeared behind a house.

I lay sprawled in the road, my face hot and heart thumping, my early-warning nerves jangled into overload, and tried to catch my breath. Then, realizing how it must look to anyone who might have glanced out a window served to release the tensions of the whole long night. I began to chuckle, and then to laugh aloud, which I suppressed with difficulty, knowing that the view of a grown man lying in the middle of the wet road giggling at the sky would be, at the very least, troubling first thing in the morning. I got up and hurried past the houses, wherein dogs were beginning to shuffle and bark, ran across an ancient stone bridge, and on to the anonymous safety of the empty hills beyond.

With the dawn, the chill began to condense out of the air, and in the declining damp, I began to feel a bit better—and then hungry. When the sun appeared I searched for a discrete place beside the road to sit for awhile and to get at the contents of the suitcase. It included two sandwiches and, among the clothes, some dry socks. Soon, between the shoulders of a narrow bridge, the road crossed a shallow stream strewn with dry rocks just where the water divided around a narrow pebbly mud shoal.

I clambered down beside the stone abutment and stepped along the shallow bank to a sun-lit patch of grass at the edge of the water. There I spread the jacket out, hung my hat on a bush, and threw the bag open to the air. I sat on the ground and drew up my swollen knee joints with excruciating pleasure.

The place was popular. It was runed all about with the random trident of crane tracks, where the birds had glided in and stalked about upon the barren mud bank. Numerous small fish, flashing silver, darted in and out of shadow and paused in the current.

I tossed a piece of bread crust a few feet upstream and watched dozens of them leap from hiding as it passed to devour it in noisy frenzy. It was fun to hear the tiny racket they made, so I did it again with amusing results, but soon decided that I was only serving to fatten them up for the cranes, who evidently found this spot to be a lively snack bar. I felt torn for a moment, trying to decide whether I felt a greater affinity for the fish or for the birds. In the end, I decided in favor of the birds but wondered idly if some giant ancestor of theirs might ever have attacked one of mine, swooping down like a great shadow and carrying him off screaming to some high rookery in the clefts of a volcano. At least that seemed a more colorful end than being dragged from the beach by some fearsome primordial amphibian.

After finishing the sandwiches, I lay back in the grass, barefoot, lulled by the sounds of the brook and the feeble warmth of the sun on my eyelids. A slight numbness tingled in my leg, and my feet were sore, but in focusing on the sensations, I forgot my wet clothes and fatigue, and surrendered myself to the vast swing of the earth. I began to experience a vision over my entirety that they say some of the blind possess in their hands and faces. An effusion of pink contentment washed over me, and floral colors pulsed behind my eyes. The moisture in my clothing turned warm. Tiny sounds came from the grass. An insect buzzed by.

Then there was a grunt. Deep-throated. I heard it and felt it at the same time. I opened my eyes instantly, sat up on full alert, and looked around. Nothing moved. My senses thrummed like wire. Then, a low snuffle in the bushes close by, and an enormous white sow emerged from the foliage. She stopped, surprised, and stood grunting softly, her small eyes winking with dull alarm. She was evidently a new mother and weighed more than I did. I pulled back. She moved her large head about, testing the air for messages with her snout. Then she emitted a loud, wet snort of disapproval. Afraid that I might be blocking the way to her favorite watering place, I moved off a few feet and waited while she continued to evaluate the situation. There was an elegance about her. She had lovely long eyelashes and was covered with white fur, like a dowager on her way to the opera.

During our stand-off, I carefully withdrew an apple from the suitcase and began to cut it into sections. As soon as it split, her nose picked it up. She stepped forward delicately, on high heels, then stopped, sweeping the area with her radar. I tossed her a wedge. It landed on the grass in front of her, and she moved back, moaning softly. Then she approached it, lifted it gently from the grass with her teeth, and trotted over to the edge of the stream, where she dropped it into the shallows and rolled it back and forth with the spade of her nose. That done, she picked it out of the water and ate it. She turned away without a glance and trotted back into the hedges the way she had come, her heavy teats swinging like a carillon of silent bells.

Sometime after I was back on the road, a bus cleared its throat in the distance behind me. It seemed that every road in Britain is served at some point by those marvelous green public transport buses. I took its arrival to indicate that a village was not far ahead, and in view of all I had invested in this odyssey so far, there would be a certain pride in making it all the way, so I decided in advance not to ride.

Gradually, the machine approached, its low growl disappearing behind the hills from time to time, the unmistakable clatter of its diesel engine growing steadily on the rises. At last it was close enough to be in sight behind me. I stopped and turned, eager for the glimpse it promised of another human being, yet wincing inwardly at the offense it gave to the tranquility of the morning. It arrived, gleaming with mechanical incongruity in the remoteness of the setting. It snorted, slowing, lifted itself heavily over a low bridge, splashed through a

long puddle, then shook itself off like a wet dog. It rolled
to me with a squeak and a sigh from the air brakes, and
silence all other sounds held themselves in suspension.

Behind the windshield the driver grinned, and with ~~........~~
hand through his vent window, invited a signal of my intentions. I
smiled broadly, tipped my hat, and waved him off. With a waggle of
his fingers, the bus roared to life again and rolled forward. As it passed,
the only passenger, a poster-gorgeous dark-haired young woman sitting at a rearward window, smiled at me with perfect teeth, turning in
her seat as the bus withdrew.

I was instantly affected and waved to her with an urgency that
must have surprised her, as it did me, for I understood instinctively
in the moment our eyes met that she was important. The generational
mandate whispered beneath her smile, and I knew in that fleeting,
magical encounter that she was someone I was supposed to know.
Perhaps the feeling had been born among the strange forces that inhabited the previous night, but somehow I realized right then that her
passing would always be detectable by the hole it left in the fabric of
my experience. I have often had occasion in the years since to wonder
about the ways my life might be different if I had taken that bus. As
the machine disappeared, a crushing loneliness collapsed in upon me.

My thoughts thronged with the young woman's face and the odd
ache it had created as the land grew stonier and more severe. Bare,
dark in odd places, and elemental, it looked like the sort of place where
only Druids or worshippers of sacrifice would hole up. It was peculiarly uneven, with trees growing sideways out of stony ground, like
the illustrations in fairy tales. Its meadows were tilted. Broken cottage
walls lay scattered at great distances. It possessed an abandoned and
haunted look, its pitted rocks like ruins, its stillness like suspense. It
had the feeling of a last stand, a lost outpost, and looked it. In this open
grassy country it was plain to see there was nothing threatening, and
yet the very openness was itself eerie and suggested invisible dangers.
It worked to deepen my loneliness and it freighted my consciousness
with desolation. I looked over my shoulder. I suppose it was the sound
of the wind, the pale light, and the flat shadows on the ground.

As the day wore on, and the village that I fantasized must lie
around each bend failed to appear, I passed through low hills with long
vistas—a strange, forbidding wilderness where occasional fat sheep
grazed unattended among the perched glacial boulders that crowded

.ıe fields. Yet the place remained singularly devoid of any people. The few cottages I glimpsed were quiet and had a mossy, buried look. They said something about Scottish self-reliance, that people willingly chose to live and farm such a remote and inaccessible place. Here they picked a wind-swept ledge or some hidden swale, built a house of gathered stones and closed their shutters on the world. "Thrawn" was the Lowlands word for their stubborn character. I liked the sound of it. It seemed to describe the action of slamming a door. I had long admired the toughness of the Scots and their rough good humor. Now I was beginning to appreciate the influence the land itself could have on the formation of a national character.

I crossed no other roads. A few dirt pathways, no wider than a wagon, straggled off into a tangle of gorse now and then, but the effect of the land was to channel the traveler along a specific way. The message was clear, and I dared not approach a house.

Then I saw someone. Far down the road ahead, the only other person I would encounter until evening—indeed, the only other person I saw actually treading the road during the whole trip from the dig—appeared suddenly out of nowhere and approached with an odd, shambling gait. I watched him come on, striding as though he had collected in his legs beneath flopping great trousers all the power of the road in its worldly meandering and now applied it to a task he found distasteful. I began to feel a rising moral dilemma about whether or not to say something. I thought, should I speak? No...I won't say anything until he does...but maybe I'll learn something if I do. No. It might be rude.

As the distance between us narrowed, I could see that he was an old man. He wore a dark tweed overcoat, and the grey skin of his determined face looked fireproof. He walked stiffly, without evident pleasure, his large feet in bulging black shoes. His hat was crushed in his hand, and he swung it for balance as he leaned forward, panting at the pavement.

He didn't look at me. As we drew level, he didn't seem to notice me at all; yet there was no hint of conscious avoidance in his stare. When he was a fraction past me, still stone-faced, impulsively I said, "Morning!"

"Och!" he replied, twisting his head around at me. "Gude marnin' t'ya!"

His dark eyes fixed me with a bright and piercing smile of discovery. If I had not spoken first, we would have passed each other ten feet apart in that lonely neglected place, without another soul around in the vibrant silence that is taken for safety the world over, without a word.

Later in the day, traveling on sore feet and with fatigue clawing its way up my right side, I entered a broad valley with white cottages scattered like geese across the verdant hills and stony fields. The masonry on a few of the houses was as patchy and colorful as a quilted blanket.

The suitcase had grown into a ponderous burden, and as I lurched along trying to swing its momentum as an aid, I wondered how many hours earlier the bus carrying the lovely young woman had passed the region. I knew that as a passenger I would have been hurried through this empty country, but as a walker, every bit of the landscape was forced upon me. I welcomed it, though, for by now I had begun to feel strangely drawn to the desolation. It spoke in a language ancient and mournful, to which, on this day, I was especially receptive.

I passed through a highland meadow carpeted with wildflowers, acres of golden groundsel, zinnia, and deep purple gentian, wild vines of blue morning glory, and a vast plain of varied small blooms reaching onward like a gingham print to the farthest serried rimlands, blue with haze, where the adamantine ranges rose out of nothing, like the backs of sea beasts in a Devonian dawn. Their perfumes crowded the air.

Toward evening, my progress had deteriorated to a wracking labor against the twin drudgery of pain and fatigue. By then it felt as though a hot cord running from my hip to my right foot was yanked taut with each step. I knew that I was nearing whatever point awaited the last step I would be able to take at the end of a long night full of misgivings and rain, followed by this day. My leg had long since foundered with its weight of pain, diminishing my pace to little more than a shuffle, and with the effort to keep going my head rang like a bead strung on a wire that stretched between my ears.

I could tell, though, that I was nearing the sea, and the realization lifted my spirits somewhat, for the sodden remnants of my crude hand drawing showed a coastline beyond what I guessed was a depiction of the ridges visible still ahead, and the breeze smelled like wet metal. But I knew I was too tired to make it. My leather case, still damp, drew down upon my shoulder with the sudden malice that inanimate things can show, and with resignation, I decided to rest.

I came upon a flat-topped stone that I took to be part of a broken wall garnished about with thistle and gratefully sat on it. A flood of relief told me how tired I was. Footsore and stiff from the swing of the luggage to be sure, but I hadn't realized how much the pain had sapped what little energy had been delivered by two sandwiches and a bit of apple hours before. I glance about at the surroundings, my attention but a thread spun of faint hope. I was very hungry and losing heart in finding an alternative to another night out, dreading especially the chance of more rain. I knew the road led somewhere, but even with promising small signs of habitation, I could not shake the sense of being lost.

Two dogs barked in the distance, sharp and poignant, shattering the stillness and surprising me with the implication of domesticity that carried in their voices. Then the silence healed itself again. In the long steep light, the umber colored mountains to the south stood deeply shadowed in their folds, a barrier to my exhausted arithmetical progression. In the sky to the east, six dark languorous birds turned in a slow carousel. I wondered dully if they were vultures.

Smooth velvet hills in the middle distance to the east, rising together from the valley, carried golden light upon their backs, while beyond the western slopes over my shoulder, storm clouds were piling up again, etched with silver and lanced spectacularly with a fan of sunbeams, but black within and pulsing with ominous lambencies. Objects stood forth in the slanted evening light as the hills, bright against the dark sky, seemed to draw near. The whole rising backdrop loomed with renewed threat.

High above, a thin echelon of cranes, winkling white against the sky, came trailing along the unseen corridors written in their blood for a hundred thousand years. I watched them until they were gone, and the last thin fluted cry, like a child's horn, floated away in the evening's onset.

Then I was surprised to hear the whinnying bleat of sheep nearby and turned to see them trailing down from the high ground on my left. Their bells clunked as they jerked their heads up to look at me, and I recalled the hay ricks of the night before. Even the sheep had a place to go for the night. For better or not, it was time to move on.

I dreaded getting to my feet again. Yet I did not want to spend another wet night on the road. Where the first night might have been philosophically rewarding, a second, especially in a advanced state of fatigue and hunger, might be irredeemably stupid.

When I stood, I noticed that my stone appeared to have deliberate facets. It was not a part of the fieldstone-and-fragment walls of the region but a singular piece of dressed stone. On closer inspection it proved to be an ancient mile stone, bearing close to the ground beneath a scale of pale green lichen the weathered roman numerals XIV. Fourteen. It probably meant fourteen leagues. But to where? From where? What place was fourteen leagues from here? And how far is a league, anyway? I wondered if the place from where the measurement had been taken still existed as a modern town. If so, it was probably ahead, to the south, since the old Roman frontier lay behind me. If not, this neglected bit of inscription might be all that was left of some vanished outpost of civilization. The Romans, with their fierce proprietorship of the known world, had left such an indelible measure of their progress that here a remnant message carried through the ages to the eyes of a traveler from a culture they could not have imagined.

It occurred to me then that we do not look back along the lines of time, but rather down through it, like water, where the more distant objects lie wavering and indistinct in the half-light of our own day. The chiseled lines on the stone echoed in my brain like words whispered into a bottle tossed upon the ocean of time by voyagers long vanished beneath the waves.

A gust of wind, rushing westward toward the storm center, shouldered past with sudden cold. Steeling myself for the walk ahead, I hefted the suitcase from the grass and stepped painfully back onto the road. I had not walked twenty yards when there occurred one of those rare coincidences whose unremarkable intervention at the time reveals none of the seeds it bears for the trellis of one's life, yet in retrospect its appearance at a particular place and time partakes so insolently from the world of fiction as to beg the question of providence.

Set back from the road, half hidden in a copse of shimmering trees, a pair of ancient stone pillars rose in support of a weathered sign whose face was streaked with tears of rust from the iron hafts on which it hung. Above the stony farm road which passed through the gateway, the words were clear in the angular golden light:

St. Edmund's
The Brothers Observant

I stepped between the abutments, and my eyes traveled the road within as it changed to a surfaced, tree-lined esplanade, winding its way upward into the hills, to end at an imposing fortress-like building on a far ridge. Against the sun's declining, tiny brown figures moved on the hillside in the slower dusk across a paper skyline. The pastoral tranquility of the place drew me in for a closer look. The distant crenellated house presented the kind of scene that, had it been revealed in the flashes of a storm at night, would have seemed eerie and forbidding, but here, in the gentle light of evening, it beckoned. I felt somehow compelled to enter—without reservation, so to speak.

I started presumptuously up the long drive without a conscious decision to do so. Where was I going? I had always regarded monasteries as remnants of the dark ages, dying vestiges of medievalism, and monks were, what? religious atavisms. English literature contains numerous references to monasteries taking in weary travelers, and certainly on that credential I felt qualified to inquire, but was it, after all, only rumor? It had never occurred to me that I would ever be in a position to find out. Such blanket hospitality did seem unlikely. What if the idea was just a carry-over from ancient times when these places were truly outposts?

Even if it were so, did it apply to all of them? What if I dragged myself up this long, winding road only to have them say no? What if they took one look at me and decided that the presence of a scruffy foreign drifter might taint the sanctity of their home? I took stock of my worn jacket and jeans and despaired to feel attired in sudden, shabby alienation. I thought of turning back, for their sake as much as my own.

I stopped then and looked out over the lower landscape behind me. Far away in the chalky haze, beneath a stain in the soft grey sky, tiny dark steeples rose among the hills; a square tower, and one like a freshly sharpened pencil. Too far. Surely the brothers would provide shelter for one night in the face of bad weather, if only in a stable. I smiled at that idea.

The leaves all about chattered noisily in the breeze. The creeping penumbra of the setting sun sent its artful fingers drifting along the cultivated hillside, into groves and across the gullies, insinuating every swale and furrow with purple shadow, silently deploying its forces for that time when it would soon claim the land. The wind was cold on my face, but this time it brought something wild and free of challenge that whispered in my ear. Again I was running under bare poles toward a reckoning as it happened whose ledgers would be drawn up and dated only long after all due claims had passed. I felt at once like a singular vibrant molecule in the long history of the world, the plaything of vaguely ancient forces, but it lightened my heart. What have I to lose, I thought, by approaching this building? I was so tired and sore that my anxiety to be inside softly picked the lock, slid back the bolts a little with each step, until it released my imprisoned spirit to the wind, into the vast blue and gold, so that by the time I had raced the advancing shades of night to the lower terrace stones, I was almost giddy with anxiety to see whatever lay beyond them.

When at last I reached the grassy level of the close, I stopped and put down the suitcase to catch my breath before hazarding an approach to the front door, despite a curiosity mixed now with a real need to get inside, where I might be allowed to sit down. The ground before the house had been leveled by hand long ago and shored with shaped stones that trailed off beyond the steps into the ground, emerging again farther out in the field like the peaks of a sunken city long drowned in the cold blind earth. Peeking from the grass around my feet were the weathered foundation blocks of a small enclosure, perhaps a vanished gate house. As always, such signs caused me to wonder what might have happened to the structure, what artifacts might lie below the surface, and what might the world have been like on the day they were lost.

I turned to see what vantage point such a structure might have had and to assess the distance I had climbed from the road. Over the line of trees the sky was fast filling with dark clouds that had opened momentarily like a great black door, where the last light of the retreating sun made of its edges a celestial map, rimmed in silver-pink. Rods of bronze slanted across the mist-filled valley below, sprinkling the hilltops with a confection of dusty gold. It would have made a great illustration in a Sunday school book, I thought, but it surprised me to see how fast the clouds had come up since I had last glanced back, how dark they were, and they grumbled with unmistakable intent.

The unlikely nature of having arrived at this place at just this time did not occur to me until much later, but there, hung with rustling ivy, the great slab sides of a lovely 14th century fortified manor house rose above me, its mullioned windows like beaten gold in the restless sunset. At the far end of the building, a ruined watch tower, complete with arrow slits, stood like a bad molar against the sky. Dozens of twittering birds exploded from the ivy, wheeled, and darted back in again.

I lifted the bag and went up the last few steps to the level of the close. There, beneath the arched entryway, a solitary figure draped in a chocolate brown cassock emerged from the shadows and stood quietly, regarding me without expression. He must have been watching me the whole time. I heard my mouth say "Hello," with a suitable lilt. There was no response. I shifted the suitcase to the left side so as to free up my greeting hand and approached him across the courtyard.

He stood stiffly, like a saint on a cathedral door, and as I drew near the image held, for his face was hollowed with thoughtful lines, as though furrowed by centuries of rain. His drooped eyes wore an expression of mingled affability and sadness.

"Good evening," I said, placing the suitcase on the ground and extending my hand. A sinewy forearm, on which I was surprised to note a faded tattoo, appeared from the folds of his robe, and he gripped my hand with a firm, leathery palm. His strength surprised me.

"Gd'en'n t'ya, sor," he said in a soft, rasping voice, modulated to carry no farther than necessary.

There followed an awkward moment of silence as he made no further remark or gesture. He seemed not the least curious as to what I might be doing so far from the main road. His pale face remained quiet as a mask against the strange still watchfulness of his body. Wind gusted through the courtyard, dropping a swirl of dried leaves nearby. The birds muttered in the ivy.

"I was, uh, hoping I might shelter with you for the night," I ventured. There was no immediate response, and in the momentary silence while I awaited a verdict, I suddenly feared that he might be hard of hearing and that through the tangle of my accent the words might have carried an unintentionally dark ambiguity. Besides, there was no backup plan if he said no.

"Of course, sor," he replied at last barely audibly, his quiet manner full of domestic solicitude. "And where might ye be bound?" He spoke with barely enough force for his words to overcome the air resistance.

Instantly relieved, I started, "Well...," and then suddenly conscious of my normal speaking voice, dropped to a stage whisper, without quite understanding why. "...To Adderlay, I think. I, uh, understand I can get a ferry there across to the train...?"

Considering this remark, he slowly shook his head. A sudden flare of fading sunlight swam across the courtyard. The birds responded in the ivy as it touched the old monk about the head in pale and spurious sanctity. He looked out over the countryside as though there was something about it you just couldn't put your finger on. His grey eyes moved over the land and sky with vague wonder. Nodding then, he gestured widely at the world. He seemed not to have a clear understanding of the idea of destination.

"I'm John Moore," I whispered, leaning in. The familiar words hung suspended from the quiet air between us in doubtful retribution, while he seemed to consider them as a kind of offering.

"I'm Brother Alf."

"Alf..?" I asked with what must have been evident surprise.

Something stirred behind his eyes. A moment of retreat.

"Oh—I'm sorry," I hurried to add. "...I, uh, don't know why; I just suppose I expected to hear something like, maybe, uh...Francis, or... Abelard...Oh, Jeez—I mean—!"

His countenance gradually changed, his eyes showing a touch of vacancy, as though he were receiving a transmission in his ear. Then his face began to break up, self-control leaking from the corners of his eyes. All at once, he threw back his head in a high and airless laugh. His mirth was genuine, but entirely contained, for no sound came forth.

"Come, Mr. Moorr," he said, stooping to grip the handle of the suitcase, the amusement lingering in the crags of his face like the remnants of a party. "Abelard...Tha's rich, tha'is!"

I tried to spare him lifting the bag.

"Here, you needn't carry that old thing," I said reaching to take up the strain. "I'm a very low-maintenance guest." He shifted the bag to his far hand, out of my reach.

"We ask only that ye mind ourr strict rrules of silence at all times."

I didn't know what he meant by that, though I had heard that some monastic orders followed a certain noise discipline, presumably to minimize distractions from higher thought. In any case, I felt sure that prowling around in North Vietnam and Cambodia had taught me things about being quiet that he could never know.

"I've got a pen that scratches pretty badly," I said as we stepped toward the entryway. A wheeze of amusement escaped him as he caressed the air with his free hand in a signal for me to follow.

I liked him. He was interesting. His sense of humor was a welcome surprise, and I found in the contrast between his outward appearance and his ready laughter a cheerful testimony to his way of life. The heavy oaken door swung easily open on silent hinges with his nudge, and he gestured me into the promising interior.

It was instantly gratifying to step at last inside. It was warm and secure from the coming weather, but my feelings were mixed. I was curious, grateful and relieved, but immediately aware that I was an alien presence where I might be regarded as intrusive, or even as some kind of vague threat to an established order, wherein I might commit unwitting blunders.

The hallway was dark. It held the comfortable smells of leather and old books, furniture polish and, faintly, of fresh bread. Brother Alf's rubber soles padded softly on the hall boards ahead. I tried to walk without putting my heels down.

Two monks engaged in lighting wall sconces by hand drifted noiselessly past, and their faces, bathed in candlelight, smiled twin welcomes. They moved along so smoothly that even their robes made no sound.

Brother Alf turned and gestured for me to enter a narrow room. I stepped in to find a sparse, clean cell with a simple wooden bed, a writing table and chair. The shape of the fading light from a single west-facing window lay suspended across the room wall to wall, as if something electric had been cored out of the space. It fell upon a particularly gruesome rendition of the Crucifixion that hung over the bed. Seeing the picture thus spotlighted, as it were, I felt as always when confronted with such images, a twinge of remorse for any religion that takes as its symbol an instrument of torture.

Brother Alf passed behind me, stirring the air, and opened a heavy plank door to reveal a private bath. He turned, mantled by the feeble light which came crookedly through two bleary panes of glass high in the adjoining wall, and grinned broadly.

Behind him, suspended from the ceiling of the little room, hung an enormous complex of iron-reinforced water tanks and polished metal accumulators. Petcocks and valves grew like mushrooms along intake, loss, and re-circulation pipes. A bulbous copper tank, linked to what appeared to be a condenser, or an expansion chamber soldered with polished brass belts, overhung a delightful little porcelain bathtub, scarcely large enough for a child, which stood on four lion's feet. A placard affixed to one of the standpipes read:

Braemar Steamship Company, Ltd.
Glasgow

As I marveled at this confusion of pipes and catch-basins, Brother Alf took up the one bedroom lamp. He struck a match. Its flare rocked and spread on the wall. He replaced the glass chimney, stilling the light, then whispered,

"Rrest here as long as ye like. Ye'rr welcome at Vespers, an' ye'll be called for dinner." I pantomimed the words "thank you" as he withdrew, closing the door softly.

Dinner, I thought. Wow! There's a good idea. I sat down on the stiff bed, feeling the delicious flight of weight from my hips, and listened to the surroundings. The place was quiet alright. In the amiable suffusion of lamplight, the ceiling and walls seemed closer. The dim corners of the room hid beyond its reach, while from the darkness of the bath, many cambered metal surfaces gleamed with a soft carnelian fire. I wondered how to go about filling the bath tanks and if the effort would make much noise. The walls appeared very thick. They flattened the small sounds of my movement and lent a ponderous sort of reassurance to the silence.

I got up and put my jacket on a peg by the door, where it hung like a person slumped against the wall. I opened the suitcase on the bed to discover that a number of things inside were still damp. These I pulled out and hung along some of the pipes in the bathroom, instantly transforming the orderly simplicity of the rooms into something resembling a gypsy camp. I kicked off my worn Topsider shoes to get some warm air into my tired old socks. With some fear that the soles of my shoes might squeak on the wood floors of the hallway, I worried about moving quietly enough in them for the rules. Housekeeping done, I sat back down on the bed and wondered what would happen next.

In minutes, a tiny scratching sounded at the door, faint as a moth at a night window. Not certain that I had heard anything, I opened the door to discover an earnest young man standing in an ellipse of lamplight. His aqueous green eyes peered at me from the shadowed hollows of his face with quick and secret alarm. I smiled, wondering how many outsiders he had ever seen. His expression softened instantly.

"I'm Timothy," he whispered. "Come."

Rising stiffly to what promised to be another adventure, I pulled the shoes back on and followed him along the gloomy corridor, where other silent figures moved in a dark regatta of pointed hoods, the lamps stirring into motion wondrous shadows on the walls as they passed. Several walked with hands invisibly joined, like those of Mandarins, in the folds of their sleeves, and the stooped faces, deep within the tunnel of their cowls, were almost completely hidden. I thought what a perfect garb for anonymity, for dispelling individualism.

I was curious to know where we were going, but as more men filled the hallway, it became clear that this was a community matter, and I began to feel alienated and self-conscious of intrusion. I was here only by chance after all and was joining them now out of curiosity, as a voyeur, an ecclesiastical window peeper. What's more, I had long harbored an ignorant suspicion of cloistered spirituality. I was dubious about men who sought changelessness to release them from uncertainty and turmoil, and I questioned a faith that has to be protected by illusory immutability. Besides, like a houseguest invited to take part in some family ritual, I was an outsider to the comforts that attended their convictions. I felt intimidated by my ignorance of their beliefs and feared that some might see me as a threat to the knowledge they held in common.

In the end, though, I had to admit that I was mostly uneasy about what I imagined went on in a monastery. I'd read Chaucer, after all. Yet, thus far, I'd been treated with a friendly and hospitable disinterest, and besides, I was growing curious to see the strange rites that must occur inside.

Timothy stopped and drew me aside at the entrance to the chapel. Others moved past us, some nodding pleasantly as they pushed back their hoods and filed silently into the great, open sanctum, taking orderly seats facing each other across both sides of the choir. Then Timothy conducted me to a low bench against the wall before he moved away and joined the others. I sat very still and looked at the faces. Quietude.

In the extended overture of silence that followed, I wondered what kind of man chooses this life? Why would a sane person sequester himself and renounce the world? How could he serve a religion that makes so much of love between the peoples and then shut himself away? What burned in these men that did not burn in me? Was it simply a difference in focus, or was it something else, something outside myself? A lack, or too much of something?

Nearby, a monk sat transfixed, eyes unblinking, and his small, tight lips never moved. I wondered about his thoughts and what it would take to know this place. As the faces gathered I thought at first that their somber, contemplative aspect made them appear unnaturally sad. Though some appeared ruddy and weathered, most looked pale in the sallow candle light, the bones of many faces close beneath the surface. Yet, though a deep hollow accentuated the shadow under many cheek bones, most of the faces seemed virtually wrinkle free, lending them a kind of creaseless, haggard calm and making it hard to guess their ages. The tranquil geography of their faces betrayed no single emotion, their downcast eyes reflecting nothing but a sedulously cultivated calmness, withdrawal and gentleness, and (though I may have been searching for it) here and there an expression of remote and hollow melancholy.

I got the impression that these men were living every day as though it were their last, at peace with the world, shriven, fortified by the sacraments and whatever liturgy was to come, ready at any moment to cease without pain. They already had the silence, the appearance, the complexion, and the noiseless movements of ghosts. The final step into the beyond would be only a matter of detail.

At a signal I did not perceive, they all stood. I rose, too, and waited uneasily for whatever was about to happen. For long moments nothing stirred. All was still, as the whole room—people, stones, and furniture—stood in quiet readiness. From one of the windows came the plaintive tapping of a wind-tossed branch against the glass, a plea in Morse from the world outside.

Then, somewhere beneath my heartbeat, it seemed as though the place began to resonate. I wasn't certain at first that I was hearing anything. It began more as a thought than a sound. Then, a barely perceptible drone emerged from the stillness. It grew rapidly, building upon itself in a continuing plangent crescendo, as sixty-some voices filled the little church with a fine, deep tone to begin the antiphonal chanting of plainsong. Voices joined and faded, replacing one another and weaving together in complicated harmony, piling up an invisible architecture of sound that seemed to move right through me, making me a part of themselves.

I had never heard anything like it, and I looked around in wonder at the faces. Some, with half-lidded eyes, stood abandoned to the music, others stared in rapt concentration. Only the younger ones looked at the hymnals. All were bathed in the warm wet light of many candles, which danced over the faces and the folds in their robes, moved upon the walls, and rose to become lost in flickering hesitancy among the shadows of the vaulted roof beams, as the smell of burning tallow and of the old wooden loft blended with the vibrancy of the men's voices in a mesmerizing resonance of the senses. It could have been the year 1200. Living history rose about me and sent its boney fingers up my spine.

Then they stopped, abruptly, the sound ceasing without departing. As the last note died away, the quiet that fell in upon us left me teetering on the edge of expectancy, as though the slightest movement might dislodge it from the immediate air in reverberant repetition. The long stillness which followed seemed to be scooped out of the very heart of sound. It was as though something had been pulled from under me, and I drifted for several minutes in a strange aquarium world of silence and undercurrents. Then the singing began again.

There was nothing but song and silences. No sermon. No threat of eternal retribution or promise of salvation, no exhortation to better conduct. There was no leader, his face solemn with the weight of what he knew, standing before them with sinister prestige. The service was entirely communal, utterly free of tasteless ecumenical excesses, and completely harmonious.

I came to believe as I sat there that if there is a way to speak into the Primal Ear—if Ear there be—then music and silence must be the key. The silences were just as important as the sounds. Besides the fact that the lulls gave the mind space in which to soar, I realized that silence itself is a vital ingredient that makes it possible for the music to exist at all. Sometimes the information came in the sound, and sometimes it was in the silence.

I thought about the monks of Tibet, whose drawn harmonic intonations were said to open the mind. I let my eyes wander among the ceiling timbers and remembered the story of how Galileo worked out the relationship of a pendulum's length to its rate while watching a brazier swinging gently from the rafters of a cathedral, timing it by his pulse. I wondered if he had been lulled, or inspired, by the hollow reverberations of vocal music on that far historic Sunday.

The chanting was buoyant. It filled the little chapel, packing itself into the high corners where it seemed to cling to the narrow places in contained and sober poignancy. It released my mind, disengaging it from logic, so that it went swimming at will in the spacious silences that followed. On that night, as well as many that followed, that space became a vibrant university of the spirit suspended in the air, beyond the reach of ordinary concerns and vexations. To this day, I think of their sound as being shaped like a peaked box.

Early music was performed in medieval cathedrals with stone walls like the one I sat against, which blocked and reflected sound, so that each note was made to echo. If a note vibrated for more than some fraction of a second, it would interfere with the next sound made. The only music heard clearly under these conditions must have been the simple intonations of Gregorian chant. I wondered if there was a direct relationship between the complexities of modern music and the development of construction materials which are better at absorbing sound.

As I listened, I relaxed and surrendered the remnants of my discomfort to the resonant combinations which filled the space. Rain began to fall noisily against the high stained glass and soon to drum steadily upon the roof. A draft swirled through the chapel, causing some of the candles to gutter and sway. It made me grateful to be inside. My apprehension at being a stranger faded, for no grace is truly isolate, and I knew from experience that it is often through those whom we can scarcely comprehend as people when we first meet that we are eventually lead into light and to some truth about ourselves.

The profound silences, punctuated by an occasional muffled cough, seemed like time tunnels back to the dark ages, and I found myself traveling within them on the fading strains of each passage of music. Life was short and cheap in those ancient times, and it has become cheaper since. The invention of the machine gun late in the 19th century becoming a prime instrument of its devaluation. It is only in specific battles for specific lives that our culture is put to the test, and with it our humanity, as we fling our youth into indiscriminate slaughter in its name. Perhaps it was this sense of purpose that had been missing in the war with which my generation had coincided — for the Thing itself now seemed to have been waiting all along, ordained in time, and it was for me and others in my generation simply to be born into it.

In a state of rapturous detachment, I began to feel for the first time a little removed from the war. Its fingers loosened upon me as the figure of death in his paper skull and suit of painted bones strode up and back before the imagined footlights of the ceremony in high declamation.

It was the first church service I could remember that I had not wanted to end. I felt that something larger than ourselves was passing through us. It lived in the ancient liturgy, smuggled down through the centuries by a succession of men long dead, men whose moss-covered graves are now forgotten. Here it was borrowing its life from us, as it must, and would continue to do, ageless and without change, until the last memory of the last man in the order passes into that conjectural realm wherein reposes the ultimate hope and fear of all humanity, beyond the time when our own epitaphs are no longer legible. I began to acknowledge the civilizing influence of historical continuity. Generation after generation of people following a prescribed set of behaviors make a culture, even in microcosm.

When at last the men rose to leave, I felt the breath of peace pass like a whispered message along the rows. I was taken up as from a dream and followed Timothy back into the hallway feeling "strong upon me," as Walt Whitman has it, "the life that does not exhibit itself."

He led me into the refectory, the dining room, which occupied the old great hall with its high stone walls, concamerated windows, and wooden vaulting. An enormous stone fireplace, large enough to turn a whole ox, contained a modest fire in the outer wall, where the smoke-blackened masonry featured a row of Romanesque pilasters with interlocking Norman arches forming a shallow arcade that bore an aura of great antiquity. Dark oak paneling rose to form a five-foot wainscoting that encompassed the room, lending a furnished aspect to the lower courses of stone, while embracing the dining space with the lineaments of an imposing and slightly mournful grandeur. Firelight danced warmly along its moldings and gleamed from the flutes of its high-relief linen-fold carving.

With their shadows mingled upon the walls, the brotherhood moved quietly among communal tables. Their uniformity of dress and orderly progression of seating was so reminiscent of mealtime at my old prep school that it made me smile.

Each man helped himself or helped another, who, because of the infirmity of age or affliction, could not. At the end of the table to which Timothy steered us sat an old man whose kindly eyes moved over my clothing with childlike curiosity. There was no dish before him, and he made no move. I smiled. His face brightened, and he smiled back. It was then that I noticed his hands. They trembled and jerked in his lap as though troubled by dreams. Soon he was joined by a friend who brought him his dinner and began to feed him with great care. The old man continued to smile warmly at me between bites. He could have been a child with pabulum on his face.

The meal was excellent. Lamb stew and a hearty nectarous wine served in hand-turned wooden cups. I felt wolfishly hungry but ate with self-conscious restraint, afraid that I might be judged presumptuous of my share. No one spoke and the meal progressed with only muted sounds of the utensils and the woolen tearing of bread.

It was not entirely unlike the military, where everyone ate together blended in common purpose and the anonymity of a common uniform. I wondered at their hidden individuality, their private hopes and fears, and what they might have left behind to enter this life. Can so many human instincts really be seized like a handful of snakes, tied up in a sack, and locked away, alive and squirming for a lifetime? When Timothy smiled his signal for us to leave, I got up careful not to scrape the bench on the floor.

Once back in my room, with food heavy in my stomach, I gave in to the fatigue of the long footslog. Despite feeling clammy, I decided to postpone the mysteries of the bath until the ache in my hip had quieted. I stretched out upon the cot with my head on the pillow and listened to the darkness and let the stillness of the little room embraced me.

I thought about the nature of the silence to which these men had bound their lives. Perhaps they were more in touch with the universe than I. For just as darkness is the natural state of the cosmos, pierced only by an occasional sun, so too is silence spread eternally, broken only by random cataclysm. I thought about the silences I had experienced, and their different meanings. There is the silence that comes with morning in a forest, and this is different from the silence of a sleeping city. There is the silence after a rainstorm, and before a rainstorm, and these are not the same. There is the silence of vast emptiness in the space between mountains, the silence of fear, crowded with imaginary sounds, and the silence of doubt. There is a certain kind of silence that emanates from a lifeless object, as from a piano with old dust upon its keys, or from anything that has answered to the need of humans, like the handle of a sword, or the stage in an empty theater. This kind of silence can speak. Its voice may be melancholy, but not necessarily, for the last notes of the piano may have been raucous and gay; the theater may have closed on a rollicking comedy. Whatever the mood or circumstance, its essence may linger in the silence that follows. It is a kind of echo. The silences created that night were alive.

My skin felt sticky with old perspiration and the oleaginous film of the road, and my clothes smelled musty and dank from over-use. Reluctant to sully the clean bed linens with all that clung to me from the long day, I remained instead on top of the blanket and stared at the ceiling, where old water stains had wrought upon the dried and crumbling plasterwork a freeform sepia map of ancient kingdoms.

Somewhere, I had read that the Hindus count three hundred and thirty million gods. I realized that their point is not the accuracy of the count but rather the multiplicity of the spirit in all things. That night, as I stared and listened, the life force of the very walls seemed to come forth and to rise about me in quiet and propitious animism.

I tried to think about the events of the day, to revisit the scenes of the morning, and the girl on the bus, about which something remained intangible and unresolved, but a ponderous weight of sleep came upon me and was soon turning out my very being, taking up all the space within me. Rain fell distantly beyond the heavy walls. The lamp light stirred. There was a settling into motionlessness at the edges of clarity around the walls and ceiling, while the vast reserves of surrounding darkness in the molding went on creaking.

Sometime, much later, I awoke fully clothed, with my knees drawn up. The room had turned cold. The lamp still burned, its feeble light struggling against the stolid indifference of the space, and I could see my breath in the shadows. I got up to pull off my shoes and looked out at the pale night. There was a whispering silence beyond the glass. Snow settled deeply on the branches of the trees. It fell like sleep.

2
Sanctum

When I awoke again, a feeble and hueless dawn etched the window from the night, where the world outside lay veiled in an impenetrable pale stillness. I groped in the obscurity by the bed for matches, got the lamp rekindled, and sat up. Achy and muscle sore, I sat for awhile watching my breath in the lamplight. When I tried to stand, I realized that my knees preferred to rest in bed a bit longer, the hip wound throbbed anew, and even the tendons in my ankles were sore. I got up stiffly, introducing weight to my joints in careful increments, took up the lamp, and limped into the bathroom to study the plumbing.

The jungle of pipes and valves with their ominous accompaniment of black shapes glared defiantly as I stood in the semi-dark trying to figure out how to persuade it to deliver a bath. The whole contraption was so over-built for its present role that I guessed it might originally have been constructed as a quarter-scale designer's model of a system meant for the bowels of a steamship, and then, too small to be serviceable yet too well-constructed to throw away, it had probably been donated to the monastery.

After a few minutes of study, the water delivery sequence revealed itself to be simple enough: a quarter turn on the upper inlet petcock handle started a soft gurgling flow toward the first downstream check valve, which took a half turn from the up position to down. This carried to the primary holding tank, which began to fill with a muffled blubbering sound. Most gratifying. I watched the rising level in a glass tube fixed to its side. It bore a red line near the top, indicating some recommended limit. By turning a round valve at the outlet end of the tank, water was then allowed to overflow via a two-inch brass spill pipe to a cylindrical accumulator for the copper boiler, which bulged importantly beneath it. Tucked around the base curvature of the boiler was a circular iron range.

Once the boiler filled, the first inlet valve near the ceiling had to be closed. Thus, spherical expansion chambers above both lower tanks could return pressure and condensation through bleed valves to the first holding tank. From the boiler, a small porcelain regulator delivered hot water through an insulated pipe that passed back through several copper-riveted brackets to connect with the down lines from both the first accumulator and upper left expansion tank. These dropped into the bathing tub in parallel, though with a cross-connect near the bottom which offered the operator a pair of ceramic knobs by which the heated line and the cold line could be mixed. A hand shower on a length of rubber bicycle-pump hose lay coiled about one of the spigots. Complex but not complicated, and simple enough to decipher without instructions, though I did wonder how many visitors to this room had gone without a bath.

As the boiler began to fill, I lit the range with one of the lantern matches. The flames popped into life and danced along its holes like a parade of miniature demons, sending their diffused orange light among the pipes and launching massive shadows to tremble across the ceiling in the flicker.

The system was fun to play with, and as I adjusted the various cocks and valves to the hiss of the water, it reminded me of something out of a submarine movie. An "ah-ooga" horn sounded in my head, and a metallic inner voice came on saying, "Dive! Dive!" It was a tinker's masterwork of self-contained redundancy, but it soon proved easy enough to regulate by ear, and the effort made a bath all the more rewarding.

Finally, by kneeling in the little tub and using the shower hose to keep the room's ambient chill off my back, I was able to achieve a delightful hot bath and a shave. Drying off, or rather "dampening off," was accomplished with two small linen face towels provided, and which I spread to dry afterwards on top of the boiler in certain knowledge that the air in the room alone would fail to wick them in a whole day.

With a change of clothes, I felt much recovered from the previous day's wear. Yet when I stood before the sink, I was surprised by the haunted face that peered back at me through the dim, fish-colored canescence captured in the mirror. I looked dark, furtive, and furrowed with broody lines. It didn't match the way I felt at all. Pulling a comb through my hair helped a little, and I tried an experimental smile, but it succeeded only in transforming the image into something like a stone with cracks in it, and I turned away worried at the impression I must have been making on my hosts.

As the room began to fill with dingy grey light from the window, I cautiously opened the door to the corridor. The hallway was cooler than the room, quiet and dark, illuminated only by the spill from a table lamp at some remove around a corner. The air that moved through it smelled strongly now of bacon and new bread.

Having been escorted about the night before, I feared there might be a policy restricting freedom of movement by visitors, and I hesitated to proceed. I prepared a face for chance encounter. I tried to look well-meaning and slightly apologetic, like a nice person who's wound up in a place he knows he doesn't belong; but for several minutes no one came by. I decided to make for the refectory hall and, still wearing my face, set out to follow the breakfast smells in the direction Timothy had shown me.

Cold air swept along the floor as I neared the entrance hall. I hesitated at the corner and then turned in, hoping to find Brother Alf on porter duty by the door. The foyer and its little office were deserted. Wintry air poured beneath the front door and curled around my ankle bones. I lifted the iron latch and pulled on the heavy door just enough to put my head outside.

Fine sleet slanted from the dark sky into the pebbly scurf of wet snow that covered the courtyard and lined the stones. It fell with a faint sound, like sand blowing against a monument, and lay piled in hundreds of little tufts among the ivy. A line of black footprints led away from the door and disappeared beyond the close.

In the distance below, the valley lay wet and green, while the slopes of surrounding higher ground, wearing mantles of white, rose into the clouds. The dark open rifts between the hills seemed to shift the dimensions of things, like spaces left for things unsaid.

I pushed the door closed again, afraid I might have let in too much cold air, and turned to find Timothy approaching with his ready smile. He beckoned with a nod, and together we went to the refectory, where, sitting close to the morning fire, I was given my fill of porridge with raw cream, thick slabs of fresh-baked toast spread with their own jam, fried eggs, kippers, and strong hot tea.

He sat across from me and ate very little, just a sparse bit of bread, his eyes glowing with amusement in the firelight, as he sipped his tea and watched my feeding with the unabashed fascination of a child at a monkey house. I smiled back acknowledgement and gratitude.

That breakfast was memorable for both its quality and the position it filled in the events of the year. For the first time in years, I enjoyed the warmth of an open fire, and felt at rare peace with the immediate future. I wished that this friendly, taciturn young man and I could tarry there by the fire for the rest of the morning, that he could answer my questions about his life, and that even in limited, whispered discourse I might be given a chance to express my thanks. Yet I had seen the evening before that this was a working farm, and I assumed, correctly as it happened, that Timothy, though he had made no move to hurry me, was wanted in the Vineyards of the Lord.

When he saw that I was finished, he conducted me on a brief tour of the main house, pointing out the library and Scriptorium, stacked with seriousness and gloom, as well as a large bright reading room, whose windows gave onto the rolling white slopes outside. He showed me the kitchens and scullery where the cooks milled about in the steam with hectic, good-natured calm. They waved and nodded.

Back in the main hall, he indicated that he had to go, and waved me off to my room. It was clear that I was being released on my own responsibilities. They were leaving me to explore the place, go back to bed, or even leave. Had I simply packed up and left, there would have been no one about to thank—no one with whom to acknowledge their unquestioning hospitality. My slipping away would have left no mark upon the duty they felt toward the wayfarer, but I would have felt the imbalance for the rest of my life. Besides, I had no wish to set out again for an unknown distance through a freezing confusion of intermittent sleet, rain, and snow.

As I stood there in the front hallway reviewing my options with leaky objectivity, I felt islanded, extraneous both to the tranquility of this cloistered shore as well as to the broad and restless ocean that had cast me up. I had burrowed easily into the cozy privacy here, and I felt unexpectedly comfortable, sheltered by walls of stone and partitioned by those of tradition. Out there in the mist, on the weather-swept road, I knew the past lay piled up, crouching in wait for me, while the furnishings of the future remained invisible still, beyond the scope of my expectations. The irony in my freedom to leave at any time was that it served to isolate me from the rules of conduct in both worlds.

A strong gust hit the front door with a muffled sound like a thrown pillow. It caused the latch to move, and sleet hissed at the window.

I took it as a sign and decided to spend some time investigating the library.

I went back to the room for a pen and my notebook. As soon as I stepped into the room, I noticed that my suitcase had been opened. It was on the floor where I had left it, but the lid was up and lay against the wall. It held a few books and incidentals, but all my clothes were missing. A hot flush filled my neck when I realized what had happened. Why would anyone take my old clothes, especially in this place?

I stepped into the hallway. No one was around. I went down to the little office by the front door. Nobody. The place was a tomb whose stony indifference stood in sharp contrast to my mounting question. There was only the sound of my own breathing in the stillness.

I felt that the theft should be reported. Surely it was just the work of a single bad apple, and whoever it was should at least know that it had been discovered. But how do you tell anyone in a place where nobody speaks? I decided to write it out with the date and time then give the note to Timothy or Alf, whichever I saw first. I went back for the notebook, then headed toward the library and its Scriptorium the way Timothy had shown me. It had writing tables and better light.

Yet I hesitated at the doorway, suddenly intimidated by the huge collection of leather-bound books, the ponderous weight of monastic history, and its stony indifference to my petty transience. I knew that the libraries of Europe had survived in the mushroom dark of the monasteries for over a thousand years, preserved in their private vaults of learning and sanctified by each order like a family fortune. The role of monks in sneaking knowledge down through the hostile ignorance of generations suddenly rose in frowning admonition before me, leaving me timid of entering the room. This was their seat of study, their crucible of learning, ponderous with rules and restrictions, even among the members. It was probably the *sanctum sanctorum* of the whole place and likely held in common reverence by the entire brotherhood. Just because Timothy had pointed it out didn't mean that I could presume to stroll in and defile their treasures with my worldly ideas and foul emanations. For all I knew the contents of this very room might hold a singular place in the long adventure of knowing. It would take only one important manuscript to fulfill that condition, and if such a document was preserved here, it would be secured in the collective guardianship of a brotherhood alert to the ravages of time and the hands of mistaken zeal.

Drawn like a child whose small feet had wandered into some forbidden chamber, I peeked around the entry and saw to my delight that it was an elegantly paneled room with snug recesses and a richly carved ceiling. Unlike the quick glimpse I had of it from the hallway on Timothy's hurried tour, seen now through the mysterious alchemy of curiosity and temptation, the fullness of its furnishings were instantly appealing. It beckoned.

I ventured a tentative step in to see more. The air felt compressed and suddenly still. It smelled of leather and paraffin wax and wool, and something else—something I remembered from childhood visits to my grandmother's house. A coal fire. The surrounding shelves were filled with ancient bound volumes arranged in neat rows from the floor to the high ceiling. The place held an atmosphere of long study, of timelessness and worry, of academic preoccupation with verities that filled the space and compressed my little complaint about a few bits of worn clothes into something small, mundane, and transitory. Here was the real heart of the contemplative life. I wondered to what extent the men were dominated by this library, by its promises and prohibitions.

The quietude of the large room served to calm my agitation, and I tried to think only noble thoughts to make myself worthy of its grandeur. I decided that if I was going to go through with a note my words would have to be chosen carefully in order to strike just the right tone of honest confusion and moral indignation. Then I realized that the clothes had lost their importance. They were old after all, left at home when I had joined the military some five years before. Their significance lay only in the connection they had given me with those gone years; they were comfortable and carried a certain residue of past experience, but in the end, not of great value. I thought that maybe I'd just write a polite inquiry and suggest them as a modest donation.

Gilt embossed bindings gleamed faintly in the uncertain light of the upper shelves, and cloth-covered scrolls, stacked like kindling, filled cubbies among the bookcases. On stepping farther in I saw that, sure enough, a coal fire burned cheerfully in the fireplace, and the faint smell of bituminous gas in its smoke gave the room an air of cozy retribution. The atmosphere in the room was warm and snug with purposeful silence. I wanted to see more and ventured another step.

There were three long tables in the center of the room at which a few elderly men were bent over their studies in the way of monks for 900 years. Their bald heads shone pink in the warm light of desk lamps. One, working extremely close to the page, looked up, star-tled from his concentration, his face lost behind heavy lenses through which his eyes seemed to lunge forward. He stared at me for a moment then squinted as though to transfer some of his diminished power of vision to his ears. I recognized him from the service of the night before and smiled. Open-mouthed, he stared at me for a long moment more, probably allowing his senses to adjust to the distance. Then, expressionless, he returned to his work, as though dismissing some minor sound. It appeared that, as far as he was concerned, if I existed at all, it was simply as a distinction without a difference, and I took his dismissal to mean I was free to browse.

I moved self-consciously, trying to be quiet, with my hands behind my back in a manner I hoped would be taken as respectful appreciation. The only other rooms like this I had ever seen were galleries full of "Do Not Touch" signs, and besides, I did not want my mounting excitement in the presence of so many old books to presume upon anyone's vocational studies.

I settled at length into a deep leather chair and scanned the shelves, my note forgotten. Much of the collection appeared to be in Latin or Greek, and most of it was religious in nature, but a few English language titles caught my eye. I saw an ancient edition of Sir Edmund Spenser's *The Faerie Queen* and carefully pulled it from the shelf. It was an early hand-copied volume, bound in dried leather and dated 1598, worth a small fortune to a private collector.

It was heavy. I turned it reverentially, cradling its spine in my hands. The dense toast-colored pages creaked and fell stiffly open in bunches, releasing the antique scent of dried gorse, old dust, and the settled smell of peat smoke from long past winters. I had read much of it in school when I cared less about such things, in text books where the uniformly blocked and centered typeface lent no more character to one poet than another; but here, between my fingers, was original Elizabethan work, printed out in a distinctive, disciplined hand free of any typesetter's margins, with lots of flourishes and trailing volutes on the taller letters, the old ink now faded to brown. I could even see points where this singular copyist had dipped his quill, three hundred and seventy-one years before, and the coarse linen rag had absorbed the excess in spidery little blobs.

The room was a treasure-trove of information, much of it a monument to superstition in my view, but their scattered collection of early works was priceless, and it appeared that I was free to wander among them at will. The orderliness of the shelves and condition of the books betrayed the pride in knowledge accumulated by the brotherhood over the years. You could hardly accuse them of the sin by which the angels fell; the collection was both extensive and beautifully maintained—a mark of prestige. Just as the nobility once displayed armor and standards, the abbots displayed illuminated manuscripts. I found a first edition of Alexander Pope, dated 1733, and took it into the adjoining room where I thought my presence might be less distracting to the men at the writing tables.

Watery gray light spilled from large windows across the upholstered chairs and made distended geometric patterns on the raw cords of the worn carpet underfoot. There were thousands of books on the shelves here, too, representing more secular subjects. In the "Cs," I saw Carlyle and Coleridge, Chaucer and Churchill at a glance.

Some incongruous old photographs hung in frames on the wall by the door. Rigid, sepia-toned subjects stared severely off, posed to avoid the lens. By their antique dress, they were people long dead, posed in sunshine on what might once have been the porch steps of this very house and seated in chairs on the grass. All their past, future, and stillborn dreams had been cauterized in that brief encapture of light within the camera's closet, their expressions arrested forever between the blinks of their eyes. In searching their faces, I found looks of vague discontent, looks of rue, as though reports of their own deaths had just reached them. I wondered if they had been descendants of the family who had built the house and if perhaps the monks had saved the pictures as a small legacy to their home.

Early photography must have been serious business, or perhaps it was just that trying to hold a grin for its long exposures made people feel foolish in an age that valued stiff collars and black clothing. Perhaps they were thinking with bitterness of things not yet come to be, which yet were now forever past. In those faces that are now nameless there was a message that can never be spoken, because time will always slay the messenger before he can reach us.

It caused me to remember again some of the friends I had lost in the war, and for just a moment the weight of their presence slumped through me. These men whom I had known so recently were just as irrevocably gone as the people in the photographs, and as with the passing of all former time, they were joined now in the great indifference. Whether they left tangible artifacts, or surrendered some trace of themselves onto film as light and shadow, or were carried only as images in fading memory, the world was hurrying on, a wet ball flung through oblivion without them.

These thoughts fell into my mind like stones. In a small chaos of discord I crossed to an alcove bench, wondering as I looked out at the weather if perhaps the reason we preserve antique photographs so carefully is because they somehow comfort our own mortal need for location in time. In a way, photography serves as a defense against loss, arresting time just long enough to pause our clocks of the heart.

I tried to close a hard fist around my mind to shut down the morose speculation that the photographs had triggered, to seal the icy hole in my chest the memories always brought, and reminded myself that I must be indeed the darling of fortune to be here at all. I looked around the room, letting my eyes roam among its details and feeling a sharp and humbling gratitude for my surroundings. I cared less just then for the grasp of some illusive cause or explanation than for mere association with rational experience by which to comprehend the haunted bone of mortality. The space around me, with its deeply carved crown molding, a filigree of rain shadows rippling across the ceiling, and the press of inaudible voices from the many volumes on its shelves, took on a wistful consciousness in the way that inanimate objects sometimes do, demanding to be fitted into the scheme of things.

As I sat contentedly there in the steely winter light from the window, feeling warm and safe from the weather while indulging myself in the rarified promise of so many books, I was suddenly effused with a genuine affection for the old house, for the profound quiet that lived in its rooms, the seamless presumption of welcome at all its doorways, for the wonderful library with its mournful weight of history, but especially for its voluptuous improbability. I could not understand the complex mystery of how my steps had been led to this place, but I was thrilled to be there, lofted free of claims on the future or the past, free to dismiss the confusion of unresolved memories, and all my failings neutralized by good fortune. If, I wondered, the *Via Dolorosa* conveys the pilgrim, not to some ecumenical homeland of spiritual reconciliation, but rather ends quietly in a little palmate fan of pacific rivulets, then perhaps I had arrived at one of these—the mysterious edge, where the slopes of knowledge dwindle, and love of being for its own sake, lacking a specific outside object, begins at last.

Company of Stone

A North Sea wind lofted rain and sleet against the window panes where it melted and ran toward the sills. Beyond the glass veils of rain seemed to herd the morning light before them. The earth and sky were drained of much of their color, giving sight a rest and allowing other senses to function more freely.

From the window I could see that the back slope of the ridge on which the house stood rose from the shoulders of sea cliffs about a thousand yards distant—as far as I could see through the rain. In the mist at its edge, a collapsed stronghold stood near the cliff, its arches like a set of broken dentures. A row of smooth foothills nuzzled at the base of the slope, rising steeply into the foreground and laced in skeins of ruined snow.

The slopes were fragmented with a delicate tracery of low stone walls, and all the fields they enclosed were cultivated. Some bore rows of staked grape vines or lines of leafless fruit trees, standing in orderly ranks like a battalion of dark skeletons. Others were open rectangles of furrowed earth, drenched into corrugated fudge.

The sweeps of sleet imparted a brooding motion to the scene. But there was something else out there that gave the sodden fields a nervous kind of eloquence. Tiny brown figures, barely visible, bent to their tasks in the appalling weather. The brotherhood was at work in the fields, conditions be damned. It gave me a shiver of gratitude to be inside—but I felt guilty, and sissified, too.

I opened the Alexander Pope, thinking how his name was especially appropriate for their collection. This was a printed volume, but an original edition, whose pages had discolored where almost three hundred years of changes in temperature and moisture had breathed a stain around the edges. I remembered reading Pope in school. He was one of the first English poets we had been required to read whose verse I found both clear and entertaining. Highly epigrammatic, which must have made him a hit at garden parties, he is still so quotable, people usually don't know when they're doing it: "A little knowledge is a dangerous thing," "Damn with faint praise," "Hope springs eternal," "Fools rush in where angels fear to tread" were a few I recalled, and finding them again filled me with a rush of nostalgia.

The ordered lines with their familiar sentiments centered on the bare field of each page, brought to me a bittersweet longing for those days when I had first read them, a simpler time of vernal naïveté, when I had been sheltered by institutions and inexperience from much of what the past year's hard lessons had taught me about the world. Reading the verses again brought back fragments of the feelings they had first given me, and served for a moment to bypass the intervening years, to cancel the chaos. I had never dreamed that the lines would echo one day, would sensitize some moment in the future, and I was both surprised and gratified to indulge the memory.

I tried to envision Pope's conservative, well-ordered age when rhyming couplets, fine manners, powdered wigs, and elaborate gardens were essential to obtain a reputation as a tastemaker. Reading from pages that had actually been printed in that era somehow impacted memories of my own life with sentiments I had long discarded. I felt a flash of longing for those gone years that now lay sheltering in memory on the far side of nightmare and fury.

At some point I heard the faint ring of a bell and noticed that the men in the library put down their pens, closed their books, and without a word, rose and departed, leaving me entirely alone with their treasure. Outside, the distant men began filing like ants toward the house. It must have been the call to the mid-day meal (*Nones*, as I would learn) and perhaps some form of worship, but I did not feel that I should attend. I was trapped in a mix of feelings about the clothes and the fact that I had been enjoying the comforts of their fireside while they had been outside laboring in the freezing weather.

When at last I returned to my room in the afternoon, it was to discover with a hot rush of shame my clothes arranged in four neat piles along the bed—cleaned, pressed, and folded. They were still warm. The notebook went heavy in my hand. It slipped from my bloodless fingers onto the bed where it flopped open, and its blank pages stared accusingly up at me from the simple coverlet. I sat there for a time afterwards, a bit lightheaded, with the sour green taste of bile in my mouth and queasy with spiritual indigestion.

3
Scullery

The weather held, alternating between lashing rains, that left a pale glaze of sleet on the high ground, and steady drizzle. On the third day, I felt guilty enough about the wordless hospitality to present myself to the kitchen staff after breakfast and offer to perhaps do the drying for whomever it was that washed the dishes.

I found that he was a plump, cherubic little man, made pink by his hours over hot water. He had a freckled nose and full, well-defined lips which hid an array of poorly distributed teeth. When I first stepped in and took up a towel, his tiny eyes looked up at me like some startled and defenseless night creature. Then, with quick consternation, he peered about in the steam for approval.

Thomas, Master of the Scullery, left something bubbling and came over, emerging like a ship from the fog. He was a large man whose baggy face bore a florid tracery of broken capillaries. Thickset and capable, he rolled like a freighter as he walked, and wiping the hams of his hands on an apron, he hove to in front of me, then stood for a long moment regarding me with the sort of listening expression I have sometimes seen in forgetful people. I smiled confidently and said that I had learned the art of cleaning and drying pots in the Army of the United States and had been expensively trained. He smiled with his mouth while his deep set eyes continued to study me. Then he patted my shoulder and turned back to the stoves. I looked at the washer of dishes, who smiled broadly, showing the pickets of his teeth, while his eyes pressed closed like the folds in a pudding.

The two men seemed glad of a little help, though neither appeared burdened by his job. They treated me with wary curiosity and a frugal sort of kindness, which warmed gradually through the day as I tried to make myself useful.

I have seldom been in an environment that could equal that kitchen for pride of workmanship. It was kept spotlessly clean by continuous effort. The faces around me held a peacefulness in their eyes that I envied, for nothing contributes so much to tranquilize the mind as a steady purpose, a point on which the soul can fix its intellectual eye.

I remember thinking that here was proof of the supreme irony in the outrageous slogan over the gates to Auschwitz, "Arbeit Mach Frei," for the right work does, indeed, free the spirit.

Late in the morning I was invited to sample some fresh pastries. The baker/pastry chef was a stolid little man about whose compact body the drape of his robe signaled an ample investment in the fruits of his own skill. From a tangled thicket of eyebrows his dark eyes gleamed with Arab pickpocket speculation, and between the twin prominences of his cheeks a pug nose was all but hidden in a wiry black beard that exploded from his face like a burst horsehair sofa. He was the very image of a picture book pirate, whose normal expression whenever his face settled into repose was an incongruous frown, but his frequent grins flashed forth like a lighthouse in a portable storm. He was called Michael and was one of the few brothers I observed who wore his hair tonsured, although he didn't seem to attend to it with great conviction, as whenever I noticed, his scalp was as blue and overgrown as a burglar's jowls.

He was glad of a new test-palate and duly proud of his work, and the offerings were warm, thick, and redolent of wild honey glaze. Prepared to show polite approval regardless of the result, I pantomimed an elaborate display of selection before trying a cinnamon roll. It proved to be delicious beyond description, the flavor enhanced by the fact that it was still so warm all its ingredients emanated in combination, rising like an answer to some exigent historic need and releasing a taste bud chorus of silent alleluias. My involuntary reaction of spontaneous delight was met with gratified smiles all around.

He soon demonstrated a delectable knack for capturing caricatures of the brothers in risen dough, to generally (but not entirely) amused admiration. He knew how to time his baking to achieve the precise degree of rise in his mixture so as to complete the carefully contrived portraits. Some of the membership enjoyed being selected for his subjects, while others, sick with restraint, managed to contain their enthusiasm. I could not escape the feeling that Brother Michael secretly enjoyed getting in his digs this way, and I liked him for doing it with humor.

It was instructive to watch Michael at his craft. He was a man of contained movement, as though long experience had evolved a path through his tasks that maximized the conservation of energy. He wasn't lazy or slow, though an outside observer might easily have thought so. Rather he operated at the studied limit of only what was required for each of his preparations. He spoke little, and in his frugality, his aversion to waste, I got the feeling that he regarded any display of emotion, despite his frequent smiles, as strength lavished on futile things.

Each time he began mixing a batch his natural scowl appeared to smooth out somewhat, as though betraying a lull in some inner tempest. I assumed that, as with any other meaningful effort, his method involved a certain sacrifice, the suppression of self-consciousness, and a temporary tilt of the will so that his awareness became transparent and hollow, a channel for the work.

I was quickly learning that there are excellences born of simplification, that the goal of perfection is approached in rejecting distractions, in paring one's life down to its minimal essentials—and should you settle in that process upon a common denominator with like-minded specialists, so much the better. The kitchen staff worked as a defining element of the whole order, and the whole, in turn, was reflected in it. Just as a single-cell animal can only exist with each of its elements in place, so the brotherhood, despite an outward simplicity, functioned under the microscope at a level which might better be described as irreducible complexity. That is, each of its numerous components functioned in the simplest way.

Unexpectedly, I was beginning to see that these were men whose inward being was so strong that they were not greatly defined by what lay outside themselves. They were whole, individuals content to be the best versions of themselves possible—or equally happy to find themselves along the road to that unspoken goal—and in their companionship I felt many of my hopes and fears for achievement, of failure and loss, the search for other men's goals, and transitory cares, rise up and swallow me down in a sweet unraveling. With all the excitement of discovery, I felt as though I had suddenly stepped aside and could see where I had been sleeping. I felt myself entering some unexplored country of the mind, where the force of the immaterial was present among much larger resonances and from which I had no desire to return.

4
Wilf

One windy afternoon several days later, when the rains had let up temporarily, I went outside to explore the grounds and to have a look at the ruined watch tower. It stood at the southern end of the manor, where it once had commanded the approaches to the ridge. Looking up from the outer stones at its base, the circular walls soared massively skyward and seemed tilted against the moving clouds. They actually rose about 80 feet above the ground and were the very image of the high crenelated bastions that children dream about after bedtime stories of castles and dragons. Yet now, ravaged by centuries of hard weather, the tower stood open to the sky, breached at last by time, and the passing clouds hurried indifferently through its arrow ports. Moss grew along the cracks, and odd clumps of grass bobbed here and there high on the outer walls, rooted serendipitously among the stones.

The masonry of its floor covered a sectioned basement of four arched chambers. They may once have served as a dungeon, but now held a store of farm equipment and gardening tools, open to the grounds. I stepped through a narrow stone doorway let into the outer wall of the tower and saw that within the encirclement of its inner walls above these rooms the old keep was littered with tumbled masonry and a confusion of broken boards, warped and split by long exposure to the ravages of weather. Bleached wooden joists on which the marks of hand-tools resembled fish scales leaned about, warped and split in disarray.

The fallen timbers seemed to be ruins of an earlier restoration of the upper floors, long since collapsed, for the original wood could not have lasted into this century thus exposed. There was a mournful quality to the wreckage. Faint curls of mist captured from the passing clouds lent a painful intimacy to the pile, standing in for the risen dust, as though the collapse had only just fallen from under the lives it once supported. I wondered how long ago it had given way and felt for a moment transposed in time, as though in the blink of history's eye I had narrowly missed an opportunity to see an intact medieval tower. It surprised me that the brothers had not cleaned the place up or put the beams to other uses. The wind moaned in its hollow like a ghost trying to find the way out.

A narrow stone stair emerged from the rubble and climbed the inner curvature of wall, winding to the left all the way up to the battlements in two sections, with a short landing half way up. I was curious to see the view from the top. Despite the absence of any flooring, which made the open space seem very large and the stairs precariously narrow, the step stones were clearly anchored in the walls. As I started cautiously up, instinctively shouldering the wall, I realized that this design would have favored the defenders of the tower. Since most people are right-handed, an attacker trying to get up the stairs would have had his sword arm against the wall, while the guy facing down had free swing.

The worn steps were covered with eruptions of lichen that splotched the grey stone like a skin disease and were slick with the rainwater they held. There was no handhold, and the tread stones were worn smooth. I placed my feet carefully, thinking that all pathways are memorialized by the bones of those who thought they knew when to turn back. The arches of my feet began to tingle.

I paused on the landing—a stone plinth projecting into space from the upper courses—to catch my breath. Backed firmly against the wall and very aware of my slender foothold in the yawning cavity, I looked around and tried to visualize the gone living space within the tower. A ring of spaced rectangular put-log sockets curving along the inner wall had evidently held the floor joists for a second story, perhaps a bed chamber, for across the empty expanse was a blackened and rain-streaked fireplace, some of its decorative masonry clinging incongruously still to warm nights and lost dreams, in a room no longer.

Hugging the wall, I continued carefully up. At the top, the sudden wind cut through my clothes, the mist flew sideways, and the wide dark landscape below, with its rocks and wind-flattened grass, looked dizzyingly far away. Proximity to the torn grey clouds gave the impression of being high under an enormous ragged canvas loosely pegged to the hills in the middle distance. The light swam past in waves, while an advancing cloudburst hung like a broken bag in the northwest.

Underfoot, the capstones of the wall itself seemed slender and unsupported. Most of the fighting platform had crumbled away, but it was partially intact for about a third of the way around the tower. It

formed an exceedingly narrow and perilous ledge, rimming the fortified wall with stepping stones in empty space.

Just short of the point at which the lip of the tower was broken off,
was a privy—a shelf of grey stone let into the original masonry along
the outer defenses, with a hole in it for the convenience of the guards.
It overhung the outer wall just enough to have served in olden times as
a kind of defensive weapon in itself. These days, it made a grand seat
with a view, and reposing on it this day was one of the most unusual
characters I have ever met.

He sat alone, suspended there in a weeping corona of mist, perched
precariously in the emptiness, with the beak of his face beating into
the wind. His robe was black with rain and it lay collapsed about his
bony frame like a tent full of poles. His wet hair was steel grey with
streaks of rust in it, and it hung about his face and ears like the physical expression of despair itself. His face was deeply lined, prized and
pummeled into a mask of melancholy, and as the rain drops shook
free of his brow they became lost among the crevices in the damaged
parchment of his cheeks.

He frightened me at first, the way shadows do at night, like some
apparition—the ghost of Hamlet's father floating among the battlements. Oh boy, I thought, here's one you won't find in the brochures.
I knew instinctively that here was the ultimate recluse, one for whom
even the monastic life offered insufficient isolation.

I hesitated as soon as I noticed him, uncertain whether to stay or
leave. I chose to stay, but at a polite distance, and stood for a long
minute smelling the wet straw and smoke carried in the gusts, looking
out at the disappearing hills and the churning oatmeal sky. There were
momentary alterations in the light, as the racing clouds permitted an
occasional softness and the fleeting clarity that came from higher layers.

"Are ye a Chrustian, then?" he rasped suddenly, his unexpected
utterance cutting through the sound of the wind.

I jumped, as startled to hear him speak as I was unprepared for
his bluntness. His voice carried in the laden air like dragged barbed
wire. His lean face was turned toward me, staring out of the mist like
some creature in a fable. The grey eyes in their red-rimmed cups were
sullen and depthless, like lead slag poured into borings to seal away
something virulent or predacious. He was scary.

I didn't know how to answer the question, despite my doubts, never having seriously asked it of myself out loud. I turned and looked these thoughts at him: I can't honestly say that I believe the universe, in all its unthinkable reaches, filled with billions of worlds and vast reserves of mystery, was simply brought into being by executive decree, or that the man called Jesus was the direct biological off-spring of the Great Initiator, but I've done some hard praying, just the same. I like the Golden Rule, but I've too often seen it used as a makeshift warning to avoid timely solutions, while trusting in the meantime to a general outbreak of tolerance and universal brotherhood.

"...I'm a broken-hearted idealist," I replied at last in a voice that, out of wonder or surprise, fluted in my throat. I realized as soon as I spoke that, while such an answer would not stand for much in formal philosophy, it held a significance for me that another could scarcely fathom.

His slab-like features made no provision for subtle nuances of feeling which show in changing muscle tensions around the eyes, mouth, or jaw line, so that I found it impossible to tell what he was thinking, but I felt that behind the bones of his face the flames of a pale pentecostal fire burned without warming and consumed without replenishing his spirit. He shifted his body, stacked his fists on the ledge, and rested his chin on them. Then he said,

"Tis nae wunder tha' w'kinna bear questions huse answers are no' available. They sit in th'mind like the holes dug furr buildings tha' nivver went oop."

He sounded to me as though he had learned English in a language lab, as I am sure I did to him. I liked his imagery though, and, took his words for the invitation hidden within them, but the uncertain stonework checked my impulse to close the distance between us. The plunging background swayed when I looked down. Concentrating then, I ventured a step closer as casually as possible and leaned my forearms on the wet stone sill of an arrow shelf. Then, with careful nonchalance, I said,

"It sometimes puzzles me why a nice chap like Jesus is supposed to have killed the fig tree."

He fixed me with a basilisk eye. I felt that if I moved my head his gaze would travel alongside me and out into space. Then, having started, I decided to hazard in addition,

"I mean...when you get right down past the surface civilities of even a state religion, you really aren't far from the jungle drums, are you?"

I looked at him evenly then, curious. I saw now that his eyes were actually pale green, the color of shallow sea water, with a core of fierceness at their center wherein burned the wasting fire. He looked away and in a moment cleared his throat. It had the dry, rustling sound of bats' wings. His laughter, I then discovered, sent more bats to flight.

"Are ye challengin' me, then?"

"Not at all."

"Och. I relish a gude challenge."

"I guessed as much," I said, grinning in response and noting the grey-blue color of his skin in the cold. I liked his comment and what it revealed about him. He remained motionless, motionless that is, as possible in his circumstances. In his freezing body, he made tiny, almost imperceptible shifts, redistributing invisible tensions in measured increments of shuffle along his joints and nerves. It seemed that even the disciplined reflexes of martyrs and hermits could be made to twitch if brought far enough from the creature comforts. I thought suddenly of a building being watched by firemen. He certainly didn't sound or seem like a stupid person, and I wondered if he was trying so hard to suppress his trembling in hope that the pain itself might at least serve him as a coherent expression of some mystic mania and thus substitute for the accountabilities of formal existentialism.

He leaned back, crossed his arms and hugged himself for a moment, swaying slightly in place like lovers in a dance hall. Then his fingers, as though they were apart from the anguish inside him, tightened on his shoulders.

"Have ye nae fear'a rretribution?" Another flung challenge.

"...Well..." I decided to plunge ahead. "I'd like to think that the universe eventually exacts its price for misdeeds," I said, "but the traditional punishments threatened in scripture seem a bit unwieldy. You know—fire, brimstone. All rather terrestrial threats. Where do they keep it all? ...I don't know if a soul takes up much room, never having seen one, though I may have been in the presence of a few. ...But the whole thing is presented to us in purely physical terms, images intended to impress the peasants. A little Earth Science goes a long way in putting some of these colorful notions to rest...And besides, I've never really liked being talked down to, being spoken to like a simpleton whose faith can be manipulated by the depiction of infernal torments."

There followed a long silence between us, during which I had time to develop the fear that I had offended him. While I worried about how to extricate myself from this awkward situation, it began to rain again. Tall grey verticals, hanging closely like wet towels on a line, moved over us, hissing dully across the fields. Just as they closed in upon us, he growled,

"Aye...Images are the literature of the layman...I've coom t'believe tha' th'whole kernel of life is t'be found in th' acquisition of knowledge...empirical an' spiritual...an' tha'in th'grey, roob'ry convolutions behind th'eggshell skull..." Here he jabbed his finger against his temple. "...repooses enooff a'heaven and hell alike as any man c'n adequately handle."

He removed his finger from the side of his head, and the pale bloodless mark it left on his skin was still there when his image began to fade in the downpour.

In far less than a minute I was soaked through with shockingly cold rain. My clothes fell against me heavily as the first of many shivers scurried through me, but I liked what he said, and I could think of no better way to have said it, and besides, I was suddenly taken by an unreasonable impulse to resist allowing him to out-suffer me. I decided to stay there as long as I could hold out. He might say something else interesting, and in truth I was enjoying the oddity.

He had expressed a liberating view of life, non-fatalistic, in which a person took his judgment with him, free of the ominous specter of Almighty Vengeance; but it seemed that for him, it meant the very heart of his conflict. I suspected that in him the two great forces of arbitration were locked in a constant battle for command of his soul. His tormented conscience was host to a relentless inquisition in which they might ramify infinitely in irrevocable convergence, perhaps finally to consume from within the very object of their struggle, leaving him burnt out with only the outer walls remaining, from whence a little ghost-like flame hisses forth.

As I stood there on the battlements with the frigid water pelting my face, I realized for the first time that, without really thinking about it, I had traveled un-returnably far from the conceptual collisions of popular culture. I had become immersed in circumstances far distant from the technical strenuousness of ordinary life, where the proper steps yielded both everything and nothing. I felt an unexpected kinship with this clean, limited man, who for all I knew, was up here trying to freeze his torment to death, while I was, what?...following some belabored effort of assimilation ecology? Anyway, I thought, men who have been ineluctably married to fatality on a basis far surpassing that of ordinary civility do not want to fritter away their lives on nonsense, even if they're going about it the right way.

"Yes," I yelled into the wild gusts, "you're right. Hell is just a condition. But it's a condition that can attach itself to place...to physical places. I was in one not long ago. A sweltering, chaotic wilderness filled with random horrors and ignominious death...I suppose trying to keep one's soul unsullied may have been a subconscious effort, but sometimes...sometimes the dirt got on you, just by having participated in the...pageant." I stared into the gloom, instantly sorry that I had said so much and angry that I had allowed the war to intrude upon the moment.

"I'm Wilf," came his voice out of the rain.

I turned, glad of his gesture, but the movement caused fresh contact with my wet clothes.

"John," I smiled aloud to his diffused form. It seemed to nod.

"Well, Brother Wilf, thank you, but I think I'll go in now. It looks like rain."

"Aye," he said, and a smudge rose in the white cascade. "Come."

I picked my way uneasily down the wet, uneven stones to the ground, with Wilf following. I was soaked, and between the precarious descent and the cold, could not control my shivering. As we approached the rear entrance to the house, he touched my arm, and in a gruff whisper, which gave me to understand that the rules of silence were in affect beyond the door, he croaked,

"Would ye care fr'a wee tincture?"

"Uh..." It took me a few moments to realize what he meant, but his invitation continued.

"Meet me dayne in the rreadin' rrume in twenty minutes."

I went back to my room and wrung out my wet clothes in the tub. Then, still in a clench of shivering, jerked on some dry ones and hurried back into the corridor and down to the library fireplace. I was warming my back at the fire, thinking over Wilf's remark about images being the literature of the layman, when he appeared in the doorway to the adjoining room. He had changed into a somewhat faded but clean, dry habit. His long hair was slicked back from his face and tied with a piece of dark ribbon, though the effort left the impression of a hastily groomed vagabond. He carried a dark crockery bottle in one hand and two small glasses in the other. With a gesture for me to stay, he crossed to join me by the fire.

He unstopped the strange-looking bottle and decanted into the glasses a cinnamon-amber liquid the color of sun-lit tea. He indicated the one for me, and together we picked them up. The fireplace trembled in the glass. I held it under my nose and inhaled its heavy, earthy smell of peat moss and something like cigarbox wood, carried on fumes which went immediately to the center of my head. I saluted him with it and took a speculative sip.

It was unlike anything I had ever tasted—complex, and difficult to compare. It had a flavor mixed of sweet cloves, leather, and meadow grass, finished off with hot swamp gas blown through tobacco leaves, and it burned all the way down. It was wondrous; so pure and strong, at first I thought it was home-made brandy but soon realized in the aftertaste that I was experiencing full strength Highland malt whisky for the first time. This was the real thing, before it is watered down to make it safe, blended away and bottled to make it identifiable, and shipped out in much diluted form to the world, where its sadly anemic descendants are popularly known by the geographic generality, "Scotch."

As its warmth spread in gentle effusion through me, I looked my appreciation at Wilf, who grinned back in the play of shadowed firelight like a delighted wolf. Despite its strength and early effect, we had a second glass each and sat staring into the fire for a long while. I felt drowsy and unexpectedly comfortable in his troubled company and believed that such moments were rare for him, too.

Then he fell asleep so suddenly that I thought at first he had died. The flesh of his face fell slack, and his mouth hung open in awful stillness. Soon he began to emit little hog whimpers. It must be exhausting, I thought, to live with his medieval torment. His words had revealed a surprising objectivity, yet he threshed in fundamentalist questions. Was he the eponymous anchorite, trapped in a commune, or simply some misplaced misanthrope haunted by the terrors of lost dreams and fled youth?

As the room turned dark around us, the dying firelight on his lifeless face could have come from the 15th century. Ochre highlights played upon rumpled browns, then faded into darkness, as in some ancient and neglected painting. The anachronistic ironies that attached themselves to him remained, even in repose, and lent their touch to other things about.

Brother Wilf seemed to be a visitor from another age, a lost spirit lodged in a place where time has stopped, where life has nowhere to go, and events unfold in ritualistic pace so slowly that a residue of everything that has happened lingers on in the surrounding objects themselves. He had shown me an unexpected kindness, and I worried for him that dreams buried alive often rise and walk in the night.

The red coals that glowed in the fire's black heart seemed secret now and improbable, like the eyes of things disturbed that had best be left alone. As I watched them and listened to the rain outside, I wondered how much more we might see if the world were lit only by lightning flashes from the Elizabethan stage. What strange insights and miraculous perceptions might our senses receive amid the crash of thunder and the hurtling flicker that give a peculiar and momentary shine to an old tree on a wet night? Our world might be transformed from its staid arrangements of laws and uniformity of expression into one where the unexpected and blinding illumination constituted our faith in reality.

That evening at Vespers the music made me cry. Or maybe it was the silence.

5
Dawning

Over the course of following weeks, with no let-up in the weather, my self-imposed confinement to the house began to tell in a gradual simplification of movement and expectation, as I began to adopt both the mood and the routine of the cloister. I enjoyed the simple pleasures of my job in the kitchen and took quiet satisfaction in the results that accrued to my efforts there. Increasingly, I learned to abandon myself to individual tasks with an unfettered intellectual absorption that focused my physical efforts to gratifying effect.

I learned to relax somewhat my hard-earned guard and my ear for small arms fire, although a few unexpected noises served on occasion to set back my relationship with this new-found comfort, and incidentally, with the staff too: once, while I was enjoying a tranquil period of scouring at the sinks, someone accidentally tipped a stack of wooden bowls onto the stone floor. They clattered down in the rapid staccato signature of automatic rifle fire. Instantly shocked from reverie, I threw myself to the floor and low-crawled several desperate feet before coming to my senses. I sprang up with my heart pumping sodden in the backwash of adrenaline even before the bowls had all stopped wobbling. I stood there, trying to cover my wracking gasps, weak-kneed and embarrassed. The brothers stood still, arrested of movement, and stared with their good open faces, not knowing what to do. I knew that I would not be able to explain it to them, and for a long moment we simply looked back at each other with tentative, indulgent smiles.

I was afraid they would think me erratic, even dangerous, and I hastened to make light of it with a series of dismissive gestures as I returned to the sinks, but the truth was that the incident had shaken me, and for a long time afterwards I was jumpy and self-conscious. I felt trapped in a bottle of smoke, unable to take a full breath and worried about what they thought of me. It mattered to me that they not think of me as some mad refugee, some quirky intolerant who had appeared among them with hidden instabilities, with anomalous discontinuities. I went about for a time afterwards trying deliberately to appear normal, but of course any artificial formality in a place so free of conceits just made it worse. I soon felt the balance to which I had offered myself careening down, and I abandoned the strenuous act.

The experience of their life was rich in unadorned truths, and in a short time there, I had begun to benefit by the lessons of simplicity that it held. As I had no wish for them to see the clouds in the background of my travels, I welcomed both the privacy and, though I didn't fully recognize it at the time, the incentive to introspection brought by the rule of silence.

In the context of society at large our lives often seem remote from the plainest and most important truths. The brothers had invited me into an environment in which this gap was seamless. Their lives were dedicated to closing it, while I often walked the edge of my perceptions, pondering my limitations, and wondering at the impenetrable nature of the world. They moved and worked with tranquil confidence, which by contrast served to illuminate my own failures, my own fears and weakness.

I thought simplistically that the reason the familiar and the evident can often seem so remote is because we have increasingly separated ourselves from nature by replacing a humanistic, emotional response to things with an analytical mentality honed by long exposure to mechanical technology. Perhaps the reason is simply that the required naïveté is not easy to retain or to re-acquire in a world filled with ready manufactured distractions. The insights of one hour are crowded out by the events of the next, so few of us can hold on to our primary selves long enough to discover the momentous truths about our own natures and those of the hurtling earth to which we all cling. Norman Angell (another appropriate name) wrote, "It is quite in keeping with man's curious intellectual history that the simplest and most important questions are those he asks least often."

In a cloistered environment, though, you come quickly to the stark terrain of your own core values where you are introduced to a rare form of seclusion in which the surface tension that binds your outward persona gives way. Proper solitude is devised from a corollary inspired by the prevailing noise discipline: that silence requires conscious management. Self-awareness, and thence broader insight, results from both the effort to find it and from the absence of distractions engendered by this ancient and simple control. For the mind never drifts free of thought. It constantly fastens itself to some point within the realm of ideas. It thinks for a living. When outside influences upon its activity are reduced, it turns inward to the nature of personal reality and the relationship that the self bears to whatever lies outside.

Without consciously deciding to do so, I found in my own silence an increasing speculation about the nature of knowledge. What can you say that you actually know from the signals you get through the senses? What does it mean to "know" something? The senses, after all, are often fooled. You can press the corner of your eye and induce double images. You can sense the presence of things unseen, hear sounds that others cannot; and what of the ghostly army that marched through me on the road? The experience was real, yet what can I say I actually know of it?

I began to develop an urge for awareness that I had not known when given the chance in school to dedicate myself to the deliberate acquisition of knowledge. I saw with sudden clarity the superfluity of most of the communication that binds greater society. Of course we all know this when we really think about it; there are countless jokes about it, but what I came to believe is that most people talk simply because they feel that sound is more manageable than whatever presence haunts their silences.

To the casual observer a monastery might seem an island of antiquated passions, of obsolete values, and indeed this was not a place that encouraged change, whose inhabitants had to adapt to every new moral perception, every whiff of theological fashion. It was utterly without pretense. I saw it nowhere stated but came to realize that truth will eventually rise from the silences induced by concentration on work and study.

Guilt was not some poison in the sacramental wine for these men, nor did the general brotherhood seem tortured by imponderables and the inventions of middlemen. These men had a foothold on the secular world as well. Indeed, I noticed that some had Royal Navy tattoos on their arms, smeared and fading with age, but still legible. Having rejected the larger world, they nonetheless lived for the most part not entirely outside it, but rather on its edge, a place where blind religious faith was confined to a corner.

In the past, the concept of perfection as an ambition had been presented to me by particularly subservient sorts of individuals, usually church people, who were so saintly that you would think boredom was just an extended pause before some eternal truth was to be uttered, and who seemed to be spending their whole lives waiting, with sickly little smiles of imminent omniscience on their lips; but here, the idea, if it existed at all, was free of this sanctimonious idealism. Here it was earthbound and rooted in the practical. You strove to disengage yourself from superfluities in the interest of becoming the best at your own work, and thus, the best that you could be.

6
Bertrand

The storm that had pursued me into the monastery lasted on and off for five weeks, alternating between ice-laden curtains of rain that flung itself through the somber hills, where it rattled on the frozen grass and beat down the chimney smoke, and fleeting, incongruously warm periods of bright breezy morning that passed like trapped fragments of summer, herded along by a dark and turbid fog. Sometimes the weather changed so abruptly that I was startled from some preoccupation by the clash of sudden rain on the window glass or by a quick fall of shadow across the page.

I was "promoted" in the kitchen from pot washer to something akin to Baker's Assistant, where I was delighted to learn that one of the perks accompanying the job of mixing dough and stirring glazes for Brother Michael was tasting the finished product. Michael's artistry was not confined to the quiet sense of whimsy with which he produced his caricatures in dough, for in his long, self-taught experience he had invented concoctions for the Staff of Life that were probably unknown anywhere else, and his "dessert" breads—sweet rolls, cinnamon buns, cakes, and flavored dinner bread—were the best I have ever tasted.

He evidently appreciated the food he made on many levels, sometimes on the basis of its density and weight, presumably also for its power to engender a certain hardy stoicism and focus, but mainly because it was fun. In addition, he was an obvious beneficiary of his own efforts at mealtimes. Although the creations were not fully appreciated by some of the more serious-minded of the brethren, it always seemed to me that a quiet compliment lay in being selected as a subject for his leavened portraiture, and even the failures were tasty.

There was a good-sized garden just outside the back entrance to the scullery, located in the lee of the house, where it could take advantage of what sunlight leaked through the hurrying clouds, while finding some shelter from most of the prevailing winds. It had been designed in cruciate form like the ground plan of a cathedral, and was a place of quiet contemplation where, I was about to learn, the paradoxes of nature were present on a scale capable of inducing profound humility.

After the kitchen was cleaned following the mid-day meal on a day of rare sunshine, I stepped outside with the intention of sitting a little while in the warmish light, and there found Brother Colum in the garden watching ants.

Colum had been sand deaf from birth, with disastrous results for his speech. His voice was atonal and without expression, on those rare and brief times when I heard it. He had no sense of modulation, and even with hard listening his hesitant, glottal pronunciation mixed with native brogue took a moment to turn from noise into language. He must have been aware of it for he spoke very little, but he had a beguilingly open nature that freed him from reservations about addressing a stranger.

He was a little younger than I, with unruly ginger hair and clear, pale skin of almost luminous clarity, like the veiny pallor of a sausage casing. He comported himself with a cautious sort of intensity that would have appeared almost comical in a hearing person, but which came, I assumed, from a reassignment of labor among his senses, resulting in the transfer of additional amperage to his electric blue eyes and red cheeks.

He was crouched at the edge of a flower bed, staring intently past the hardy highland blooms. I sat on a bench nearby and watched him. He flicked his eyes at me in quick recognition, then returned his gaze to whatever was demanding such concentrated attention. There was something careful about his manner, as though he had once been badly scalded and so would approach all things tentatively for fear they might be boiling, yet his affliction had transferred to his face the habitual appearance of deep focus. He hunkered there with his hands on his knees, staring at the ground between the rows of flowers.

It was a fine, clear day for the appreciation of gardens, and I saw nothing unusual in his posture. I assumed that he was just assessing in his strange way the progress of his plantings. The plants were healthy, too—hearty and strong, as though they had burst from the ground full-grown. I wondered if they grew so vigorously because, in this land where even the ground held memory, they knew their season would be short. The robust blossoms nodded on an intermittent breeze and glared with fierce color at the sky. On a distant hillside beyond, the wind and sunlight made the long grass flicker like fire.

Colum spoke suddenly, in a blare of gibberish—a strangled, peevish hiccup, sudden and unintelligible at first. When I turned, he looked hard at me and repeated what I then realized were the words,

"How much noise do ants make?"

What a wonderful question. Wonderful in the true sense of the word. Other than having heard their relentless chewing and the skittering tramp of their armies in the jungle, the question of vocal noise at their level had never before incited my curiosity. I had thought I was as familiar with the kingdom of insects as I ever wanted to be, having left some of the Southeast Asian ones enough of my blood to keep a small animal going for some time, and having encountered a few that were as dangerous and unpredictable as humans had set me somewhat against them. Flies in particular had long seemed to me a waste of an improvident god's creative energy.

I looked at him and smiled with a shrug. Curious though, I began idly to scan the earth at my feet. It is true that sound enhances visual perception, and some things, like music, can only be clearly understood through sound—or, as I had enjoyed learning in the chapel, by the silence that fills the spaces between the notes and then rushes in to take over when they stop.

Soon I began to see that the ground around the flower stems stirred with tiny movement. A few black ants were hobbling past along the grains of soil in what, for them, must have been pretty rugged terrain. It became evident that they were following a traffic pattern of sorts. Not a formal one, in that they were leaving a discernible path in the dirt, but even a brief study of their movements revealed that there was a certain trail discipline in their progress. Despite wide separation between individuals—sometimes long minutes would pass before I would see another—those bound toward Colum's end of the garden always passed the opposing traffic to the right. Just the reverse of British highway rules, amusing to think.

I watched them for a while and began to see a kind of intelligence in their behavior. If not intelligence, at least a more or less predictable manifestation of instinct, and it aroused my curiosity. Despite having spent much of my life in countries that harbor a wild profusion of insects, I have always had a decidedly uneasy relationship with them. Here, though, I became intrigued with the tiny progression, and putting my childhood fear of even small monsters aside for the moment, I decided to back-track their movements.

I got down on my hands and knees and crawled along the garden verge, eventually arriving at the opposite end of the flower bed from that where Colum was now engaged in some close inspection of the cut bank. After a few minutes I was able to pick up the tiny trail where it emerged from the wild grass that fringed the scalloped tool cuts along the edge of the bed. Soon a small black, segmented body with its feelers whirling, picked its way out from under the blades of grass and moved down the striated precipice left by a trowel. It hesitated at a clod of dirt, turning first one way and then the other, before deciding to pass it on the right, and continued south.

No matter how close to the creature I tried to place my ear, I heard no sound. Its tiny scrabbling progress emitted nothing that reached my hearing. I wondered if whatever sound vibrations it might be releasing were simply too faint to overcome the air resistance. Or maybe I was catching it at a time when it just wasn't muttering to itself.

Colum's question had introduced the intriguing notion of scale. Surely, the world of life that existed in the few millimeters of dust that covers the earth was just as vibrant and dangerous as our own, filled with challenges and with the croaking and cackling, creaking and ticking of insects in their thousands; shrieks, hoots and grunts, all against a deep background of steady mysterious sound, not to mention the air above, filled with the whip and lash of grass and the ghostly panting of butterflies—all of it beneath our hearing. There must be a vibrant world down there that we simply can not hear if it doesn't howl or snort along frequencies compatible with the gasses that comprise the air.

The little ant moved constantly, with minor hesitations, though not always straight ahead. He wasn't carrying anything, so I assumed that he was outbound, perhaps on reconnaissance. He behaved like a person under threat. There was an urgency to his movements and numerous little diversions to the sides, as though scanning nervously the unexplored terrain which bordered the trail. The Forbidden Zone? I began to sympathize.

When do they rest, I wondered. I could never remember seeing a resting ant. Perhaps they have to stay in motion for some reason, the way it is said that sharks do. Maybe movement is necessary for their survival, for surface cooling, or perhaps it is simply in response to some impenetrable evolutionary mandate.

Once he dislodged a tiny bit of dirt which moved as he brushed past. I wished that I had a simple paper drinking straw to use as a listening funnel. Even that diminutive side-swiping collision must have compressed enough air molecules to have loosed a single, short-lived sound wave. It made sense to think so. After all, sound is simply the product of colliding molecules. His antennae were probably bombarded constantly by invisible particles that were ringing his swiveling head like a bell.

I tried to imagine what it would be like at the lower micron levels, constantly peppered by whizzing spheres, humming with atoms in constant collision. Down between the quantum particles there is just the icy vacuum of empty space. Life at even the molecular level must be cold and hazardous. I saw a frozen world in which all surrounding space was filled with colored spheres connected by sticks—enormous versions of the wooden molecule models from school room physics class—clattering about like errant Tinker Toys. Of course ants are unimaginable magnitudes larger, but I couldn't help wondering if their relative proximity to quantum levels gave them any experience of that invisible universe—any rumblings underfoot. Trying to see the world from the scale of what I imagined an ant's reality to be began to personalize him. I began to think of him as "Bertrand."

I wondered if he could feel the breeze, if the movement of air currents reached him that close to the ground. Electromagnetic radiation reaches us from wherever in the universe a collision or explosion has compressed gases at such high temperatures as to release energy in the form of waves that radiate out across the empty reaches of space as from a pebble dropped in a pond. Pulses crested with the microscopic fragments of dead stars, fungal spores, and charged particles that interact with earth's magnetic field to hit us as radio waves, along with molecules of atmospheric gases spun across the vastness from the interiors of distant stars in tiny supersonic shock waves. Yet when they get here they simply bounce off, or pass through, our unfeeling skin after drifting in cold space at over 1000 miles per hour for billions of years. What irony, to arrive unnoticed after all that. I had read that some of them, reduced to about a 25th of an inch from crest to crest by the time they hit us, have been traveling since the beginning of time, just after the Big Bang.

I wondered if Bertrand could hear them, or if he had to struggle at all against the rhythmic pressure of their bombardment, or if they burned him the way the longer ones that whip in from the sun can burn us. Maybe that's the reason he kept moving. What might cosmic waves feel like, slamming into the ground at every hand? Could they account for his odd, high-heeled gait? What might their incessant plunge sound like to him?

Even though the pulses pass below the spectrum of human hearing, one can actually listen in on them when tuning a common radio, because the static between channels is part of their amplified noise. The ceaseless racket would be maddening if we could hear it all the time. Could Bertrand?

Along with all that, we're constantly hammered by a lot of human-generated radiation, too—the faint and distorted signals that pass through us from almost every radio and television station on earth. There are bursts from taxi dispatchers, airline pilots, Morse code from distant ships—and even the dying fragments of mindless word salad screamed into a combat radio by some despairing countryman of my own, half way around the world.

All this electromagnetic commotion pushes the air molecules around with an unseen hand. This must be why sound waves do not carry very far. Since they are just the brute movements of air molecules themselves, then of course even a cross breeze quickly batters away the refined shape of the wave. This would explain why noise carries better through certain solids and better inside than outdoors. I thought again of the voices in the chapel and how the stone walls bounced their tones back in distended reverberation, a condition that would render any but slow, prolonged intonations unintelligible.

Bertrand put on some speed and got out ahead of me while I was distracted by all this garbled speculation, and I crawled into the first furrow of the garden to look for him. In the lower stillness among the tall flowers, I became aware of the wavering hum of bees. Pollen drifted between the shadows that fell in purple semaphore across the rows. The dry earth at the base of the stems was sprung like cracked tiles, as though the plants had, indeed, been thrown from the ground.

From below, it was clear that most of the blossoms favored the east. Why do they do that, I wondered. Could there be something in sunlight itself that actually inhibits their development, so that the shaded side grows faster, thus forcing the stalk to bend in the direction of the longer, or the more refracted, light?

Bertrand was two or three feet away, negotiating a curled leaf which obstructed his path like a fallen log. I ducked back out and moved along a parallel row to keep up with the little creature, whom I was coming to admire for his singularity of purpose. He seemed to know his orders. The fragrance of the blossoms must have been hitting him like factory smoke, while the dust of flowering anthers fell on him in chunks.

Actually, the same radiation that stirs the air floats the pollen and suspends visible dust particles, too. All this energy passing by, gives support to some other stuff that's large enough to see, things which move about us constantly in hovering transport, because the air molecules collide against them from all directions in such numbers and at such high speed that it forms a constantly gusting micro-wind. If something is light enough, it can become suspended, bobbing along for hours, as if on a buoyant sea. This is how certain life-forms get around, too. It is an ideal open ocean for bacteria and viruses to migrate upon, until they encounter some unsuspecting host on his way home from a mini-mart in the rain.

Even Bertrand's steps were probably stirring up a multiplicity of particles I couldn't even see: launching invisible bits of soil, broken leaf hair, skin flakes, and tiny desiccated insect parts in considerable numbers. He moved in and out of shadow and passed behind a leafy stalk upon which a tiny grey spider had anchored one filament of its web. I wondered at the din of all this detritus crashing into its delicate net. How does a spider ever get any sleep?

Spiders, even small ones, have always given me the willies, and one of my defenses is just not to think about them, but here I realized that they also make heavy contributions to this remarkable warehouse of odd floating items that we, with high nonchalance, lump together as "dust." Pieces of their fur and minute chunks of their legs float about in great profusion, because spiders don't have exterior muscles on their joints and have to walk like robots, by hydraulic bursts of fluid into their hollow limbs. It's an ingenious but fragile system, and when they die, they simply fall apart, and their empty fragments dwindle away on the air currents.

I enjoyed this imaginary juxtaposing of magnitudes and thought what a harrowing life all this gave Bertrand. Being bombed by interstellar microwaves, and sidestepping tumbling body parts must make for a hard day. Since coming out of the twittering shadows of the grass, I figured he had covered about sixty feet of cosmic and terrestrial hell. I tried to estimate how far he had ranged and realized that, depending upon what time he set out, he could probably cover about 100 yards in a day, constantly beset with the warble of incoming particles and with intergalactic pulses thundering into the molecular soup all around; bacteria and cold viruses cackling eerily as they sailed by on the constant gale, not to mention the strange calls in the jungle, or the earth tremors from passing humans, or the sway of towering objects that blotted out the sun.

Eventually, he began to encounter traffic, as other ants converged with him in growing numbers. Some were carrying things, shouldering huge crumbs gathered from somewhere. Some carried bits of leaf that rocked in their progress like tiny sailboats, while others were simply plodding along the way he was, chin down as though burdened with dreadful information.

I looked up and was surprised to discover that the shadows had lengthened and that I had somehow inched my way along the entire garden to the end where Colum, now on his hands and knees, was engrossed in the activity at the entrance to a nest. Two small holes, worn smooth and bibbed with a fan of tailings, terraced beneath an embedded rock, had been mined out of the cut bank of the garden and stood like dark nostrils, breathing in and out the streams of scrambling insects.

So Bertrand was actually homeward bound after all. I wondered what he had to report. Whatever he knew, he'd come a long way with it. I crept around and joined Colum as little Bertrand emerged from the flower stems. He moved with greater surety now that he was on familiar ground, his articulated suspension system carrying the bulbs of his body delicately over the granulated surface in a rapidly seriated pattern of steps in which at least three legs were always driving. There was never a sequence in his pace which left unsupported time, as when horses and people run.

I wondered if our designs for tracked vehicles came from observing the movement of ants and held for a moment the amusing vision of military scientists in their lab coats, lying around on the ground in attitudes of close inspection with desktop magnifying glasses. Perhaps the image isn't far wrong, for indeed gun turrets do have an eerie resemblance to the magnified hip joints of insects.

Through how many less-efficient variations could that simple structure have evolved? Biochemists hold that evolution proceeds by random genetic changes—errors—and that each living thing is an experiment within the continuum of trial and error and temporary success. In nature, "correct" means whatever breeds survival. Always to demand established routes and habitual ways, then, is to go against the grain of life. To engage in continuing experiment is to reach for the only practicable definition of harmony that we have. So we are all just experiments on the part of nature, a gamble within the unknown, maybe for some new purpose, maybe for nothing. Our only task is to allow this game on the part of the primeval depths to take its course, to feel its will within us and to make it wholly our own. It would follow that our destination, both as a species and as individuals, is never a place in physical terms, no matter where we travel, but rather is a new way of looking at things. Given the interconnectedness of learning, then, a true journey, no matter how long the travel takes, has no end until the mind fails.

Nature always seems to deal in coordinated whole values, distributing even numbers of limbs to insects, birds and animals, providing balanced opposition in leaf growth, the helical array of willow blossoms, and setting the golden mean of 4:3 in the proportions of the nautilus shell the world over. In synergetic geometry there is no such thing as pi—that awkward, irresolute expression for the circle that is never truly squared, but wanders off the page in a gaggle of digits, carried to infinity. We are so used to applying certain physical characteristics to the world of nature that we lose track of the fact that it is we who impose them. In reality, nature is soundless, senseless, and colorless, merely the hurrying of material, endless and meaningless. It is we who create from the jumble of external physical phenomena the sounds, sense, colors and meanings that make up our emotional and intellectual lives. It is we who assign value and such notions as balance, quantity, and order to the world for reasons rooted in our own need, and it was only I who dictated independently that Bertrand moved in a certain fashion, that he was busy, curious, or determined. It was I who decided what "he" was, based upon my own perceptions.

Here the question returned of "what is knowledge?" Perhaps, despite the flaws of Cartesian logic, all things depend for their very existence upon a mind to perceive them. In such case, I would be Bertrand's objective correlative, for what can be said to occur unobserved?

Bertrand entered the congestion that thronged toward the entrance. I was struck by the extent of the population. It seethed with frantic purpose, in places even overrunning itself. There is something awe-inspiring about the sight of any living creatures in uncountable numbers. It stirs some atavistic chord whose note belongs to the distant days when we were a true part of the animal ecology; when the sight of another species in unthinkable hosts brought fears or hopes no longer applicable. I tried to keep track of the little creature, but he soon became absorbed in the anonymity of the crowd. Then he was gone.

I looked up, suddenly alone. As I emerged from the conjectural adventures of Bertrand's world, and my own reality reasserted itself, I felt momentarily displaced and somehow abandoned. Yet it had been fun, and realizing that I had been free for the first time in a long while to luxuriate in such childlike imaginary speculation made me smile.

The air was cool. I breathed it in and looked around. Long shadows fell eastward as the sun broke beneath late afternoon clouds for what promised to be a long, well-lighted evening. I had spent hours in another world, unaware of the passage of time, and returned now to my own reality as though from a journey. I sat there on the ground with Colum feeling content but a bit remote and tenuous. I thought about little Bertrand, underground somewhere, gasping out his report and being debriefed by the elders. ("...Now let's get this straight, Number Seventy-Nine Thousand, Six-Eighty-Three. You say there's an endless jungle a half day's march from here? Preposterous! Now go get cleaned up, and behave yourself.")

The ant's patrol had been an adventure for both of us, one in which for me the outer eye had opened an inner one, and I felt an unfamiliar kinship with all the life that swarmed about me. When your cares are sufficiently pared of their outworn chattels, then a grain of sand, or a blade of grass, or the movements of an ant, can take on the significance of the finger of Jehovah on the Sistine Chapel. There is a therapy in observation of the ordinary and the obvious. I recalled the old railroad crossing signs that warned: Stop, Look, and Listen. Walt Whitman called it "the profound lesson of reception."

New ways of seeing can disclose new things: the radio telescope revealed quasars and pulsars, and the scanning electron microscope showed us the whiskers of the dust mite. So, what if you turn the question around? Do new things make for new ways of seeing? The answer has to be a resounding yes. The discovery of America sent shock waves through the Church's interpretation of the Old Testament, just the way modern geology has impugned the mosaic account of creation. The invention of television, and in particular its live coverage of both the Vietnam War and the space program, has altered our world view in one generation. When before has time, its chance gestures, its gratuitous orchestration, been captured in the form of an instant replay?

The Americans were working up to the launch of a manned mission to the moon. I wondered if it would affect the way we perceive our world as profoundly as did Galileo's telescopes. For now there could be no church-imposed recantation.

I sat in the grass at the head of the garden and tried to absorb the scene. The flowers shouted out their color to the grey stone walls and the now darkening winter sky. This was one of those moments, rare in adulthood, when some of the wonder of childhood briefly returned. I gazed about, filled with delight and stirred by vague longings and hopes. I realized, sadly, how much I had lost the capacity to be exhilarated by natural beauty and the occurrence of little things. The enchantments of adolescence had become eroded, stifled by the obsessions of an adult world. I gradually became infused with a delighted tranquility. I wanted to be nowhere else, to hold those moments for as long as I could, to try to let what I saw and how it made me feel become a part of my being so that it might lodge in memory to remain there as a sensitizing influence on my judgment for as long as I lived.

The amusing landscape of thoughts that I had traversed with Bertrand renewed my conviction that the world has a purpose more profound than its description, and that we ourselves have an existence separate from our day-to-day experience, somehow deeper than our circumstances. I looked at Colum, who sat nearby with his knees drawn up, alone in the rapture of his privacy, and wished that I could talk to him about these things.

I lay back on the ground and turned my head to the side. A little clump of wild flowers waved gently nearby, magnified to a prehistoric forest by their closeness. Twenty feet away a small bird landed and strutted about, busy with its affairs, rustling its feathers and calling unmusically from time to time, like an impatient customer in a deserted store. Behind him, the rapid rise of low clouds, scrumbled into wadding and vaporous with drizzle, announced the end of what had promised to be a golden evening, but I welcomed the restless pulse of uncertainty they imparted to the air.

I was learning that what appeared to be a monastic life of narrow seclusion in fact hid riches of discovery and an enviable kinship within the chancery of nature, and I found the brothers to be courteous, hospitable, hardworking, pious, and funny. My comfort in their company grew, and along with almost daily indulgence in the library, I was drawn into a deepening respect for the greatness of their enterprise, the essential civilizing influence of their order:

For centuries men like these had seen the hordes burst in, both barbarian and royal; had lived through the sacking of their abbeys, the burning of their fields, and the murder of their brothers in frightful circumstances. Even the invention of the printing press must have dealt the monasteries a painful blow, usurping their leadership in learning and delivering the power to produce books into the hands of secular interests, whose copy work was thus faster and whose output was greater.

Yet, rising in darkness to pray at length before first light, awaiting the workday while illuminating the shadows with the flame of their devotion, they had gone on cherishing fine books, parchments, and manuscripts, and they had continued to read, moving their lips over words that have been handed down for hundreds of years and which they will pass along for the hundreds to come.

I was among men from whom a daily unflagging stream of worship, or at least profound contemplation and a volume of prayer, ascends, from which, if it is efficacious, we are all the beneficiaries. Among people pledged to these spiritual allegiances, "Bless you" and "Pray for me" are not just polite formulae, but declarations and requests for definite, effective acts. I tried to imagine the value and fame in ancient times, before the growth of skepticism, of men whose lives were spent hammering out in silent factories these imponderable but priceless benefits. These are the anonymous well-wishers who, in both thought and deed, attempt to reduce the moral overdraft of mankind.

In my increasing admiration for their discipline, I came in surprise to the realization that my own planes of need were shifting. Their quiet ways offered a kind of solace, and I found unexpected contentment in their domain of prudence and sanctity. Gradually, my interest in good traveling weather diminished to the point where I realized one day that I had stopped checking.

For my hosts, the place was a springboard into eternity; for me, a retiring place to rest awhile before returning more contentedly to the hurrying world. Strange that the same habitat should prove favorable to ambitions so glaringly opposed.

7
Harvesting

On a clear, breezy afternoon, while the North Sea wind held a mountainous accumulation of grey clouds at bay to the west, I was feeling confident enough in my new surroundings to explore a bit further the grounds of the old manor. At this time, despite my feelings of compatibility with what I was learning about the lives of these men and the curious acquaintanceships I had with some, particularly brothers Wilf and Colum, I remained very much aware of my "otherness." In striving always to see myself as they might, I kept my movements contained, modest and silent. For this reason I had been unwilling to presume upon whatever freedom there may have been to investigate beyond the main building.

However, on this day, emboldened by natural curiosity and drawn by the sunlight, I ventured forth with a vague hope of finding evidence to enrich my conjectures about what life on this isolated hill might have been like in the 14th century. Among the ancient grey outbuildings that fronted the woods behind the manor house I was surprised to discover within a small stone barn, not a cache of medieval weaponry, but an apparently serviceable black Woolsey automobile lurking in the shadows beneath a confection of dust. Faint splinters of light winked from the chromed grill and headlamp rims. A forlorn little four-seater French Citroen slumped dejectedly beside it, partly hidden under a dirty tarp. The packed earth beneath them was redolent of oil and atrophy. They seemed to look up at me with expressions of fading memory and lost opportunity.

Nearby, a tin gasoline can of questionable integrity sat propped off the bare ground on bricks. It was far too small to be of much service to automobiles. I lifted it by the carry handle and shook it. The liquid inside thunked, hollow and distant. I was surprised and amused, and oddly moved, in the presence of this equipment. Here, shut away from group consciousness and drafts, was the brotherhood's lifeline in case of medical emergency. Here was effortless access to a wider realm of products and services that might answer to their needs, and yet the machines were but flotsam cast up and abandoned on the shore of a hurrying world. The cars had been long neglected, settled upon cracked and flattened tires but with their keys ready in the ignitions. They had been relegated to sacrificial symbolism and beached before their time. Even the extra fuel was but a naive contingency.

I was oddly moved by this discovery, as though I had found two guard dogs being slowly starved to death. Though I could understand the brotherhood's rejection of the technological playthings of greater society in the main, I could not help but fear that in its selective isolation, the monastery might be found one day to be a bit too far removed; to be standing on its own air hose.

I backed out of the garage in a small chaos of sympathies and closed the doors again, partly to protect the cars and partly to shut away their sad whispers.

Later, while investigating the storage vaults beneath the flooring of the old tower, I came upon the parts to a relic from a by-gone era—an old horse-drawn harvester—the kind of tool known in the States as a dump rake. It pointed up the amusing generational gap to be found between the only mechanical conveyances I had seen on the place.

This device consisted of a long row of crescent shaped spring tines mounted on an adjustable rack between two tall, radially-spoked metal wheels. The driver, reins in hand, would sit on a scooped pan seat mounted on a flat spring to the rear, with his feet on iron foot pegs. Hay was collected until the tines of the rake were full, whereupon the operator tripped a lever that tilted the tines and dumped the hay. By continuing to rake and dump across the length of a field, long field-wide windrows could be created.

Clearly long discarded, the wheel assembly, including its solid ten-foot axle, had been separated from the frame and stood alone near the other parts, the rusting metal covered with a powdery orange rind. The curved tines of its raking mechanism had been dismounted and, draped in skeins of dusty spider webs, lay stacked together in the corner like a rack of collapsed ribs. The seat and other parts of the frame were propped carefully against the wall, as though the machine had been stored in mid-repair. Except for the rust and other garments of neglect, the individual parts seemed to my unpracticed eye to be in pretty good shape. Perhaps it had been delivered long ago in pieces, and there had simply been no one to assemble it.

Thus released from its attachments, the free-standing axle bore an incongruous resemblance to an Olympic bar bell. I rocked it speculatively with my foot and judged the assembly to be light enough to lift. I bent to the center of the bar and took a wide grip. An old familiar strain tugged across my shoulders and lower back as the wheels broke free of their crust of dried earth and came easily off the ground. Despite its length, I liked the heft and the grip afforded by the axle.

I lifted the wheels clear of some other equipment and carried them out into the grass, ribbons of cobwebs trailing from the spokes. I positioned them to give myself plenty of room, took an underhand grip on the bar and tried to curl it. The rims themselves were hefty, but their size and wide separation imparted a certain momentum to the effort, and I was able to lift the bar up to my chin in a more or less fluid movement. The wheels turned freely on their old grease, so the axle itself did not twist in my hands, and I was pleased to find that the bearings didn't squeak.

After some minor initial difficulty in balancing the long bar, I tried a few more. It was fun to discover that I could curl them about eight times, and with the work, the blood began to pump into the muscles of my arms and upper body with an old familiar pulse that warmed my skin and pounded in my temples. My upper body fibers tightened, and I began to slip into my old workout breathing rhythms with pleasure. Military presses proved much harder than the curls but served to convince me that the harvester wheels and axle were a good weight for general exercise.

Except for the monks who plied the fields far down the slope toward the sea cliffs, nobody was around. It was a pleasant cool day. The afternoon sunlight made the sky slant like a pale lid, and a gentle easterly breeze brought the scent of the sea and with it a hint of meadow grass and newly-turned earth. I decided to stay outside and try a whole routine.

Just inside the rear entrance to the residence was a hallway containing a few ancient wooden benches. I retrieved one of these and carried it into the yard where, lying back on it with the axle placed at the head of the bench, I tried a few triceps pull-overs.

After awhile, in the midst of a set of bench presses, I heard some giggling. With the axle poised overhead on trembling arms, I looked in the direction of the sound to find that I had an audience. A group of five young monks were watching with great amusement. They were grinning delightedly and hopping silently in place with barely-contained exuberance, their gestures and the play of their habits giving them the appearance of a girls' cheering squad. Colum was with them. He jumped and stamped his feet, pointed, and made excited speechless sounds. It reminded me of how the Vietnamese soldiers ("Indigenous Personnel") had gathered to watch us work out with old railroad axles, babbling excitedly in their incomprehensible gibberish.

I stopped and invited the brothers to try it. They grinned and huddled together, unsure but curious. Soon two were persuaded to come forth. Colum held back initially but squealed and danced about with childlike glee. I demonstrated the proper position to take on the bench, and carefully lifted the axle to each in turn, while standing by to guard against mishap. Eventually, all but one of them tried their hands at the bench press, with universally gratifying results. I was surprised at their strength. They were, too, and it pleased me to watch the joy of their discovery.

One takes a certain amount of natural leverage strength for granted until it is applied experimentally, when it is tested in some unusual way from time to time. Lifting dead weight is different from the daily use of tools designed for scratching in the earth. Trials in lifting can be dramatic to watch as well, and it amused me to see how happy they were to indulge in good-natured competition.

The workouts often drew an audience after that, along with a number of cautious participants who came apparently to test the validity of reports. At times they made me feel the author of something grand.

8
Terra Incognita

From the first morning I had seen it from the library windows, I had been curious about the old ruin on the cliff and hoped for a closer inspection. One early morning dense with fog I followed the field workers across the slopes. Their dim, hooded shapes, with cowls raised against the damp and with long tools riding on their shoulders like pole arms, they resembled a ragtag medieval army, gray and wordless as ghosts, trailing off into the ancient mists from which it had come. The damp grass brushed at my cuffs, while the air, weighted with moisture, fell wet upon my face and absorbed some of the sounds of our tramping.

I felt happy to be with them. On an adventure to hike down the hill for an exploratory visit to the old ruin, joining the brothers' daily tramp out to the fields seemed a good way to get there. I enjoyed the solemnity of their company, although their silent purposefulness served at the same time to emphasize my complete lack of responsibility and to isolate me in a dilettante's quandary. They had important work to do, and tagging along behind them made me feel like a politely-tolerated parasite. I thought again with mildly uncomfortable gratitude how carefree it was to be here among these anonymous, taciturn men, in contrast to the experience of other company only scant months before, burdened with the awful responsibilities of combat command.

Part way down the ridge, the still white miasma of fog began gently to separate at the seams where it transformed into slow billows traveling just above the ground. As the land dipped further away, we descended out of the mist, and our ragged line began to divide as the men decanted into various fields. The fog base that enveloped the higher ground from which we had come lay protectively overhead like a ceiling of concrete, grey and thick as architecture. It drifted in from the sea like a living thing, capturing the long rays of the rising sun beneath it and focusing their slanted light on the hillsides, where it spanceled the tiny figures that moved upon the green land with golden spikes and shadows.

I continued down the long slope of the ridge toward the ruined stronghold that, as I approached, took on a glowering aspect where it stood upon a grassy mound littered with tumbled stone at the edge of the cliffs. Even at a distance, it was an imposing defensive structure, standing now in ruins—silent sentinel to a time when an enormous tide of history was chased out by social upheaval and the invention of the cannon, leaving such places abandoned and stranded along civilization's shore like an isocline of death.

It proved to be farther away than it had looked from the higher ground, and by the time I approached to within a few hundred yards of the walls, the long downhill trudge had reawakened the edge of pain where the bullet fragment rode against my hip bone. I stopped to rest just inside the ruin's long, damp shadow at a place where a slice of ancient curtain wall cut diagonally into the hillside.

With the breeze-flung grass sighing all around, I sat down on one of the remnant base blocks to rub down the pain and to look over the outer defenses of the massive monument. Even as a forlorn and crumbling artifact standing in for the glory of a by-gone era, the placed seemed to leap from the ground before me. I tried to visualize the workers who had built it, wrapped in scratchy woolens and moving high upon some fantastic wooden scaffolding, slowly lifting the stones into place one at a time. How could such huge constructions be accomplished by illiterate workers in an era in which less than ten percent of the population could even read a plan, and most of those who could, pretty much ensconced in the religious houses?

The very mass and weathered age of the thing made me feel a tiny transitory creature whose fleeting life was even now passing unnoticed and would be long unremembered centuries before this structure would fall. I realized with a twinge of frustration that I didn't know enough, that I lacked the mental equipment to sufficiently divorce myself from my own era so as to escape the probability that I was pushing my own interpretation, conditioned by the present, onto these ruins. We can strive for a certain scholarly objectivity, but we are all programmed, be it ever so subtly, by our own times, when everything seems to matter intensely, even as it is disappearing. People who are interested in history, like kidnap victims, must try to learn where they are from the chinks of light that reach them through tiny holes in the blinds of the present.

Terra Incognita

While the building threw the powerful light of its long past into the yellow gleam of the new day, I felt myself in the presence of one of those rare slits in the curtain of time, when the stage lights come up and someone is about to speak. I continued to sit there admiring the old stone work and tried hard to understand its message long after my initial impulse to get up and look for an entrance had passed. I was a timid ambassador from another world awaiting instructions in a language I couldn't quite understand and was afraid to break the spell by moving.

Perhaps it stemmed from this feeling of displacement in time, but after a while, I began to sense a mild tremor of foreboding. At first it was intriguing, and I stood up. I could see nothing especially off-putting about the building. In fact, I wanted to explore it. That was the reason I had walked the better part of a mile down to see it. Yet I felt a passing but undeniable moment of strange reluctance to approach any nearer.

The angled tower, a high square donjon, rose with picture-book majesty before me in the morning sun which, pausing beneath the cloud deck, lanced through its cracks and upper loopholes. There were dark places in it, too, openings to the interior, which beckoned like the doors of a museum, yet held an odd promise of dread. It made me curious about what might have happened here.

I stepped to the side and ventured a few paces closer to change my angle of view. The upper stones of the tower suddenly seemed then to grow taller and, in an old trick of perspective, to begin moving against the scudding clouds. It was momentarily dizzying. Cracks in the ancient stonework were tufted everywhere with grass and little bushes that had managed to root in the crevices where the masonry was slow to drain water.

It was hard to tell if it had ever been battle damaged or was simply worn by wind and rain. Over it all hovered a palpable atmosphere of antiquity and the permanent solemnity of a graveyard. There was something intangible about it, remote in other ways than time. It was as though the place had intent, that it was somehow capable of withholding a certain psychic sensibility.

Its original entrance was a jagged black hole, inaccessibly high in the west-facing wall, its ramp and portal casements long crumbled away. I shook off the odd feeling and decided that I had already invested a considerable hike in coming to see it, and turning back in its very shadow would both invalidate the effort and leave me forever curious. Besides, how often does anyone get to explore a genuine castle that is not listed for tourism?

I walked up to the massive foundation stones, and stepping over some of the fallen masonry to the south, I entered the gutted remnants of an arcade, carried on slender columns and extending along a southward-lying pentice wall whose former symmetry stood delineated outward into the grass by a line of broken pillars, the ghostly bones of once-secluded ambulatories, now long cloaked in silence but for the wind. Here they presented another entrance. I stepped into the arcade and approached what must once have been an interior gallery to the great hall. The finished stonework was finer here than the solid blocks of the keep and appeared to have been added during later centuries when the occupants must have had more money and the leisure time for such refinements.

With some hesitancy I peered around the entrance in a small effort to reach back through the centuries, to share, however tenuously, in something grand that had once pulsed with life, with all the ideology, religious zealotry, greed, hate, fear, and love that animated its conjectural generations, their heraldic pennants presumably fluttering gaily in the sunlight of a bygone era.

Yet inside, the place bore an atmosphere of eruption and collapse. Its voluminous dark interior all but swallowed the misty light that spilled from breaches in the upper walls upon a wreckage of arrested history. Large portions of its roof and upper floors had fallen in ages ago, leaving its open stones to grass, its walls to sky and the weather. It was a mysteriously alien place in which order had been slowly fractured and linearity broken until human beings no longer fit.

I took two cautious steps into its roofless gallery, where I was startled by an explosion of small birds that cried in alarm and shied away, chittering down the wind, and a large black rook labored up with wings that went whoop, whoop, whoop, like a child's toy swung on a string. I caught my heart-beaten breath and laughed inwardly at the unexpected sounds. But the sudden activity and damaged silence seemed like illegible messages.

A few steps farther into the huge hollow, and the heavy walls barred almost all sound from outside as a black damp closed around me like a fist. The tiny crunching sound of my shoes on the flooring stones leapt and vanished through a sudden wall of darkness. Stacked blocks and giant stone columns soared into the abyss overhead, launching remnant ceiling beams into the vaulted gloom. The place held a sort of nightmare charm, not exactly scary but eerily without precedent in my experience, as I advanced tentatively into a dreamscape of remnant architectural achievement.

Much of the structure inside had fallen, the dead masonry jumbled on the floor, leaving in places a few broken buttresses that arced into empty space like unfinished thoughts. It looked like the setting of great intrigues, a place where the past and my version of the present were inexplicably woven with invisible links of iron that events themselves had forged while the world wasn't looking. Had happenstance, in league with a fleeting moment of awareness, brought me to stand alone at the precise point of their ghostly convergence?

The sea fortified the captive air with the tang of ocean-washed rocks and lent its weak light to a high row of shapeless clerestory openings through which it leaked onto the edges of things in faint metallic highlight. It was cold. Everything smelled of dampness and quiet desolation. The crumbling stonework in shadow was silver-black, like charcoal, with the same frail sculpted look of burned wood, but where the uncertain daylight struck the stones they were reddish and porous as cake.

At the far end of what must have been the great hall, about 20 feet up the wall, was a small arched bay that projected like a martin's nest, accessible in its time by some hidden stairway or a now gone story. Some breach behind this hanging pulpit allowed filtered daylight to hollow a glowing alcove out of the dim penumbra of the interior, and it was mostly this light that enabled me to see objects close by.

As I crept cautiously into the further darkness of the main keep, then paused to let my eyes adjust, a lid seemed suddenly to descend around me. It was probably just moving cloud cover outside, yet with it a palpable silence issued from the shadows. But for the spooky vibrancy the place had of things gone yet still there, all was motionless except for the stalking movement which my imagination imparted to the changing light.

Then, from high among the ruined arches came the watery gurgling sound of pigeons. I was unexpectedly glad of their familiar noise and surprisingly comforted to know that I wasn't the only living thing around. Just as I was thinking that perhaps it was only me that lent the place its gaunt restiveness, I was startled by the violent rush of the pigeons' sudden departure. I jumped and a faint squeak caught in my throat as they went flapping through piers of misty light, to disappear by some unseen opening. In the sault of adrenalin that followed, I heard my gasps and wondered if there was something besides my presence alone that had frightened them. I felt a fleeting need to lean on something to steady myself but then just as suddenly decided I didn't want to touch anything.

I stood still for a time, fighting the impulse to turn around. I tried to think about what those distant people had been like who occupied this stronghold in ancient times. I saw them now as dark, brutish survivors in an age lit only by feeble sunlight and fire, who slept with their dogs and ate with their hands. I could almost feel them moving about me. Was my anxiety, I wondered, simply due to an over-wrought imagination, or had it indeed been provoked by some unseen presence?

I was distracting myself with this image when it began to give way to the very real, hard-edged feeling that I was, in fact, not entirely alone in the place. I was unexpectedly overcome by a sure and irrational conviction that "they" were somehow still there. It was then that fear placed a dead hand on my shoulder, and I froze, standing still, instantly alert. I don't know where the idea came from, but it took hold, sending out quick rootlets of despair as my blood whelmed in its courses within me. I tried to swallow a sudden dry pain in my throat. Something crept up the back of my neck and through my hair.

I remembered the haunting I had experienced on the road weeks before and how it had been preceded by the same implacable kind of dread. There I had been outdoors, but the seeming threat had made me feel trapped inside the unseen structure of its malevolent intent. Here, I was inside, but in the cavernous and shadowy interior I felt the emptiness spread out around me in a vibrant silence, a silence in which the building seemed to be whispering to itself. The void overhead weighed down upon me, and the surrounding air felt compressed and still.

Then from the dark shadows and whispering corners, I thought I could hear the rustling of robes and muffled footsteps. I turned quickly to face the specter, only to find there a skulking creature made of fear. When I turned back it seemed that everything around me had just jumped back into place and now was gradually returning my stare.

I tried to gather my wits. After a moment more of hard listening, and hearing only my breathing and the surge in my ears, I got hold of myself. I felt silly at the power of my imagination and ventured another cautious step. But I knew in an instant that even movement was unwelcome. The shirt moved on my back. Something wanted me out of there, and the feeling was as real as any sentient, waking-state presence. I stood still, unsure, listening, and searched about among the effects of time's slow violence upon the silent architecture.

Then, with my whole being on alert, awed and fearful, and following the mandate of my need to escape, I decided I had to go ahead and move through the main hall toward a broken seaward wall where the morning light shaped a number of openings to the outside. I stepped carefully on among the lunging shadows and the wild flowers that grew incongruously between fragmented flooring tiles, my face burning, and with a child's fear that the slightest noise might dislodge from its dark recesses an echo of lost voices, or worse, some smoky vision.

Anxiety fled in little tremors along the surface of my skin as I crept past an inner-wall beehive fireplace. The broken capitols of two small support columns hung from its hooded vent like blunted fangs. Just then, a faint moan of wind from its hidden chimney heightened the life-like effect of a wide mouth drawing breath to scream, and just as I glanced at it, a terrifying image leapt into my mind: a splintered mirror suddenly healing itself to reveal a dreaming woman tucking up her hair! My throat caught as I stared into it, stunned to complete immobility! For long seconds, the vision was so vivid and of such shattering intensity that I could not tear myself away from it. It held me in utter thrall until at last, my breath burst from me in a loud animalistic yelp I had never heard before.

The sound of my cry broke the spell. It hummed about me in the empty room as I sprang to a window casement pursued by the hollow sound of my own breathing. A flutter of birds burst noisily overhead when I scrambled across the broken sill into the daylight and fell onto the ground outside. I wanted to call out for help, but the cry remained a voiceless echo in the back of my head.

Breathless and with my heart working hard in my chest, I scrambled to my feet in the rush to get away from the place. I hurried on toward the edge of the cliff, but there I was trapped between the end of the land and the looming consciousness behind me. I knew that if I turned suddenly to look it would not be there and would only come closer when I turned away again. Even if it spoke just at my ear, as it seemed at times about to do, when I turned there would be nothing there.

I gathered my breath and looked hard out at the North Sea, trying to calm myself by staring at something familiar and keeping my back to the building to make it go away. I wondered again what could have happened in this place. What event could have imparted such tactile creepiness to this neglected corner that it clung so, impervious to the centuries? The sea below, dishwater grey beneath a dreary sky, shifted heavily like a slowly heaving vat of slag.

From the base of the cliff came the noise of the water lifting smooth stones on the beach and then draining back through them with a hollow, swallowing sound. A large, disorganized flock of seagulls turned overhead, mewing, yapping, and shrieking with the living voices that mariners claim are of souls lost at sea, the wind tearing at their urgent, rasping cries, while far below a few cliff-dwelling birds, flying tangents to the land, wheeled on the updrafts and barked in the hurrying air. I took some reassurance from their racket. Yet, the sea had a darkling, marbled look, like bad meat, and lacked its customary power to console. To the north the mountains rose straight from the water, as though newborn. To the south they stood bleakly against a smudged violet sky, while farther out to sea the endless water glistened dully with the cold, leaden hue of base metal.

For long moments I felt surrounded by symbols of fate. At my feet the cliff face showed that in the tide's relentless push and pull, there was always more loss than gain. The land on this little promontory was doomed. Very slowly to be sure, but it was returning to the sea as certainly and inevitably as death. I wondered what would happen to the spirits when the ruins began to slough into the water. Were they somehow attached to the stones and compelled to follow them down, or would they simply move to the nearest habitation—the monastery? Or did they depend for their existence entirely upon my vulnerable imagination?

I walked along the edge of the cliff admonishing myself for being silly, but still uneasy and disconnected at the turn my excursion had taken. From a small crescent of beach in a cusp of the cliffs, the slap of waves on the sand below came like the sound of grieving. The air smelled faintly of bracken and linoleum.

I made a wide arc back toward the fields, purposely avoiding the stones that had fallen from the ruins. Perhaps they retained some of the dreaded consciousness. Some of their fragments lay sunk in the earth, dulled by centuries of weather and sediment, while the sunlight gave others a pale and bony gleam. Although half buried, they preserved in their skewed positions a heavy motion, as though thrown. I stepped carefully away from them and hurried circuitously back toward the anonymous companionship of the brotherhood.

I felt an urgent need for contact with their humanity, as though by cloaking myself in the company of these wholly private men it would somehow cleanse the eerie metaphysical defilement through which I had passed; that within the mantle of their severe benevolence it could not find me, and I hurried through the grass to declare my place among them.

Before me there rose a comfortingly benign quality about the landscape, which, as though I were seeing it for the first time, seemed to smile in welcome with the promise of refuge. The feeling probably sprang from my own need for company, but the geometry of the fields and the uniformity of their hand-built stone walls hinted at moral rectitude and Bible-reading probity. It lay in the angles where the cultivation fit together, in their pleasing symmetry, and along the borders of color, where the varied green countryside met the granite sea. A sourceless light seemed to brighten the land from underneath, as though the undulant sprinkling of yellow flowers on the fallow portions of the hillside were leaking into the air.

The wind gave their neat patches of winter wheat the look of a riptide, and when it lessened to a breeze, silken currents stirred along the grasses making their tassels luminous and vibrant, as though the fields were trembling a foot from the ground. Carried in the gusts also were the sounds of the shore behind me where the tide still rattled the pebbles like marbles in a jar.

The highest object in the scene was the monastery itself, where the solitary crag of its broken tower against the sky lent the hills a kind of sanctifying touch that could be seen for miles around. But it was an illusion of course, just like the apparent *dis*order that makes jungles seem savage to missionaries.

One of the details which imparted such an idyllic character to the fields was the extraordinary uniformity of the native stone walls that separated and delineated them. These were low, square-shouldered works, wherein art and engineering merged uniquely in balanced proportion. Each was level, about two feet thick, and was traversed here and there with elegant arched stiles. They snaked across the contours of the hills, occasionally allowing some minor hump or dip in the earth to roll past unnoticed. Most importantly at that moment, they marked the presence of my own kind.

One of the lower fields was being cleared of boulders in preparation for planting. Four monks using spades and crowbars were engaged in dislodging rocks from the ground and then carrying or rolling them across the slope to where two other men were using them to build onto a section of wall. The two wall builders, being farthest down the hill, were the closest to me, and I made straight for them.

Besides my overwhelming need just then to hide in the sanctuary of human company, I was curious to know how the construction was done. Yet, mindful that they might not care to work under the prying eyes of the idle, I approached but then kept somewhat apart to watch from an outsider's respectful remove. It was here that I met the Brothers John, stonemasons, and it was here that I learned to my surprise that I had acquired a nickname.

The older man was also the larger. He had a full, ruddy face softened like beaten copper by experience and age. It sagged at the sides as though it had been flung onto the peg of his nose to melt there slowly in the sun. Round blue eyes nested in his bushy eyebrows like robin's eggs. He was a tall, well-built man with sparse white hair that stood out across the top of his head as though electrified and with a long fringe that surrounded his freckled pate like a bad grass skirt. He had the rugged worn look of an aging piece of garden sculpture. This aspect disguised an intellect of insight and piercing good humor. He had a deep voice, raspy as a dirty phonograph needle, which he used sparingly and with the long habit of modulation. Nonetheless, when he spoke, the sound of it fell through the air like timber.

The smaller John was a saturnine man of middle age who spoke little. His cowl, which was raised, cast a shadow on the pallor of his face and gave a certain suffering quality to the melancholy of his eyes. There were what appeared to be traces of many passions in his look that his will had disciplined but that seemed to have frozen the features they had long ceased to animate. Sadness and severity predominated in its lines, and the timeless intensity of his penetrating gaze seemed almost to read my thoughts. There were occasions to come when it would be uncomfortable to tolerate their inquiry.

The two men worked together wordlessly, selecting the stones piled by the diggers and turning each one in their large hands to find just the right point at which to strike with a rock hammer. The use of the fragment that resulted was determined by its shape. Further refinements in shape or size were also achieved with the hammers.

The wall, I noticed, was actually set into the ground some six inches or more, founded on heavy flat stones. I remembered there was a passage in the Bible somewhere about building on a strong foundation, and I enjoyed seeing the work which, for all anyone knows, may have been the very thing that inspired the scripture.

For a while, though both men were aware of my presence, neither acknowledged me with more than a glance. I smiled interestedly whenever they looked up, and I watched with admiration the neat fit they were achieving with both the heavier pieces and the sherds. Finally, the larger man waved me over. They both continued to work.

"So, ye're "The Reaper," ay?"

I didn't understand."...Uh, excuse me?" I asked.

"In tha' war coontry," responded the smaller man without looking up from the hollow of his cowl.

I was momentarily shocked by all that their brief comments had revealed. First of all it seemed I had somehow acquired a nickname, and secondly, I couldn't understand how they could have learned anything about me, especially about the events of my recent past. I had told no one. Then I remembered the incident of the spilled bowls in the scullery and wondered if there had been other times when I might have inadvertently revealed similarly provocative behavior and how readily they must have interpreted the evidence. In view of my self-conscious efforts to remain unobtrusive it was revealing and bit disconcerting to realize that at some point I had become the subject of some discussion, even in an atmosphere of prevailing silence.

Then there was the surprising reference to "that war country" itself. How strange it was to meet someone so removed from the baleful reality of my own experience that he didn't know what to call the place which had dominated my life for so long, the very name of which was impacted with such malevolent feeling that to be reminded suddenly shunted me for a moment in time.

Then the other voice added, "Th' woon tha's been flingin' th' harvester aboot, aye?"

"...Oh...'The Reaper'."

I understood then that the name was intended to convey both meanings. It made me laugh, but I wasn't sure how to take this news. In my experience nicknames and other cutish endearments usually became attached only to the most popular, or most unpopular, people. In seconds, the idea that I had somehow acquired a discrete label within this arcane community, whose view of the world I did not even fully understand, grew profoundly uncomfortable.

I had assumed that by keeping to myself and by helping out where I could, I was remaining as inconspicuous as our outward differences would allow. Of course I had failed to appreciate the full effect of a stranger's protracted presence among them and worried now about where I may have been relegated along the nuisance scale. I chuckled a bit self-consciously. "...Do they call me that?"

The big man rested his hammer, then wiped his fingers on a small towel and extended his hand to me.

"Aye," he said with a flat grin and added, "I'm John." Then, indicating the other mason, "...An' tha's John as well."

"So am I," I offered, and shook his big leathery palm.

The second man raised his hand in a vague gesture. His sleeve fell back, and I was surprised to notice a faded blue tattoo hidden beneath the rock dust in the hair of his forearm. It appeared to be a nautical design, and the incongruity of it caused me to wonder if perhaps the Order served for some to cloak the past.

"John?"

"John."

"John..."

"...John." We all smiled, enjoying the coincidence.

Their heavy woolen cassocks were ragged at the hem and sun-bleached across the shoulders. Their hands were large, rough, and horny, like the feet of shoeless people. They worked well, kneeling together in the black soil, going about the selection, breaking, and fitting process with such wordless coordination that it took me a long time over many subsequent work days to realize that they hated each other. Both were bound inseparably in a companionship of specialized skill, but they couldn't stand each other, a phenomenon that is possible anywhere but reaches heights of subtle paradox more outrageously in age than at any other time.

I don't know how I first came to realize this, for their cooperation appeared complete, their shared movements so familiar to one another, and their mutual eye for the shape and fit of each piece of stone so exacting, that I mistook the perfection of their creation itself as evidence of harmony between them. The wall grew beautifully straight-sided and so well chinked that no light was visible through it anywhere. Theirs was an unspoken language of inexplicably correlated vagaries that told through a glossary of fleeting mannerisms of an animosity as elaborate and well-tended as a termite castle.

I watched them with growing admiration for a long time. The taller man, who I came to think of as "John of the Hoary Fringe," seemed the more personable of the two. He spoke a few times as softly as his helicon voice would allow while he selected rocks from the pile and turned each in his hands to find the relationship he sought between its outer shape and the breaking planes within it. He was a man whose honesty of purpose shown through his speech and his silences alike.

The shorter man shared this work, too, but also served to align their progress with plumb cord which he stretched between long wrought iron nails resembling giant knitting needles. He kept the nails in a leather bag beside the trench, and he set them, delineating the course their work would take, entirely by eye. A dark, taciturn man who appeared always to be hiding within his cowl, and who, had it not been for the frequency of his providing just the right fragments to complete a section as tightly as a jigsaw puzzle, might have seemed to the casual observer to be working alone. It made me uncomfortable from time to time to feel him staring at me with something akin to suspicion. He became "John of Nails."

"So...ye b'lieve in killin', then?" he asked suddenly, apropos of nothing.

The question surprised and alarmed me. No one had ever asked me that before. So they knew, and here it was. The very issue on which I would surely be judged by some for the rest of my life. The point on which subconsciously I had refused to reflect, myself. The core issue of all human conflict.

My mood fell. My soul, or what I thought of as the character of my person, seemed to vanish suddenly, and my throat checked under a swallow. The truth was, I didn't know how I felt about it. I only knew that I had survived to be there because of it, and I did not want to become engaged in a philosophical argument I could not win against any adherent of inherited opinion, or any student of scripture. This was about war, about death in war, and only those safe at home with no experience of desperate outrage and its attendant demons could enjoy the luxury of moral reflection.

His use of the word "then" was curious, too: "So, do you believe in killing, *then?*" I had heard it at the end of sentences before, but here it implied that his question belonged to some previous dialogue between us, that it fitted a slot within some secret dialectic pattern. It revealed the course of his thinking, and it told that he held his own ideas in readiness. I hesitated, not knowing what to say while silence mingled with inertia and despair. John of Nails watched for his answer from the shadow of his cowl. Finally the deadweight of his sedulous gaze pulled me back from the slopes of lubricious speculation.

"...Well, no," I said slowly, trying to find a clever way to retreat from the question. "Once a man indulges himself in killing, very soon he comes to think nothing of robbery; and from robbing he sinks to drinking and Sabbath-breaking, and from that to procrastination and incivility."

I smiled and looked him hard in the face. John of the Hoary Fringe began to chuckle out loud, revealing a row of teeth as big as old beach stones. He looked down at his companion, who smiled in spite of himself. John of Nails placed the head of his rock hammer against the ground and then pushed himself laboriously to his feet using the butt of the handle. He rose, laughing quietly, and slapped the dust from his hands. His eyelids were sealed nearly together, from whence a thin tear of mirth trailed out. Working its way along the cracks in his face, it ended as a shine against his prominent cheekbone. Yet he barely made a sound.

I felt the mixed relief of the reprieved, for though I was glad to have amused them and felt the situation saved, I knew that someday I would have to reconcile his question to myself. In the meanwhile, I had been granted an interval in which its ecumenical imperative would settle into the context of my life, to stand in dress rehearsal for the inquisition of time.

Their demeanor was amused but remote, and I was pleased when they invited me to join them in a short tea break. Plunging their dirty thumbs through the crusts of fresh loaves, they handed me two large pieces of smudged wheat bread. John of Nails produced a folding knife from somewhere in the folds of his robe. He took a paper package from his tool bag and unwrapped a block of cheese that resembled in color and texture a large bar of lye soap, from which he sliced three generous slabs and extended one to me on the blade. It smelled like an old sneaker.

As we munched the bread with its surprisingly tasty cheese and sipped strong honey-laced tea from a thermos, they pointed out some of the techniques they used to achieve the high quality of their work: how fragments with smooth facets became outside pieces, and how they prized a near right-angle break for use at the shoulder of the wall, for nature strove to prevent it. I became quite interested and began helping afterwards in the selection process by ranging through the fields to find rocks with the visible striations they looked for in achieving straight-faceted breaks.

John of Nails proved to have a wide-ranging mind, unfettered by what I imagined were the dictates of any consecrated church. After some time spent gathering stones for them, I asked about the old stronghold where I had been so frightened in the morning. I can not quote his remarks exactly, but the essence of what he told me would take deep root in my elemental view of the world, enduring to this day as ambages of received perception:

Nothing that has ever lived has truly died, it is merely changed. Nature is a grand library of all that has ever been. You cannot find your way around in it, and yet it is all there, somewhere. Often humans can catch a fleeting glimpse of something as it passes by on an odd wavelength of their consciousness. A moment of comprehension, a spark of light, is all that is necessary to briefly illuminate previously unsuspected places in unknown worlds or long-past times. Everything is available to everyone, sometimes only inches out of sight.

Then he ended by making an expressive gesture with his hands, indicating the mutability of all things.

I worked with them all that day, and for most days afterwards, either digging and trundling rocks to be shaped by their hammers, or splitting and fitting, as they willingly taught me the secrets of their craft. I learned the heft of the hammer and how to find the angles within each rock, and I learned to keep the third-dimensionality, the inner facets of the wall itself, in mind at all times so that every fragment found a secure fit throughout the structure.

They soon revealed an interest in philosophical speculation that came as a surprise to me. We often talked about the nature of knowledge and the question of personal reality, an epistemology which I felt sure was not encouraged by the ecclesiastical doctrines to which I assumed they were sworn. Both men held insightful, unconventional views, and I was often amused to hear John of Nails dash his tumultuous waves of thought against the other's great genial, comprehending silences.

By the end of that first day together, I was well aware of the profound differences between them. Beside their physical disparity and their unspoken personal animosity, the characters of the two Johns represented both halves of the mandala, the Yin and the Yang of human nature. They were paradoxes. The congeniality of the taller man masked a deep, black realm of introspection coupled with a language of gesture so eloquent as to have created an order as true to the impact of external reality and as sensitive to another person's being as ripples in touched water. The brooding demeanor of the shorter man, which had so discomfited me initially, gave way to a passionate, insightful garrulity. Yet they were inseparable, conjoined by a shared pride in their work, mutually invested in the walls they had built together with their own hands and which in turn lent form and meaning to the very landscape itself. Together, they were leaving their creation on the world, and in a thousand years time, their signature will still be legible in this remote corner of the crowded canvas.

By the evening bell, as we made our way up the hill beneath a crumbling sky, the masons settled back into an introspective silence. I walked with them, listening to the sounds of our shoes in the grass, and breathed in the rich chlorophyll smell which rose from the trampled stems. I thought about the wall and what sort of influence working in stone might have upon a man's values over time. How do the conventions of an abstract faith square with the hard, tectonic disciplines imposed by their kind of work? Perhaps some balance between a formal apostolic orthodoxy and an almost pagan respect for monument serves to evaluate our innate capacity for spiritual freedom in which, unchained from the dogmas of the church and the dictates of others, a man is led by his own moral intuition alone.

There was another thing, too. Robert Frost's verses about good fences took on new meaning. Here were men living within a closed community, and as with the Johns, often thrown together for hours each day by specialty alone, the vagaries of personality aside. They were like islanders surrounded by the grey waters of otherness. One does not risk giving offense in a closed society, for an island imposes certain conditions and duties foreign to outsiders. An enemy on an island is an enemy inescapable. There is no blending into an anonymous background once offense has been taken, no neighboring society toward which to flee. Islanders are required by the very limits of their land to watch their steps at every moment. No one treads easily upon the emotions of another where the sea licks everywhere around.

This is both good and bad at the same time. Good because it means that people take care with one another but limiting because it can bring an inbreeding of the spirit—too much held in, periods of regret and silent brooding. So, considered and considerate, formal at every turn, they remain shut off from the deeper interplay of their minds, focusing together only on the "safe" matters of work and religion. They cannot speak freely because they are cornered—everywhere they turn is the outside world, a limitless expanse of it in which to drown. They held their breath and walked with care, and this made them who they were inside—limited by choice. Good neighbors.

As the Johns and I had started home from farthest away, we were in trail as the brotherhood with shouldered tools made their way in a thin bedraggled file up the slope for dinner. The brown cassocks, bent against the hill's declining, shuffled quiet as shadows of the men inside them. Their shabby line moved with such wordless gravity that it could have been the ritual procession of some dread new dispensation.

9
Hellfire

Late one restless night as black clouds mewed up the slack gloss of an early moon, wind tore at the branches all about, and the cold air felt electric when I stepped outside. I had planned to walk along the ridge and to watch for a while the moon shadows race across the fields and out to sea.

However, as I made my way along the back wall of the monastery, I noticed an eerie orange glow flickering among the trees about a hundred yards distant. It came from an area where two stone huts were built into the hillside within a steep belt of woods that sloped away from the garden and which I had never visited. It roused my curiosity. Not only was it strange and unexpected, but it seemed at first that the woods might be on fire.

I stopped and watched. A yellowish light moved wavering and inconclusive through the stems of the trees, sometimes lofting on a narrow beam to sweep among the leaves, one moment haloed and diffused, the next a hard bright point. It appeared that someone with a hand light was out there in the woods near a fire, and I decided to investigate who might be defying the customary hours for sleeping—or worse, trespassing on ground for which I was feeling a certain share of responsibility.

The tops of the trees dipped and swayed in the gusts, and the old growth thrashed noisily in the diffused moonlight. I started across an open meadow and approached the wood line cautiously. Searching the lower darkness, I entered the woods and crouched in the underbrush from where I could see through the trees that there was indeed a fire. Deep within the tangle of roots and stems, occasional rags of flame burst out of the ground and fled downwind, broke and vanished like a shout in the night, while small coals scampered away through a break in the thicket.

Uncertain about what was going on and still worried that I might be approaching an unattended fire, or worse, the work of vandals, I began to plan what I might be able to do. I could circle around for a better view, but that would risk stumbling in the unfamiliar woods and giving away my position. I might opt for a frontal approach, counting on anyone close to the fire being at least partially blinded by its glare.

Thus hidden in the forest's fingered shadow, I knew I was at least surrounded by a supply of stout pieces of wood. Peering through the trunks, I was able to make out the rim of a long pit around which the silhouetted trees stood like crude fencing, and in it a hidden fire burned below the ground like some secret glimpse of the earth's core broken through into the darkness.

At its edge a tall hooded figure moved, casting its enormous shadow into the lower branches. Shimmering lightly in the heat, the image wavered, separated, and rejoined like some mythic being, some fearful attendant of Hell conjured forth at hearsay by priests for the purpose of frightening their supplicants.

Instinctively, I checked around my position to determine if I could be seen against the lighter background of faint moon glow behind and searched the nearby ground for something hefty enough to be used as a cudgel. I looked up to check for head clearance. Overhead the oaks leaned forth with limbs like bones. The midnight stars, coined out of the dark coping through fleeting rifts in the clouds, winked through the bare wickerwork of the trees, while the light of the hidden moon lay in a sulfur haze over the eastward hills behind me.

The whole scene could have risen from the pages of Dante, whose portentous touch was completed when suddenly I recognized the lean and haunted figure of Brother Wilf himself. From deep within his cowl a pair of eyes glowed red in the sockets of his face like the coals they reflected, while he moved about the pit with a long-handled rake, goading his fires like some demonic sorcerer. I was both glad and relieved to recognize him, and amused by the consistency of unearthly images in which he always seemed to appear, I stepped into the light just as he moved down into the pit.

"Stealing yourself for the celestial interview?" I asked. He looked up, startled.

"Och...," he said. "The Reaper himself emerges from the shades o'night t'plague m'high an' secret study." He was in good spirits.

"I thought trolls had set the woods on fire," I said.

"Hah! Trolls. Tha's ye're own tormented mind. Ye'r oon-repentant, an'ye kinna sleep."

"Hah!" I snorted back. "There. Did you hear that? That was the snort of the righteous."

"Ah. Well...in tha' case, ye'll be wantin' a wee dram, will ye no'?"

The fire sawed about in the gusts. He leaned his fire rake against the pit wall and stepped back out of the gap in the ground, rising like a dark messenger from the underworld. A fine sleet began, falling slant upon us out of the darkness, and it hissed in the coals.

He beckoned me to follow him to one of the low huts defiladed into the earth nearby. We ducked into his workshop. Inside, the smoky interior was warm, and while the after-image of the fire danced in my eyes, quite dark. It smelled of things burnt and of wet burlap. The center of the room was dominated by a large bellows and a brick forge. In a shallow fire pit atop what appeared to be an oven with a small iron fire door, a few bleached coals glowed orange beneath a grate, while the rest of the room lay sleeping in soft, quiescent shadows. A low ceiling beam and two tiny windows lent a fairytale wicked-witch kind of Disney geniality to the place. I gradually became aware of tools, buckets, tongs and bars, and other assorted implements hanging in the gloom along the walls.

He lit an oil lamp, and as he hung it objects around us leapt from the gloom and swayed gently on their shadows. He reached into the darkness and brought down an unmarked bottle like the one he had shared with me before, and from another shadow he produced a worn crockery mug, chipped all about the rim, as well as a small glass clouded with scratches from which he dumped a number of metal washers into a pile on a workbench. He handed me the mug and blew some dust out of the glass, then poured a whisky dark as maple syrup into both.

It tasted very strong, again like brandy. It was dry and leathery, and it burned its own welcome on the way down, spreading warmth through my chest and back. Yet it left a coolish, eucalyptus sort of after-flavor in my mouth the way cough drops do. I asked him the name of it, but the noise he made in response didn't sound like it belonged to any language I knew.

A double row of plank shelves surrounded the room, and assorted work in various stages of completion lay upon these in no evident order. Several vises of varying types were clamped to the work bench, and two large anvils of different size rested on heavy upturned log ends in the center of the floor.

I learned that Wilf's iron projects ranged from the large—gate hinges and farm equipment—to the delicate, including fine silver and gold repair, which he accomplished with the aid of assorted magnifying lenses. He even made his own tools, skillfully laminating the cutting edges of trimmers, scythes, and axes.

The fire pit just outside was where he carbonized wood before bringing it inside to cook it into charcoal in the oven for eventual use in raising the temperatures he needed for heating and forming metals. It's proximity to the hut worked to Wilf's immediate advantage while keeping his sometimes noxious, and often loud, activity at some remove from the main house.

Points of yellow light glinted dully from a number of small metal objects on a back shelf. There was something intriguing about them, and I took one down and held it to the lamplight to discover that it was a highly imaginative little figurine: a whimsical creature with a toothy grin and oversized hands and feet. Amused, I brought down another. They all proved to be comical little monsters, gremlins, and assorted beasties, carefully handmade in brass. Their anthropomorphic detail and charming expressions defied both the seriousness of the man and the utilitarian nature of his work. When I admired them Wilf muttered something self-deprecatingly about scrap and dementia, then dismissed them in a manner which told me they were none of my business really, but their sheer secular incongruity, along with his discomfort at my compliments, made me suspect he did them strictly for his own amusement, and I liked him all the more for it.

We braced ourselves with a generous second pouring and took them with us back outside so that he could tend the fire. I watched him work the rake through the coals to assure an even burn and thought about the great skill he had revealed. I thought about the spiritual torment in which he had struggled the day we met on the tower, his ready generosity toward me, and his surprising sense of humor, which he loosed so sparingly, like a trickle charge to his humanity, and I came to realize that what Wilf saw with clarity is that the world can indeed be silent and cold and bare, but in this, too, lies its terrible beauty. He might be killing himself with religious melancholia, I thought, but he is probably making better progress along the road to enlightenment than I am.

I stood contentedly in the warming smoke of the pit and watched the demonic vision of Wilf at work with his devil's fork, stirring the coals into faint ceramic collision. A profound release of all care settled upon me as I stared into the bed of glowing remnants and breathed the sharp smoky air. I enjoyed the poetic effusion of the whisky and the intermittent sleet pelting gently into my hair, while silvery moon-spun clouds fled past the gap in the surrounding branches.

Then, quite unexpectedly, and I think for the first time, I experienced one of those rare euphoriant moments when a limitless view of the world suddenly opened within me, and I became imbued with a sense of being at one with the entire universe. I could almost hear the cosmic hum of atoms in the ancient dark beyond, and with it came a flame-lit glimpse of my deep interrelatedness with all things both animate and inanimate. In a flash I understood that every single incomprehensible thing is but a composition of star dust, a complex mix to be sure, but one held in universal common.

Like many (if not most) people, I had carried around since school a purely academic acceptance of this rumor, relegated to some closet of memory where other facts of no immediate practical use are stored, but here suddenly this fundamental truth about physical reality rose out of the night and moved in, animating the strange paradigm that insists all things bear the basic chemicals that make up the stars and that seed life throughout the vast silent vaults of the cosmos, to an extent yet beyond the reach of our minds. I felt an unfamiliar comfort in the realization that many of my genes were like those of both gorillas and mushrooms, and that my makeup differed from that of plants and minerals merely in molecular arrangement, not in essence.

I must have chuckled out loud in the grip of this amusing revelation, for Wilf looked up.

"Och...Ye'r droonk," he observed, probably correctly.

"Nope...I'm sober as a...mineral."

"...Daft!" he finished, turning back to his work.

The contentment I felt in those moments induced a release, as though some of the slag had suddenly been poured from the crucible of my experience, leaving a lasting access to a chamber of thought that to this day provides a balance of contrast with those times when I lose track of this deep commonality and withdraw into the limited horizon of my own individuality. Perhaps we are all programmed to lose our grasp on this perspective from time to time for the reason that each of us needs a sense of singular identity, too; or maybe it's just because, when examined up close, the world seems all dirt and rocks, and since we have to get on with the day-to-day chores of living, we get tired, we lose the pattern.

I thought cheerfully about the unexpected compatibility I felt with Brother Wilf and wondered whether, at extremely subtle levels of the cosmic connectivity of things, the quantum energy given off by every individual might carry with it some residuum of that person's entire experience. Perhaps we carry around in both the essence of our spirit and the atoms of our physical makeup all the life experiences of our years, such that those energetic particles are imparted and stored in the shared consciousness of the universe. It may be that we feed this great reservoir with all our thoughts and feelings. We don't ask to be included in the pool, at least not consciously, but there we are just the same, accessible by clairvoyants and psychics, even sometimes by departed spirits, and subject to the serendipitous insinuation into our lives of others whose imprint upon the great canvas is enough like our own to form attractions. Whether or not we may be aware of the process, we are equal participants in the exchange with all other conscious things—both those who know how to tap into the resources of this vast non-local information system and those who simply have a passive susceptibility to its universal power.

It would never before have occurred to me that I might find such amusing commonality with a self-tortured monk, much less to have encountered this person along the far coastal reaches of northern Scotland. The improbability of the occurrence of any event suddenly assumed a purely theoretical existence, independent of the imperatives by which they are calculated. Whatever laws govern chance convergence seemed but the products of naïve conjecture, for the realities of such congruencies just go on without them.

Gradually, perhaps released by the whisky, this carefree indulgence in philosophical speculation gave way, as it often did, to recollections of the violence and uncertainty of the year before, actions independent of my control and indifferent to my puny sanction. This memory was a chain attached to the leg of a monstrous nightmare, dragging me back down a trail of mournful images and tethered still to remorse left unspoken. I tried to flee the sadness that slept uneasily in the corner of my mind like some vengeful beast that awaited only my inattention, and I resented its tendency to stir anew whenever I wandered into those sunlit uplands of the mind where hope and joy were attempting a comeback.

In a deliberate effort to regain the mood of the fire and the keen sense of being alive that the night's encounter with Wilf had produced,

I deliberately concentrated on his studied turning of the coals. As he raked and mounded the glowing bed the flames gradually subsided until he seemed like a man prodding a small dragon to stand still. Hot cinder-flecked smoke sheared from the pit and ran before the chill gusts, while bright sparks darted upward to vanish into the infinite hush of night.

I stayed there enjoying Wilf's company, the whisky, the chill, and the singularity of equivocal truths that fell like magical fruit from the night, until a flinty blush of morning haze began to congeal through the trees.

In the end, I decided it was better to be whole than good.

10
Thanatos

In April, old Brother Philip suffered a stroke from which he did not recover. I didn't know him, but I knew who he was, as we had nodded pleasantries from time to time. It happened in the refectory at dinner time. He was sitting a few tables away, along the outer periphery of my attention, when he suddenly stiffened. His elbows dropped off the table, and he slid down on his seat. He jerked suddenly and fell forward, his chin banging down on the cloth. Only his head could be seen, eyes closed, like a serving of John the Baptist.

There was an immediate stirring and shuffling to help him. Benches scraped back and numerous muted voices grunted and caught as he was toppled into strong arms and carried from the room in ironic parody of a death scene from grand opera. It was over very quickly, and he died later that night, quietly, surrounded by his friends. A vigil had been set up around his bed, and when he finally slipped away he was among the people with whom he had been closest in the world. Lucky man.

I went by his room to pay my respects while he lingered unconscious, but I did not try to enter. The tiny candlelit cell where he had spent so much of his life was full of contemplative brown figures whose enormous shadows leaned bear-like over them from the walls, as though their very souls had been loosed for a better view of the ritual. Theirs was an ancient summons, a call to arbitrate the final generic entropy coded within us all.

I found myself drawn to the watchful assembly. The event within the room held me in gentle thrall. The sort of death to which I had grown conditioned was always loud, bloody and chaotic, numbing in its rich ferocity. Yet Philip's peaceful withdrawal gave pause, providing time for reflection and an opportunity to place the fleeting experience of life in some kind of perspective. I stood against the wall in the dim hallway, nodding to the brothers who came by, and tried to sort through my feelings.

I recalled how, in Vietnam, we had kept each other at arm's length, bound by the secrets of our elitism yet afraid to get too close, squatting on our hearts like toads in order to protect ourselves against loss. I remembered my first few days in-country; how fearful and stunned I had been at the sudden and evocative incomprehensibility of death shock by gunfire, even as I had lain trembling in the midst of it. Yet, as it continued over the furious months that followed, it had come eventually to leave me strangely unemotional. Where at first the stupefying immutability of the violence had evoked a protracted clutch at my heart, later, if I allowed myself to dwell on it, there came nothing but vague, dull-edged thoughts.

In historic times, death had a solemn social importance. It was not regarded so much as the moment when a body shuts down, as it was a dramatic climax, a moment when the soul made its entrance into the next world, passing in full consciousness into some unknowable place. Among the watchers there was always the hope that the dying man might reveal something of what he alone could see; that his countenance, if not his lips, would speak, and on his features would fall some light or shadow from beyond. The last words of great men, like Napoleon and Lord Byron, are still printed in gift books, and the dying murmurs of every common man and woman were listened for and treasured by their neighbors and kin. These utterances, no matter how ordinary, were given oracular significance and pondered by those who must one day go the same road.

Here, the brotherhood was assembled in respectful legacy, sustained by the energy of their idealism and uncorrupted by disputation, by any quodlibetical conceit that would subject every mystery and their traditional secrets to scrutiny. They remained silent, prayerful, expectant.

I wondered at their faith in a formal hereafter. Does an abiding confidence in some spiritual promise serve to lull the serene and eventless vigil? Traditional concepts of heaven have always seemed to me conditioned by our earthly experience. If Paradise is to be this world purged of disaster and nuisance, if immortality is to be this life held in poise and arrest, and if this world purged and this life unconsuming is regarded as world and life restored to their proper natures, it is no wonder that we tantalize ourselves with ideas about other hands reaching out to greet our departing souls and voices raised in welcome from another shore as we take our leave of this one.

Yet as a myth it is a benign illusion and useful, and I found myself wishing hard for a rebirth of innocence enough to believe in it again. In the attentive huddle of Philip's room I saw that the distance between us could not be crossed. I knew that the time of my untrammeled acceptance lay unreachably far behind, beyond the crucible of fire through which I had passed. Never could I know such innocence again. A hot wave of remorse for lost ideals, for flown nescience, rose in my throat and broke over me in a fervent wash of emotion.

With Philip's passing the brotherhood began the age-old process of knitting back the hole his absence had left in the texture of their lives. He had evidently been well-liked, a keystone in an arch whose other stones were other lives. As the central stone trembled, its warning carried along the whole curve, and when it fell, the arch fell, leaving its lesser stones heaped together for a while without design. His death altered the pattern of life for a time, but it was remade again, as lives and stones are, into other patterns.

Discussion began even before his simple interment ceremony of what to do about the problem now of being left with only one valid driver's license among them. For several days the need of a second qualified driver was generally discussed and agreed, although selection of the candidate was the subject of some concerned whispering. In view of the neglected cars I had seen, the argument made me smile.

11
Terra Nova

As I made my way up the old steps of the house tower, the fog was so dense and still that it was easy to imagine a man could run his hands through it, separating it into tendrils that would gather themselves languidly once more into the whole and disappear without a trace. I had grown fond of the harsh tower stones. The place was like a fierce-looking monster that offered me protection. Even when hidden in a heavy press of mist, being there was like having a pet dragon.

I often found Wilf on the parapet where I had first met him, and our long discussions had given the place a further life. Rained upon for centuries, it was worn by both weather and attention, for though in architectural decline, the walls still made an edifice wherein the spirit grew. It was sumptuous of mystery and enchantment, and I enjoyed the metaphor I came to see in its perilous climb.

This morning, hours before the brotherhood stirred, I had risen early hoping that, alone on the battlements, I might watch the day break from its pink satin shell. Instead, I had crept outside only to enter an impenetrable fog that filled the night, opaque as a solid object. The sea-chilled mist dropped upon me lacing my face and dampening my hair with its cold purity.

I liked the unexpected conditions, though, and began to grope my way carefully along the back of the house to the foundation courses of the tower. Feeling with my foot for the bottom step, I started gingerly upward on each of the dew-soaked footings in turn, keeping my shoulder against the camber of the wall and questioning the white darkness with my hands.

Near the top of the stairs, the casemate against which I leaned came to an abrupt end as I stepped into the emptiness above it. The air smelled cold and full of the conflicting odors of chimney smoke and wet stones. I sensed the surround of open space and gravity. It caused a tingling sensation in the arches of my feet. Entirely sightless in the fog, I eased down onto my hands and knees and began inching along the slippery rim of the tower in the direction of the old privy seat, tracing the edge of the capstones with my fingers. I knew the wall dropped away on both sides of me and was grateful for once that I could not see. I groped cautiously forward holding my breath, as though a lift in the chest might undo my weight upon the narrow stones.

A dark figure suddenly congealed in the grayness beside me! It seemed no more than a shadow in the night, a thickening of cloud sensed without seeing, but its presence sent me reeling. I gasped aloud and dropped onto my stomach in a panic of sprung equilibrium, my legs straddling the top of the wall and my brain full of heartbeats. A disorienting wave of fear broke over me. Had it not been for the mist that masked the emptiness around me, I might have lost my balance on the ledge and plummeted forever into the spread heart of silence. As I clung trembling with my chest pressed against the wet stones, something vaguely familiar seemed to linger from my glimpse of the shadow.

"Wilf??" I barked into the dark.

"...Ay," came his familiar rasp from close to my ear. I couldn't have been more than a few feet from him. I let out my breath with relief, but it left me weak and shivering from the scare.

Once again, there was a dramatic and mystic quality to one of Wilf's appearances. It was perfectly explainable by the fact that each time I saw him I, too, was in those places quite as a course of natural events. Yet understanding the powerful signature of this coincidence did nothing to relieve the impression he gave of belonging to some force-field of phantasm, of moving always in circumstances which lent something fabulous to his arrivals.

His was a king's solitude, unique and inviolate, and I was instantly sorry to have disturbed him. He grunted and moved over by way of invitation, and I rose weakly to sit beside him on the slab. His robe was heavy with dew and the wool in it smelled musty. He must have been sitting there for hours, exactly where I had seen him many times before, just thinking. I wondered for a moment if he was one of those who believed that to continue a dream you must lie down the next night in exactly the same position you awakened in, where the body parted from its images. Did he seek in this unlikely aerie some inviolate coordinate that provided physical continuity for his ruminations?

"Sorry, Wilf. I wouldn't have disturbed you."

"...No' t'warry, laddie," he mumbled absently, facing into the void, there to resume floating in the black realm behind his staring eyes.

He appeared to be troubled again. The high solitude of the tower seemed to lend vitality to the frightening equations of his unfathomable mind, and he sat thunderous and regal, like Zeus on his mountain. Yet I could feel him shudder slightly from time to time, as though he stowed pockets of unrest in various parts of his body. Even though he was motionless, I felt that if he'd had a tail, it would have been whipping around our ankles.

Acting on the assumption that he would have given some indication to the contrary if my unexpected arrival did not provide him with some measure of comfort or distraction, I decided to stay with him there a while and settled in to await the dawn. He had shown me an easy friendship despite his deep and conflicted struggle, and it pained me to see him in his distress. I often wondered what could have brought him to these periodic seizures, these intervals of philosophical paroxysm. Had there been some singular event in his past, or did he harbor some atavistic predisposition to the problem of finding a workable compromise between the sublimity of his ideas and the absurdity of the facts he knew about himself? It has seemed to me ever since that only sorrow can bring a man to such an anguished view of things. Yet a sorrow for which there can be no help is no common sadness. It is some dark sister traveling in sorrow's clothing.

We sat together for some time in unspoken pendency while the opaque and languorous stillness lay all about, isolating us entirely from the world. No sound came from any quarter, and no thing stirred. Time and all of life itself was held in suspension by the unmoving fog.

I do not know how long we remained there, together and yet alone, for as the quiet gathered itself around us it thickened until its presence leaned in upon my awareness, becoming a palpable thing that demanded attention. With it came a sense of vast abeyance in which everything outside ourselves seemed held in universal suspension.

In this strange miasmal stasis I came to realize for the first time that without some form of movement, I had no gauge for marking the passage of time. As I sat, listening for any small event which might announce itself from the deep quiescence, I began to see that indeed our whole concept of time was inextricably dependent upon notions of space.

By twitching a finger I could cause an event locatable in time and then feel it recede into the immediate past. But soon the moments piled up again, and without some additional trick of movement, or without fixing upon my own pulse, I could not retain a sense of position within the endless flow of, what, seconds? Are there such increments if there is no measure?

I suddenly realized with an amusing burst of minor enlightenment that where there is not some kind of motion there is no time. The inseparable nature of these concepts had never occurred to me before. All our techniques for measuring time involve some movement—of gears, shadows, crystals, or electrons—and movement means distance, however small, and thus, space.

We have become so dependent upon timepieces that we tend to think that they somehow contain the time. We say that a watch "keeps" time. Yet time refuses to be bottled up like a genie in a lamp. Whether it flows as sand or turns on wheels, time escapes irretrievably while we watch. Even when the bulbs of the hourglass are broken, when darkness withholds the shadow from a sundial, or when the mainspring winds down until the hands hold still, time itself, like a caravan, packs up and moves on. The most we can hope for our clocks to do is mark its progress, to keep up with its relentless, imponderable schedule, if they're able. The vast ineffable continuum we call Time is never kept. Like a heartbeat or the swing of the planets, its tempo is set by forces far outside our own. Time is to clock as mind is to brain.

The quietude continued to mount. It swelled until it became the silence of Time itself—so great that I could almost hear it; so dense that it changed from a concept to something deeply audible—and in it I saw that space, too, is ultimately indefinable. Since we humans have entered the cosmic theater so late in the show, there remains no finite point in the universe from which to begin measurement. The glittering swarm has played to an empty house for uncountable eons, and its vast complex of relative motion continues without end and without regard for any of our quaint and pitiable instruments. All of human life is conducted on guesswork amid the infinitude of hurrying material.

Between my own heartbeats, the earth on which the tower rode hurled us about its axis some 1800 miles through space each hour. I wondered why this didn't produce constant, remorseless winds at the surface. How can fog settle about with such stillness? Yet, my brain reeled on, even this heliocentric wobble is compounded by additional tangents, other gravitational vectors: our hurtling ellipse about the sun, itself a minor place whose travels within an outer splay of the great galactic wheel constantly inclines our orbital plane, so that every several hundred thousand years or so we go "upside down," while the entire incalculable mass caroms away from its own fantastically remote center. The planets move about like hands wringing themselves, and the whole thing is flung across nowhere.

Thus wordlessly entertained by our human need to locate ourselves in time and space, to measure the brief spark of our lives within this swirling indifferent mass, I began to fantasize that I could actually feel the roll of the universe around me, its hurrying centrifugal matter tugging at the socket in the base of my skull, as the world tilted beneath its curtain of hidden stars. I came to feel that I leaned not against the tower stones but against the quiet and empty air behind me, drawn helplessly into the silent stream of immutable laws.

I tried to cudgel my imagination across the vast inestimable reaches, but the effort brought me quickly to the outer boundaries of my own intellect. There I glimpsed for a moment the awesome blackness, whose ever-receding infinitudes hurled me back from the edge of theoretical abyss, back among the quaint pavilions of my own limited contingency. Like a blind man translating an invisible warning through secondary senses, I lay confined by my petty hopes and fears, deposited where I had begun, breathing gratefully in the wake of my own humbling improbability and awaiting the trivial pulse in my arm. Perhaps, I thought, our survival within this immensity of forces is due to our collective slightness, to our very lack of significance.

Eventually the fog seemed to unlace its fingers ever so slightly as the shapes of things nearby grew slowly out from the darkness, and a gentle grey suffusion of light made outlines visible. I felt Wilf relax slightly. That is, he emitted somehow a small telegraphy of release; something invisible leaked out from the vitality of his inner conflict, and he made a sniffing sound through his nose, though I couldn't tell if the air was drawn or expelled.

"Tha' was no dream, I'm thinkin'," he muttered.

"...What?"

"Ezekiel...Tha' was no dream."

I didn't know what he was talking about and thought it best to wait for whatever else might come. He put his fingers to the edge of his mouth pensively, as though debating whether to peel the truth from his lips like a band-aid.

"We're told tha' Ezekiel had a vision of God, are we no'? ...The wheel within a wheel?"

"...Oh...yeah," I said, remembering vaguely the expression. "That's not exactly the picture I have of The Creator of The Universe... It seems more mechanical than—"

"Exactly! Mechanical! ...An' d'ya no' think it extravagant tha' he would spend fifty-two verses describin' but a dream?"

This was an unexpected subject, and his slant on it was immediately interesting. I was unfamiliar with the scripture he was talking about and had only a dim recollection of the reference from long ago, but the idea that this troubled rebel, this clean, hard, limited churchman who dealt in universal skepticism, was actually postulating a reference in the Bible to a machine which came out of the sky—in essence, a UFO—filled me with a keen curiosity mingled with amused awe.

My mind leapt with irreverent implications. What then about the Star of Bethlehem? I had long wondered about that. The conventional wisdom summoned to explain it had always seemed a bit lame to me. Has it ever been possible in that part of the world to see a star other than the sun in the daytime and all day long? Could not this reportedly much-witnessed event have been a low-altitude phenomenon? And if, as the Bible account goes, it was actually moving for several days before it stopped—stopped, mind you—over a village, the only rational conclusion is that it must have been something non-celestial and under intelligent control. Indeed the scriptural account indicates that it sopped over a particular *location* within the village. There is no other rational conclusion. To believe otherwise is to accept the profoundly unreasonable idea that the physical laws of the universe simply suspended themselves.

When I asked these questions of Wilf, his casual affirmation gave testimony to long and comfortable thought on the subject.

"Of course, laddie. Have ye no' rread of the sons of God brreedin' wi' th' dahters of man? It's rright there, way back in Genesis?"

That there was a scriptural distinction between "Man" and the "Sons of God" was new to me. The more I thought about it, the more it fed my curiosity about all the rarified dialectics of the Old Testament, and for the first time, I grew excited about reading the Bible. What Wilf was telling me conflicted with what my reason had long been poked and prodded into an effort at belief, and this new interpretation soon gripped my imagination in a howling rage to know more.

I thought about it all that day while digging and lugging rocks for the two Johns. I would have liked in particular to know how John of

Nails felt about this idea but was afraid to bring it up for fear that under un-anticipatable questioning I might somehow compromise Wilf.

Any obsession is a hunger for experience, and when at last I was back in the solitude of my room that night, I anxiously took up the guest Bible from the night table and found the passage in Genesis to which he had referred—Chapter 6—where on the delicate brown paper, soft as old skin, it was recorded that:

"...*when men began to multiply on the face of the*
earth, and daughters were born to them, that the
sons of God saw the daughters of men,
that they (presumably the daughters) *were beautiful;*
and they took wives for themselves of all whom they
chose.
...*There were giants on the earth in those days,*
and also afterward, when the sons of God came in to
the daughters of men and they bore children to
them. Those were the mighty men of old, men
of renown."

I liked that "*came in to*" phrase and decided that there might be more to Bible reading than I had realized. I wondered about the reference to "*giants*," though, and made a mental note to ask Wilf about it. Goliath is described as a "giant" in the story of David as told to children, but this passage made me wonder if there might not be more to the term than previously suspected. I knew of no anthropological evidence for giants, though the ancient Egyptians left some pretty impressive over-scale architecture.

Freed of its doctrinal significance the book of Ezekiel proved to be fascinating reading. Its unexpected verses carried me through what he saw, heard, and felt so compellingly I came to believe the man had written for our times, creating a record of events which would have to lie dormant for centuries, awaiting the dawning of rocket power to be fully comprehended. No one living before the 20th century could have brought a sensible frame of reference to these entries.

The writing, despite multiple translations down through the generations, makes it clear that, whatever did happen to him that day in Chaldea, it was no dream. The first twenty-eight verses of the book are entirely taken up with a detailed description of some kind of manned craft which came down out of the north with a roar, with smoke and wind and fire. I read with rapturous attention that it had a hard shiny surface and metallic feet and that it could maneuver close to the ground without turning. From within a bubble canopy a man-like figure dressed in reflective clothing addressed him, calling him "Son of Man" (the same distinction made in Genesis) and gave him instructions. Later, Ezekiel was taken up in this machine and transported to other places.

I found the writing remarkable for its richness of detail on matters he could not have imagined in his own age. The sheer magnitude of the events he recounts evidently went so far beyond those of any dream that the truth of his experience transcended the limitations of his language.

The following evening, when there had fallen a wistful twilight, I met Wilf on the tower and told him excitedly about my reading in Genesis and Ezekiel. He listened with a kind of watchful repose, like an experienced cat. When I asked if he thought we might be a seeded race, cross-bred with extraterrestrials, he laughed. At least I think that's what he did, probably for the first time in years. His mouth spread in a gargoyle grin, and the sounds that came out were like the pounding of a machine when one leg comes loose from the floor.

"Och! Of course! ...`Tis all in the biblical rrecord!"

He was as close to glee as I ever saw him. It was as though a Special-Ed teacher had just got through to an idiot. When I asked him about the distinction between the "giants" and the sons of Man, he said,

"There were no giants, lad...I dinna ken wha' they use tha' werd. In th' original Hebrew the werd is "Nefilim," whuch means `Those who were cast doon'. Tha' is, those who descended to the Erth."

His words were a bright blow to my brain. While I tried to take in their meaning his eyes rested upon me expectantly, with all the charge and intimate grate of rubbed animals.

Wow, I thought, this is great stuff! If this got out, it would make the dogma of the church almost comically groundless, while enlightening a new generation on the basic tenets of the original Christian record. If one of their bright objects was in the sky over Bethlehem, it means that the man called Jesus was himself of special interest to these Nefilim who *"came in to"* human women. I scrolled excitedly through the possibilities while the soaring choral voices of Handel's

Messiah sounded in my head with, *"Won-der-ful!...Mar-ve-lous!"* Stag-ger-ing, I added.

"...Of course..!" I said aloud. "The Annunciation..."

"What?"

I could feel myself smiling.

"Jesus...was a spaceman..!" I announced speculatively and looked toward him. Wilf just grinned thinly in that sinister way of his, the wet lusterless eyes gleaming in the half light.

"And this would explain the origin of our notions about angels as people who can fly..!"

Wilf looked over, his mouth open in what went for a grin. He reached into his sleeve and withdrew a small silver flask. Extending it to me, he asked with amusement, "Would ye care fr'a wee tincture, laddie?"

"Brother Wilf," I said, as I took the flask without looking, "...every moment with you is a feast of utterance received."

"Och! Ye'r daft," he muttered turning his ambiguous smile to the shadows.

To this day the flavor of certain smoky single malts reminds me of that wonderful moment on the tower with Wilf when I hung suspended like a trapeze artist between paradigms.

With further reading, I was soon to realize that these "forbidden" references spill over into the New Testament, too. Matthew, Mark, Luke, and John, who start the whole thing, tell with a few variations many of the same stories as they recount the life of Jesus, albeit many years after the events. In the 9th verse of Matthew's second chapter is the crucial passage:

> *"...and behold, the star which they had seen*
> *in the East went before them, until it came and*
> *stood over where the young child was."*

This is one of the most famous entries in the whole book. Hymns and carols have long celebrated this time when the physical laws of the universe supposedly did something weird. If it is to be believed, this is a description of a witnessed aerial event—but a celestial impossibility of course. Whatever the source of light these people saw, it could not have been a star if, a.) it was moving along, and then, b.) it stopped. Even a mediocre high school physics student today can not think otherwise.

My respect for the unfettered thinking of the brothers in this place grew exponentially. Was I visiting an enclave where the evolution of consciousness had collapsed the old world view that placed human-kind at the epicenter of intelligence in a cosmos perceived as else-where largely lifeless and meaningless? After all, belief that mankind has a special relationship with a more-or-less humanized God is cen-tral to monotheistic religions. The existence of alien beings, especially if they are further advanced than humans, intellectually or spiritually, disrupts this cozy view.

I began to see that as a species we are hide-bound by our comfort-able illusion of mastery and control over nature and that if we can surrender this limiting view, we might discover our place as one spe-cies among many. Even if our gifts of the capacity for caring, rational thought, and self-awareness were to prove unique, if we can get over our notions of pre-eminent intelligence, we might open ourselves to a universe filled with life forms different from ourselves and to whom we might be connected in promising ways we do not yet comprehend.

It seemed that if extra-terrestrial beings exist, indeed if they had taken a hand in the creation of human beings, then our traditional Christian concepts of "angels" and "demons," which may well have evolved from their activities, places an unfair, possibly even irrel-evant, moral code upon these beings. If, instead of "demons" or "an-gels" we used such words as "inter-dimensional realities," "inter-ga-lactic travelers," or even "Jungian archetypes," it would free us from the ethics-burdened concepts of "God" and "Satan" while leaving us more receptive to any second coming of biblical revelation. It might not serve us to prejudge any foretold arrivals with these limited and naively fearful images.

Special Note:

According to the recently discovered Gospel of Judas, known for centuries to have existed, but only brought to light and published by the National Geographic Society in the spring of 2006, Judas attends the final Passover meal, as usual in the New Testament version, but then departs from the customary script. When Jesus appears to pity his other disciples for knowing so little about what is at stake, Judas boldly says he knows what the difficulty is. "*I know who you are and where you have come from,*" he tells the leader. "*You are from the immortal realm of "Barbelo*." This "Barbelo" is not a god but a heavenly destination, a motherland beyond the stars believed by an obscure sect called the Sethians to be something akin to a home world. Judas believes that Jesus comes from this celestial realm, but is not the son of any mosaic god. Instead, he is an avatar of Seth, the third and little known son of Adam. Recognizing that Judas is at least a minor adept of this cult, Jesus takes him aside and awards the special mission of helping him shed his fleshly form, and thus return heavenward. He also, incidentally, promises to show him the stars that will enable Judas to follow him on. This is, at the very least, a strange and provocative exchange to be found in scripture.

12
The Message

Some days later there occurred one of those germinal incidents that one looks back upon years afterward and says here was a point where my life diverged. Here was the very moment from which sprang the events that placed my feet upon a different path. I was quite unprepared for the sort of comical zeal which Fate displayed in leading me on and then elbowing in to become an over-zealous agent of change.

At some point I had been given one of the robes to wear while working outdoors with the Johns. It proved to be surprisingly practical for the weather. At first I had to get used to wearing what seemed more like a dress than I was used to, but the fabric tightened when wet, holding the moisture and thus served as a windbreak while reducing the loss of body heat for the wearer. There was an additional benefit, quite subtle, of this ancient style of garb: by blocking one's peripheral vision, the deep cowl served to direct one's attention upon whatever was pretty much directly in front—the work.

Thus cocooned on a morning wet and drained of its color, while I was digging to remove the slick, gun-metal stones imbedded in a hillside planned for tilling, a grey rain squall whispered in from the sea. All the grasses lay down before it, lightless and artificially distinct, spread upon the hill like fine spun metal. Their every detail of stem and blade shone in matte finish from which the tints had faded, until the pale cascade drenched them all and made them shine, glistening as they dipped and thrashed in the breaking wave of air that rolled ahead of it.

I was learning to like the rain again, after the misery of Southeast Asian monsoons. I had come to hate the rain there, where even my sun-conditioned skin went grey and drawn in its relentless torrents, my jungle sores festered, and my weapons grew rust. Here, though, the rain was welcome to fulfill its traditional role again. Freed from the freight of bad feeling I had imposed upon it the year before, it now presented itself comfortably in its timeless, life-supporting context. Thus, as the lowering morning sky darkened further, I stopped to watch a curtain of fresh rainfall coming up the hill. It sounded like spilling sugar in its progress, and when it arrived my woolen habit and scapular quickly grew heavy and pendulous in the gentle soaking. The robe stayed warm, though, and I had the feeling while viewing the scene from within its cowl that I was peering out at the world of the fifteenth century, as in a steel engraving.

In that moment I was swept with a wave of nostalgia for a true glimpse of past ages and thought how limited we are by artifacts and the monochrome work of long-dead artists for our grasp of what has gone before. Quiet tapestries with their faded blues, and worn implements gloomy with the patina of age, have all conspired with the desiccated leather books of bygone times to veil the vibrancy of the past, to present it in stopped action, and to impart a dulled and hueless tinge to its images. Even the hesitant, yellowed newsreels of the more recent past have forced the early decades of our own century into a muted kind of resonance, as though the events they recorded happened mechanically, out of focus, or under water.

Herein perhaps lies the whole burden of the inquiry. In a way, the great limitation to human understanding is that objects which survive over time are held in hard evidence as to past events. Yet it is a false authority which clings to all those artifacts, antiques, and weapons that I have personally always liked to touch and to think about, for even though they have endured into a subsequent era, they have done so simply by escaping destruction—usually through neglect—and not by some connective imperative, some generic set of rules. Since, ultimately, no direct witness to the ancient past survives the witnessing, in the world that came to be, that which has prevailed can not really be held to speak for what is gone but can only stand in pretended symbol of the vanished reality. In fact, except in the case of rare artifacts that can be directly traced to specific events in history (and even these can only whisper about the gone reality) it is neither. Maybe it is just this incompleteness of the message that intrigues us, that attaches our need for location in time and, ultimately, exaggerates the force of the past.

I stood alone there with these thoughts, one arm resting atop the handle of a shovel, the other tucked inside its sleeve and armhole for warmth, and watched the landscape innocently like a fool, like a diver caught in the rapture of the deep who plays on the bottom while his air runs out. In the years since, I have given much time to thought and reading in history, but standing in that rain, wrapped in ancient garb, I experienced a fleeting transcendental moment in which I felt flung to another time. I was participating in a movie of hillside grasses filmed in the Middle Ages, my thoughts narrating the evidence.

Then the portentous moment arrived—the singular event from which the crowded contingencies of an unknown future derived—disguised, in that way that nature has of keeping us off guard, as a moment of pure buffoonery. It began with the sharp cry of gulls. The sound brought me from lofty reverie, back through the centuries in a flash, and the immediate awareness overtook me with a start. It was unusual for the birds to be aloft in the rain, and as I turned, looking up, I slipped on the wet grass. The handle of the shovel went up the right sleeve of my robe so that as my weight pitched downhill, the spade dug in, the handle caught in the heavy fabric behind my shoulder and began to lift me off the ground. Thus pinioned as from a tent pole, and unable to free my arms to break the coming fall, I felt myself levered through the air in a slow arc. Flailing helplessly, I watched the wet earth rising until it hit me in the face. I landed with a splat a yard or two down slope, and lay stunned and unbelieving for a moment, with the wind knocked out of me. In the next instant, I became aware of a lancing pain in my hip.

I tried to roll over, but thought better of trying to get up, and just lay there for what seemed a long time, resting and sorting the sensations, while the neural nets clashed in my brain and the rain fell into my face. Finally, I realized that I was lying on the shovel handle and had to squirm about like a beached eel for several embarrassing moments, trying to get the shovel out of my clothes.

I have often wondered what that must have looked like to the others and tend to recall it whenever I seek the virtue of humbling thoughts. A man standing perfectly still, who suddenly wheels and hurls himself downhill like some loosed bedlamite upon his face in the wet grass can hardly be an image that inspires trusting work habits among his fellows.

Once free of the shovel, I knew I had a much bigger problem, for the fall had torn the deeper healing tissue around the bullet wound in my leg, and the pain rumbled through me like the muffled thunder of an avalanche, obliterating there, somewhere beyond me, all the structures of my imagination, all the landmarks of my conscious self. The world went red for a moment, and then my peripheral vision began to close in. It felt as though I was passing out, and I rolled to my knees, trying to prevent it. When at last I realized it was bearable and tried to stand, the effort released a bolt up my right side, and I had to sit back down.

Soon two of the brothers came toward me across the hill, their kind and curious faces borrowing a grim pallor from the depths of their blackened cowls. I waved them off with elaborate nonchalance and then finally, unsteadily, got to my feet. I felt woozy and breathless. Tiny white specks swam before my eyes. I was worried that the banshee pain meant the wound had reopened. I put my head down, which made me feel a bit better. Then, probing the sensitive new tissue gently with my fingers, I was relieved to find that I was not bleeding.

When at length I tried to resume the work of freeing the stones from their grip on the soil, I found that the leverage it required was now too painful and knew that, at least for a while, I could not provide it. I limped with increasing uselessness and with growing concern for my footing on the saturated hillside through the rest of the day, resting often and trundling the rocks I would have carried. I could tell that the Johns noticed, but either for reasons of discretion or for the sake of the work itself, said nothing.

Though their hands kept busy, it appeared in the rain that the men moved slowly, as if conserving remnants of their energy from the wind. I did the same out of transparent necessity, and thus each time I returned with a stone they deliberately engaged me in what became an ongoing intermittent exchange on some neutral subject, such as that perennial favorite, the folly of Man, in a kind of broken conversational Morse throughout the rest of the day. I realized that they knew I needed the rests, and I suspected that they had surmised the initial cause of my injury, but to acknowledge their kindness at the time would have meant opening myself to another troubling discussion on the morality of war, or worse, inviting their sympathy.

Once, as I struggled up to their supply of rocks with an especially promising stone it had taken a half hour or so to prize out of the ground, I tried to show its clear striations to John of the Hoary Fringe.

"Look at these fracture points. It just invites the hammer, doesn't it? ...Here, and here..?"

He acted pleased, making a small "O" with his mouth, and indicated that I should drop it near his knee among the ones he was selecting at the moment.

By now the rain had let up to a fine fog drip, which moved against the dark fields in faint veils of mist. I sat for a rest on the pile of muddy rocks and stretched my right leg outward gratefully. John O' The Fringe saw the movement, and as his eyes searched along the stones at hand, he made a remark to John of Nails which I took at first to be a continuation of something between them, but on later reflection I came to see was meant for me.

"God does no' require tha' we give oop our personal dignity, tha' we throw in our lot wi' random people, nor tha' we lose oursel's an' turn fray all tha' is no' Him."

Here he paused, tilted a rock up on its narrow end, and with a single downward blow of his hammer, cleaved it open into two flat segments. Then, as he turned his attention to the wall,

"God needs noothing, asks noothing, and demands noothing fray us. Like the stars...'Tis only the life *with* God whuch demands these things."

Both men worked in silence with their bodies canted somewhat away from me for several minutes following these pronouncements, so I took his comments to have been relevant to something they had been discussing in my absence. Several long seconds into this oddly poignant silence, I felt that I might be intruding and rose to make my way back up the hill to work. Nor did I want to be seen as taking undue advantage of an unspoken interval of rest. As I started away, John's voice came on loudly.

"Experience has taught tha' if knowledge a' God is th' end, then these habits a' life are no' the means, but th' *condition* in whuch th' means operates."

I stopped and turned to find him looking hard at me, his silver locks hanging in dingy wet strings along the sides of his ruddy face.

"Ye dinna' have t'do these things, ye know. No' atall. God does no', I regret t'report, give a hoot. Ya dinna' have t'do these things— unless ye want t'know God. They werk on yoo, no' on Him."

As I watched his face for any further sign, he suddenly broke into his broad, toothy smile and waved me away into the darkling mizzle with his hammer. I thought about those words for the rest of the day, wondering what he meant exactly about knowing God, my physical difficulty always inserting itself through the effort to grasp his illusive message, which seemed to remain abstract, hidden in the middle distance of an evasive idea.

Toward the end of the day, anxious for another excuse to rest again before trudging back for another rock, I sat heavily on the pile again and said, "You know, I've heard some pretty dull sermons over the years. ...John, I think I see what you mean about there being no need to join up with a group of like people or to live according to ritual. In fact, I get more of a sense of spirit, if that's the word, from sitting out here with you chaps in the drizzle with the smell of the earth than I've ever had in a church."

"Ay. Troo enough," he said without looking up from his work. "But do ye want to know God?"

"Well, I, uh..."

"It doesna' matter t'God...But there are conditions tha' moost be met if ye'r t'pursue any kinda' learnin'."

Then John of Nails spoke from beneath his rain-soaked cowl.

"D'ye think y'd know God if ye had perfect knowledge?"

Oo, I thought, that was a good one.

"Well...," I said, "yes, if you had perfect knowledge, you'd know… everything..."

"Ye kinna' get perfect knowledge without discipline. Ye c'n coom oot here an' sit in the rain all ye like an' take in th' evidence, but if ye'r no' willin' t'meet the standards a' greater insight, ye'll remain ignorant a'joost tha' bit a' knowledge."

The idea of striving for perfect knowledge was delicious in its simplicity. As the logical extension of any education, it was easy enough to grasp in concept, but I wondered why it had never occurred to me as a goal of life—perhaps the very *purpose* of life. If you could achieve perfect knowledge, you would surely know God—hell, you would *be* God. What better definition of godliness could there be?

It began to occur to me that they were giving me the central creed of their order—that it is not necessary to seek a knowledge of God, but that if you are going to, there are requirements. As for God Himself, He's too busy and powerful to be bothered with us, but there are nonetheless certain benefits to us of reaching for this kind of complete awareness. Their theology offered a refreshingly simple and direct route to higher consciousness, unencumbered by the fog of dreary senselessness that pervades the liturgy, or the vacuity of sermonizing. It was an intuitively sensible approach which would certainly allow for an unfettered interpretation of the Old Testament. It also went right to the heart of my own niggling guilt about church-going, and it clarified for me why people in churches always seemed like cheerful brainless passengers on a package tour of the Absolute.

It made me chuckle at the utter insignificance of humanity before the infinite courses of the universe.

"Do you think that Christians really understand the conditions we are taught?" I asked. "I mean, if it's true that God brought the vastness of the universe and all that's in it into being by a single act of will — by just lifting a finger — does anybody have any real idea of the unimaginable power we so blithely invoke? What does the hymn say, "...*come abide with us*"? ...I mean, you can't abide for long near even one of our puny industrial generators. They have to be shielded."

I thought I heard a muffled snigger. I could tell by the twist in the folds of their cowls that the Johns exchanged a glance. Then the deep voice of John O' The Fringe said, "...Get ye back to werk, Reaper!"

By the end of the day, I felt certain that my physical capacities had become so reduced that the others must surely think me too soft for the work. The same reason I'd left the archaeological dig had returned to haunt all the good of staying in this delightful place. It was increasingly difficult to negotiate my footing on the slick grass of the hillside, particularly while trying to carry any stones that required both hands. The faces of both Johns by now acknowledged that I was having some kind of trouble, but I feared that any attempt to explain would sound like an excuse, especially after all our good-natured talk about greater things.

That evening, back in my cell, I examined the smooth new tissue of the entry wound, much changed by the surgeon's scalpel and now pink and delicate as a baby's skin. It had knitted smoothly, sealing the gouge with a bloodless membrane, but which appeared now as an enigmatic groove across a purplish green nimbus rising beneath the skin, and the injured muscle trembled fitfully.

The following day it was not much better. The constant bending, lifting and moving about the grassy slope kept jabbing the demons awake in my thigh. By the end of the second day after my aerial tour on the shovel, my diminished capacity had become a nuisance to others, for I saw they had wordlessly begun to take up the slack.

Convinced that I was now perceived as a hindrance to the work and worried that continued efforts there were aggravating my wound, perhaps beyond healing, I finally resolved with reluctance that I had to stop trying to move about on sloping ground. However, I did not want to change to another job. The digging suited me, and I enjoyed watching the Johns transform field stones into smoothly chinked walls. Besides, the wholesome combination of physical labor, along with their open intellectual latitude, helped to realign the detritus of my experiences over the previous year and gently to adjust my planes of need.

They had never countered anything I said from high canonical principles, nor espoused abstention from something called "sin." They had never made reference to retribution for fear of some idol, either, though if pressed they might have given it the name of a saint. They lived in conditions designed to provide a shared experience of the means to an exalted end; regimented and contained, yet with their brains free of it, and I enjoyed their surprising encouragement to face whatever lurked in the unknown darkness beyond the pale and limited circle cast by the lamps of inherited opinion.

Saddened and tired at the end of that day, I dreaded even the long climb up the ridge toward shelter and supper. When at last the bell sounded in the distance, I decided to remain behind, to rest and pretend to be watching the sea until the others were all far ahead, so that no one would feel he had to wait for me.

I had come to love the far tinkling knell as it sounded across the quiet fields at all times of the day, but especially at dusk. It always held a message of peace and a certain promise, and like the voice of a favorite dog, it penetrated until it was heard in the heart, lodging there where it remains a fond memory to this day.

As the others shouldered their tools and began the trek back up the hill to dinner, I sat upon the unfinished wall and listened to the final notes of the bell, plaintive and poignant on the evening air. John of Nails hefted a canvas tool bag over his left shoulder and held it there with his right arm across his chest. He hesitated, his eyes traveling restlessly upward along the line of walls.

"Coomin, Lad?"

"I think I'll wait just a bit, thanks, John...Let this thing stretch for a while. I'll be along in a few minutes."

"...Ye dinna wan'ta miss ye'r supper, noo," he added, while fleeting indecision tugged at the corners of his eyes.

"...John," I asked, "What do you think it was that Ezekiel saw?"

He looked at me without expression for a moment, wearing his weariness loosely, standing upright in his faded folds and controlling his breath. Then he squinted into the distance and wiped his free hand down his side.

"Ye'r warried aboot the wheel within a wheel are ye?"

"Yeah...and I'm leaning toward the, uh, unconventional interpretation."

"...Whether he saw it or he dreamt it, it was a vision all the same."

"Well...I don't think it is all the same...There's a qualitative difference between dreaming and what we call external reality, don't you think?"

His response was singularly memorable, as indeed were most of the thoughts he carefully meted out.

"Well," he said thoughtfully, "You know, religion is simply th'veil tha' man draws over his soul t'hide the nightmare of his own inadequacy. Ye'r interpretation of the werd matters less than whether it gives people soomthin' greater than themsel's t'b'lieve in."

It was inarguable, of course, though it surprised me to hear him say it. I envied the evident freedom that his views bestowed for living open to time and fate and to heretical opinion painlessly, noticing everything, yet choosing the given with a fierce and pointed will, yielding every moment to the freedoms that accompany a single purpose.

As he limped away, I turned and watched the breezes fanning the grass. Shadows spilled into the hollows and gullies as though draining into a vast pool of dark beneath the ground. Gradually the grey twilight deepened, and the evening spread its dusky robe over the sea beyond the haunted ruin on the cliff.

I felt no appetite that night, probably due to the gentleness of the evening and the nourishment of the soul the Johns always seemed to leave with me. Besides, I was in some pain, and discomfort of that magnitude tends to supplant the pleasures of dining.

As night came on, I remembered John O' The Fringe's words of the previous afternoon about the means to a godly life, and while I listened to the wind in the emptiness and watched the stars trace the arc of the hemisphere to fade in the black veil at the edge of the world, I saw his truth for myself: you do not have to wear a hair shirt or anchor yourself outside in the cold dark. If, however, you want to look at the stars, you will find that some darkness is necessary. But the stars neither require nor demand it. Hell, they don't even notice.

In spite of themselves, my friends were gradually peeling back their layers of reserve, revealing the secrets of their order like a nest of Russian dolls. I was honored by their candor and uplifted by their ideas. I was grateful that they never preached. They simply dropped an occasional conceptual stone in the stream and then amused themselves by watching my efforts to retrieve it. It felt good to be alive. I looked up at a river of stars overhead and in their tangled thickets of light found myself wondering if God was mighty enough to stifle His own laughter.

Even though my performance for the last few days had been below the standards set by the others, I knew it was nevertheless expected that I should report to the fields for stone-clearing each morning. Where the work had begun casually, as a natural outgrowth of my first meeting with the masons, I had come to look forward each day to the combination of exercise and camaraderie that it offered. Over time it had, I could see in the others, become my job.

However, I came now sadly to admit that if I was to get off the hill for any healing time without seeming to shirk responsibility, I needed to contrive a change of duties. After a bit of soul searching alone in my room, I decided to request an audience with the Abbot for the purpose of seeking his advice in what might well be an entirely imaginary dilemma, but one which for me radiated channels of discomforting possibilities. Besides, I hoped that whatever might result from an interview with him might carry the appearance at least of his endorsement.

I had in mind to explain my reluctance to leave the Johns for temporarily lighter work, perhaps for a spell in the orchard, where I thought I could be of help for a while with less risk to my footing. Accordingly, even though I had never even spoken to the Abbot, I wrote him a short letter, pleading an appointment at his convenience in hopes that he might guide my selfish resolve, or better yet, serve to intervene in some diplomatic way before I had to spend another day dragging myself around the hillside.

The answer came that night in the form of a small note, which appeared on my night table, ink-dashed in black on monastery letterhead, bearing simply the time, 5:30 AM, and his florid initial. There was something both exalted and quaint about its simplicity. But it unnerved me. It made him suddenly real. I had been in residence there long enough to have fallen formally under his unquestioned authority, and the spare efficiency of his note left me with unexpectedly complex reservations about meeting him. He stood now in regal disproportion to all that had happened to me in this hospitable place—everything, from the surprising informality and discretionary anomalies, to the food, shelter, humor and intellectual freedoms.

Suddenly my problem became small, unworthy of his attention, and all I wanted then was to remain quiet, to shrink if possible into greater obscurity. After all, people heal, but the land must be tended, nurtured every day. The seasons don't wait for men to feel good. What is an outsider's sore foot to a general, a chieftain whose people have endured centuries of slaughter at the hands of heathens, whose role as keepers of learning was usurped by the barbarous printing press? What an unmitigated wimp I would seem before a man whose character has been forged in the crucible of harsh discipline, of silence and celibacy, a lifetime of denial, thought, and who knows what other obscure vows of conduct and learning. The little square of paper with its clear, ominous numbers grew ponderous with ambiguity, irony, and paradox.

I put it down feeling foolish and uncertain. My heart screeched to withdraw the request, but as I was to find out, the Abbot had his own reasons for the interview.

13
CEO

In the early morning before first light, I slipped out of my room and limped along the darkened corridors to the Abbot's office at the south end of the manor. The hallway ended in a small foyer bounded on both sides by full bookcases and a plain writing table of the sort that was in each of the rooms. There was a stark and macabre formality about these things that a pair of very fine and colorfully gruesome 19th century paintings of martyrs in their suffering on the walls at each side of the large office door did nothing to relieve. The art, like most religious painting, with its secret meaning that I could never quite formulate in thought, though it often touched me with a vague sort of pathos, was dark with age and graphic in its depiction of sacrifice and pain.

There was St. Sebastian tied to a tree, his doleful eyes rolled heavenward and his pale European body shot full of arrows. The other was of a woman, evidently being prepared for a public drowning just ahead of a thunderstorm. In my mood of morbid apprehension, I found it all quite depressing. I wondered if those who went before the Spanish Inquisition had been treated to anterooms like this.

The heavy wooden door to the office was richly carved in high relief of biblical events, seriated over some eight panels. The work was old, very high quality and opulent of detail, on which the urgent figures emerged from each section as though spilling out of boxes. It looked to me as though they were all trying to escape.

I approached the door and searched for a place on it to knock, wondering if the small sound of my knuckles would carry through it. I rapped unconvincingly and waited. It was quickly opened by Brother Timothy, the Abbot's secretary, who had been so hospitable when I first arrived. He gestured for me to enter, a permanent evangelical smile underlining the hypnotic mildness of his green eyes, which lay like quiet pools beneath the high ridge of his brows.

"Good morning," he squeaked as he closed the door behind me. His voice was high and elflike, carrying his whispered words on gossamer breath, while his hands grasped each other as though for reassurance.

I nodded an edgy greeting and stepped into a warm and darkly furnished office with linen-fold paneling around the walls and a scattering of Persian carpets on the floor. It smelled of tallow and wood and lemon oil, with a certain sweetness hovering at the edges. A heavy desk stood centered before an enormous stone fireplace whose sculpted mantel and tooled facing rose to the ceiling where it met a spread of vaulting beams. A fire burned cheerfully, launching strange penumbral shapes from chair legs across the rugs, while numbers of fluttering Presbyterian nymphs peered down from the high shadows of the crown molding.

From an antique clock on the mantelpiece came a hollow knocking sound, like a knuckle on a box. The room was perfection—a delicate, almost allegorical, suggestion of a fairy tale setting. Except for the fire, all was a motionless tableau of expectancy. Rank has its privileges, I thought, even here.

An amber lampshade cast a rectangular pool of subdued light onto the center of the desk, while faint ribbons of starlight lay upon the cushions of a large sofa beneath the latticed window, revealing to my surprise a large black dog that lifted its head as I entered. I turned to find that Timothy had slipped out noiselessly. There was no one else in the room.

The dog's tail thumped quietly on the sofa cushions, and I crossed to make friends. He smiled widely up at me, his eyes narrowing happily, with his long rose-colored tongue hanging out moist in the lamplight. He readily submitted to having the back of his head scratched and quickly dropped into contented guttural breathing while I administered shiatsu behind his ears.

While thus indulging ourselves, a low side door opened from the outside, and I turned to see the entrance filled with a hooded figure in silhouette against the night. From it came the single edged word, "Bernard—."

Evidently, the dog was forbidden to climb on the furniture, and at the sharp sound of his name, he closed his mouth and stared. His face turned mournful, and his body became immobile. Then, slowly he climbed down, his weight sinking heavily from shoulder to shoulder. He paused and looked accusingly up at me, then plodded despondently from the room and into the outside darkness, his toenails clicking on the threshold. His departure left me feeling wronged and vulnerable.

"Good morning," said the Abbot quietly, closing the door behind him and stepping into the room.

"Good morning, sir," I said. "It's good of you to make the time to see me."

He moved without another word to his desk and pushed back his cowl. There he paused to examine something on the desk, canting his head oddly into the narrow light and touching his chin to the big knuckle of his right fist, while the fingers of his left hand moved delicately over the papers. I couldn't interpret his reticence and watched him closely for any sign of what might be expected of me.

He appeared to be a man of something more than sixty years with a lean, muscular head on which the dark skin seemed less to hang than to be resting upon its prominences. Around his shadowed eyes the flesh had been molded by decades of wind and weather into meridians of scrutiny, while beneath the catenated curves in his cheeks the sinews that worked his jaw flexed visibly. He pursed his lips in thought for a moment, which gathered the lines around his mouth as though drawn by strings. The steel-grey hairs which haloed his forehead in the lamplight had probably started the morning groomed, but the cowl had left them standing unruly and transparent.

"Bernard thinks I sold him out," I ventured, trying to joke and hoping the sound of the words might be easier to manage than the ponderous silence. After a few moments, he looked up suddenly as though he had forgotten that I was there, smiled, and stepped from behind the desk into the firelight.

It was then that I noticed he was partially blind. The clouded and shadowy pupil of his left eye was useless. His right, though, as if to make up for this deficiency, seemed preternaturally alert and observant, and as he peered around the room with the jut of his face, motes of light winked through it.

He gestured for me to sit on the couch recently vacated by the resentful Bernard, and then he drew up a captain's chair. He sat down carefully, with a studied precision. Then, placing his elbows on the armrests and leaning slightly forward, he enlaced the fingers of both hands and held them as though wishing to contain an internal tension.

"I often think," he began softly in a refined and curbless accent, "that our civilization has fallen out of touch with the night..." He glanced past me to the first hint of morning beyond the window. "With our lights, we have driven the night back to the forests and the sea."

I was relieved at his thoughtful manner and the way he chose to open our dialog indirectly. There was a polite circumspection about it which implied that he understood me to be at least as uneasy about coming to see him as I actually was. Besides, his observation struck me on a deeply personal level, and I shuddered to remember why.

The night had provided the enemy in Vietnam with a great psychological and tactical advantage. In a third-world country that has little or no electricity, life, including combat operations, goes on uninterruptedly after nightfall, while a modern aggressor who has never known a world without artificial light must stop at the darkness, must pull in and contain his activity. He becomes small at night. He gets surrounded.

It chilled me to remember those twittering hot nights enshrouded in the manifold black wrappings of darkness, tension, paradox and fear, but I did not want to address the complex of details that would be necessary to explain this truth, or to introduce talk of war to the quiet gentility of the room.

"Yes...," I said softly, "I agree."

After a thoughtful pause, he reached into the shadows and drew forth a small table that held a bowl of whole pecans which he placed between us, as with a wry smile he said,

"...It seems that we are enjoying your use for the old harvester."

I chuckled to realize that, of course, he knew all about it, that indeed the friendly contests of strength which were still going on with the harvester axle would not have been continued without his tacit approval.

"...As if there wasn't enough exercise around here," I offered, hoping he would credit me with being aware of the irony.

"All effort nourishes the spirit," he said.

His long fingers rattled among the nuts in the bowl, then withdrew two, which he began turning together in his hand like Captain Queeg's ball bearings.

"You have been working to clear the lower east field for some time now. ...What have you learned?"

I was surprised by the question. Was I supposed to be learning something? What had I missed? Was there a quiz? His query pushed me more off balance.

"...Well, I've, uh, learned that there is no shortage of material for the walls...and, um, that gravity is indeed an immutable law."

His eyes remained downcast, and I was immediately sorry for what I had said, realizing that whatever his reason for asking, it did not deserve the indignity of a flippant remark. He smiled flatly, the corners of his mouth jabbing at his sunken cheeks in the sebaceous orange firelight which played along the side of his drawn face. I knew that I was being patronized and deserved it.

He made a fist around the pecans, and I heard the muffled crunch of their destruction. Then he opened his slender fingers, picked among the sherds, and extended his hand to me, wherein lay an unbroken half of the nut. I took it gratefully and made another attempt to respond to his question, partly to grapple some dignity from the silence.

"...Um, from the first...I have been conscious of a force of... custom...a tradition—yet these are not quite the words—that exists here almost independent of men. It simply borrows for its life from the ritual which people have created to nurture it, so to speak, to maintain its continued existence—a kind of energy that passes through us and along each generation of those who've come to live here...I have wondered if it is simply the accrued inertia of long practice, or if maybe I'm just imagining something..." When I realized that I was personifying the thing I stopped, embarrassed.

In the tenuous blue light from outside the window, I began to make out details of his features. The prominent cheekbones appeared at first to be bruised, but I soon saw that a network of tiny veins in his cheeks were broken and smashed flat, appearing like a blue paste beneath his skin. It looked like the result of an old injury, and seeing it brought back my uneasy feeling, intensified now by the realization that I was in the presence of a complex man who bore the markings of an impenetrably rough past.

I watched as he fingered the segments of the nuts in his palm, separating out the hulls. He held up a smooth fragment of shell, pinched gently between his fingers like a broken bird's egg.

"Here in the delicate fissured hemispheres `tis writ, we must believe, each feature of the tree which bore them, each feature of the tree they will come to bear..."

The appropriateness of his metaphor struck me so suddenly that I had to wonder if he had brought forth the bowl of pecans in the first place precisely to illustrate this point.

"...Just as," he continued, "the history of the Earth is written in the stones which you have come to...discuss."

Everything he said struck me like pillows, leaving soft wounds of introspection on my defenses. How could this detached and remote little man, whom I had seldom even seen, know so much about the lives of each of his charges?

"Well, um, I'm just having a bit of trouble holding up my end of the hillside lately," I began. "It's just temporary, and I was hoping that you might advise me of some other way to make myself useful for a while...as I don't want to have the others feel that I am shirking...Uh, I was thinking perhaps the orchard..."

His grey eye rested briefly on something behind me and then traveled out the window.

"Our clearing efforts are always short-handed," he said rising from the chair and passing his spread hands along the folds of his robe in the manner of a woman smoothing her apron. There was nothing feminine about the gesture, simply practiced and familiar. He stepped around the sofa to the window and looked down to where the misty fields had begun to take form in the eastward dimness.

"The rocks seem to grow from the ground," I said. "For every one we dig out, the earth seems to throw up two more to take its place... Heh, heh."

"Of course, it is the earth which grows from the stones," he all but whispered without turning.

I rose and joined him at the window, looking down on the fields where I had spent so much time digging and carrying and philosophizing with the Johns. Just outside a flowering tree grew beneath the window ledge, its blossoms like a form of brilliant knitting—bright stitches of white yarn, blown open and fastened onto rain-blackened boughs. From this high remove, the fields beyond seemed insignificant, lost in the broad panorama of sloping headlands, with the North Sea spread like an endless sheet of metal into the haze beyond. Our fine fieldstone walls, assembled with such meticulous care, were reduced and softened by distance to rambling black lines, like dark string gently flung.

"Do you not hear the Aeolian music when God and Man work together to make fruitful the fallow plain?"

It seemed an odd way for him to phrase a question. It sounded unlike his normal speech, as though he was quoting something, and I took it lightly, misunderstanding his tone.

"Well...," I said somewhat distractedly, admiring the wide stillness beyond the glass, where the absence of wind seemed to prolong the early twilight, making the shore calm as a lakefront, "...I thought the field was doing pretty well when God was running it all by Himself."

The Abbot made no reply, but in his profound silence I knew instinctively that I had again misjudged the moment and had said the wrong thing. He had given me to understand earlier that my humor was inappropriate, and in a crippling effort to relieve my discomfort, I had forgotten myself already, had lost track of my tenuous position. A void opened between us, and a hot sense of woe sagged through me.

"Oh, no..." I muttered unconvincingly. "I'm sorry," and glanced over at him.

His face held the calm and settled purpose of a man expecting the worst, whose every fear has been instantly gratified. He sighed, and looked up at the ceiling as though something of rare interest were going on up there.

When at last he spoke, though, he did not seem to be angry. Well, not exactly.

"How long have you been with us now?" he asked with a look of mournful indulgence, though the disparity of expression in his eyes made it troubling and impossible to guess what he was thinking.

"I, uh...," I began and had to stop. I realized that I actually didn't know how long it had been. I had so abandoned myself to their sheltered ways and to repaying them in their only discernible currency, that a sense of the passing weeks had become lost in the daily work.

"Well, I—"

"Are you happy here?" he asked.

"Oh, yes, sir...I've tried to make myself useful...I don't want anyone to think that I would presume on your hospitality..."

He held up his hand in a dismissive gesture, accompanied by a weak smile.

"Do you belong here?"

His question rose before me like a sudden wall. Was this very issue one that I had been avoiding subconsciously since long before my arrival? Did I really belong here, or anyplace else for that matter, simply because it was, what, safe?

Could the physical labor and intellectual freedom I encountered here have held such voluptuous appeal simply because they offered an alternative to something that was happening on the other side of the world? I wondered then if I had been seeking in the company of the brotherhood some balance to the artificiality of comradeship enforced by combat, and whether I was truly so simple-minded as to have remained with them out of fear.

He must have read my dilemma, for he added, "Perhaps we possess some deficiency in common, you and I, which makes us subtly un-adaptable to the ways of a wider world...But we are not excused the task of seeking within ourselves the truth of being a force of nature...instead of a feverish little clod of grievances that the world will not devote itself to making us happy."

I looked at him to see if this last was directed at me, but his good eye was seeing inward, the frosted gaze of the other, fixed blank as a cat's in the half light. I wondered if he was going to qualify his statement, but he stood remote and silent as a wax figure staring through the glass, his form in the grey dawn still as congealed grease. In the silence that ensued, I became aware again of the mantel clock, its repetitive wooden clunk grave and resonant.

"Without this knowledge," he continued quietly, "we can never truly be of service to others."

I could only guess what his words meant to himself, but there was a confessional sort of intimacy in the way he spoke them with his powers of action momentarily suspended, which made me feel as though I had somehow strayed past museum guards, into a forbidden gallery of ideas, kept hidden from the public for the dangers they entailed.

His implication that directing one's life outward, toward usefulness to others, could be a conscious goal came without warning. That is, the idea itself wasn't unfamiliar to me in a catechismic, poetical sort of way, but this was the first time it came with sufficient portent to yield a feeling of personal displacement. This time it came, without the slightest hint of admonition, from one whose life was the very embodiment of its aspiration, and his words settled upon me an uncomfortable benediction.

With a growing sense of inadequacy, I could at first relate his words only to my recent past and asked naively, "Do you mean that you can't really serve a common purpose unless you know your own...?"

I couldn't finish, torn between wanting to say "job" or "self." I knew instinctively that his meaning was deeper and more grand than that, but this was the only substitute for a good idea I could come up with on short notice, while the affective meaning of his words continued to crowd my mind.

"...Yes," he said distantly. "...Something like that."

"How does anyone know where he belongs, really?" I asked.

"Self-knowledge is a subset of all learning," he replied, turning his face full on me for the first time since we had stepped to the window, "Knowledge determines character...and character is always destiny."

His voice was modulated, but this sentence was delivered carefully, distinctly, like links in a heavy chain. It sounded at first like an aphorism—one of those cute summaries of the human condition that are fed to children as collective generalities—but his demeanor was serious, constraining me to consider what he had said more carefully than I might have.

I was beginning to see firsthand the briskly intelligent reserve that characterized his leadership and to appreciate the magnitude of personal experience that loomed behind his words. I smiled to realize the subtlety with which he had assumed the role of teacher, revealing his precepts with all the delicacy of touch and allusive circumspection of a fable.

I liked the syllogistic relationship he drew between knowledge and character, character and destiny. Of course! We are all products of our knowledge—at least products of what we *think* we know. I remembered John of Nails asking, if you had perfect knowledge, wouldn't you know God? The beauty of the question is that it applies no matter what your concept of a supreme being might be. It follows that the acquisition of knowledge, and not the vagaries of "goodness," is the road to godliness! I was beginning to see the point that knowledge was the root course, if not the very purpose itself, of living.

"Heh!" escaped involuntarily as these thoughts jelled. I was surprised to hear my voice break the stillness. "Well...at least I know of some places I *don't* belong."

"Yes," he replied with a fathomless calm that foretold nothing of the gold to follow. After a short pause, he added a simple declarative statement that has continued to resonate within me through all experience ever since: "...All knowledge is good." Pronounced with the barest hint of emphasis on the word *all*, concise and profound in its simplicity, it launched me into a minor tempest of quiet speculation.

"What about knowledge of evil...or what you might call 'negative learning', like knowing how to do harm or to kill?" I asked him.

He reached out a finger and ran it along the latticework before him, then turned his hand to examine the tip, perhaps for dust, as he spoke.

"Unlike mercy," he began slowly, "the quality of learning *is* strained. It is always conditional upon circumstances...the challenges, disappointments and opportunities which we encounter every day. Even as we move from moment to moment. Learning is constant, but it is not like a coin which remains physically whole even through the most infamous transactions."

I recalled again that John of Nails had said learning required discipline.

"Yes..." I said. "So if all knowledge is good, but we can be corrupted by the getting of certain knowledge...then we must not only learn, we have to, in effect, learn learning. So the epistemology of our condition..."

I looked to him for approval, but he had turned away without a sound, retreating out of the slant greying light to the interior of the room, and my thought went incomplete, like a hole in the air. He did not need to know the effect of his words nor hear how I might choose to direct his *principium.*

I had the feeling that in this lay the essence of his power. He served as a hidden catalyst, the man who worked behind it all, a movement in the shadows of the candle, who, avoiding directive, served rather in other ways to cause the changes through which his charges might grow. This was why I had so seldom seen him in all the time I had been with them. He was known not so much by his presence, as by his effect.

He stood with his back to the fire, glancing at the papers on his desk, which I took as a sign that our interview was over, that I might be detaining him. The economy of his words gave them a delayed effect, a slow-curing formula which set their truths within me over time, though their immediate influence upon how I felt about being there at all was profound.

He had raised the question of my objectives, and I had to face the grim fact that I had none. At least none that I could articulate beyond the humbling portent of my own survival. I had none, and the brothers had all. They lived and worked with singular purpose, which left me to suppose that I had only been trying to borrow from their communal sense of mission in order to cloak myself with bogus intention, to wear the badge of manifest resolve.

I did not like having to recognize this about myself. I liked even less having been lured into the fact. Still, this was not, after all, a great epiphany, no Saul-on-the-road-to-Damascus kind of revelation—for single events rarely awaken within us a total stranger—but he had left me feeling numb and uncertain, my powers of adjustment temporarily exhausted. I knew that he was right to question my presence there, but I could not suppress a flash of irritation at his device for getting me to question it. In so doing, though, he served to set my thoughts on new courses, for which I am grateful to this day.

When he spoke again, it was with his face still turned in the direction of the desk.

"The acquisition of knowledge," he said, "is not unlike making a clearing in a forest; the greater your progress, the greater your exposure to the unknown."

I sorted through the implications of this metaphor to test its basis for the other things he had said and found that I enjoyed my susceptibility to its imagery. Long conditioned by direct illustration, I suddenly recalled the stick-up visual aids on felted easels I had seen as a child in Sunday school.

As I crossed to the door, I said, "It would probably all be too easy if we could just go about borrowing ready-made souls."

"Yes," he replied with what I thought was a slight chuckle. Then he added, "...For who can flourish in an atmosphere of compliance?"

As usual I didn't quite get what he meant at first. Like much of what he said, the meaning was initially illusive—intuitively true, yet it left me feeling for a moment that I was grasping for wet soap.

"...Sir," I began with some difficulty, not quite knowing how to complete what I wanted to say. "I hope you do not think that I have tried in any way to take advantage of your good graces. I have not meant to overstay my welcome..."

"You are welcome here, John. If this is what you want. Look at what you know of yourself, so that you can bring known assets to bear upon the questions...And remember that self-criticism is also a tactic for remaining ineffectual. It contains permission to surrender."

Then he added, somewhat wistfully, almost it seemed in afterthought to himself, "...Many people are content with temporal success because they lack the aspiration to strive for something truly noble enough at which to fail."

While I sifted through these remarks for hidden insults, he looked up and smiled, I know, with all the warmth in his heart, all of its remnant that his damaged face could show.

"Good morning," he said by way of ending.

"Good morning, sir...Thank you."

I turned and let myself out the heavy door, somewhat confused and a bit melancholy. His words had left me feeling embarrassed and manipulated and fraudulent, rekindling the sense of isolation with which I had first arrived. He had presented me with issues which would eventually have to be resolved, one way or another, and I had now to turn the question I had often asked on behalf of the brotherhood upon myself: was this sheltered life truly productive of a higher sort of existence, or was it after all merely a ritualized escape from what it professed to celebrate?

For myself, I really did not know, and in order to shelter myself from further philosophical speculation which might lead to discomforting conclusions about my own integrity, decided at least for a while not to care. I understood only that their life was good for me in multiple ways. It cleansed and inspired, sanctioned and forgave; and I resisted having to formulate alternatives. Though I held no formalized intention of joining the order, of taking vows, I had gradually relegated to that compartment of the mind that we no longer keep on active duty the realization that I would eventually be moving on. Yet the Abbot's good words would serve to tinge forever afterwards my memory of events there with a vague and lingering sense of failure.

Back in my room, my petty and temporal concerns aside, I wrote down as much of what he had said as I could remember, and I thought about his advice for the rest of the day. Gradually the full weight of his insight emerged, and it was then that I realized the time for my departure had come. I decided to address another letter to him, thanking him for his time and his kind attention, and letting him know privately of my intention to leave the following day.

An answer, written in his even foliated hand, came back. In it he expressed his support of the decision and added the following:

"Thinking independently and acting without
reservation upon one's own moral convictions,

you begin to serve a higher order than those
who march with the unthinking majority and who
must suffer the consequences of believing what
they are told to believe."

It was like him, I thought, to have put such a bullion thought on paper, rather than telling me directly and risking the loss of its details. I pressed his note in the pages of my journal, the way maidens of the last century saved wild flowers. Like the other things which he had found in his thoughts and taken gently out for me to see, it would grow in relevance to me over the years. I have saved the things he told me, caressing them from time to time with the fond hands of memory.

14
Exodus

The morning came softly hazed from the sea and filled with the steady hiss of falling water. It rained all that day and the next, windless and soft, and fog hung deep in the trees, caught in the branches like fragments of uncertain day.

The postponement caused by the rain became a mixed blessing, for the physical pain in my thigh rose unexpectedly to the point of near immobility, then gradually subsided over the next day, settling at last into a distant noise, like living by a river, though the my hip remained stiff and quite sore to the touch. I suffered a loss of appetite, which sometimes accompanies pain but always seems to inhabit the foreshadow of imponderable events. I was more anxious than I realized.

The weather kept drawing my thoughts outside. I missed the work, for it had come both in reality and in metaphor to represent all the good of my sojourn. I even missed the weight of rain-soaked wool across my shoulders while searching the ground for the rocks that revealed evident breaking points.

My thoughts were mending at a different rate. Though I welcomed the delay that the weather imposed, I felt since the decision was now fixed that I had become a stranger again, an interloper whose right to use the facilities lay compromised. I didn't know how to say goodbye, and like a nervous man who finds false security in keeping his hands in his pockets, I sought refuge for most of those two days in the quiet of the library, where I would be safe from encounter with the brothers I knew to be at work outdoors. This provided some recovery time by minimizing the need for movement, but I was haunted by a growing sense of impotent nostalgia and the poignant distractions of comforting grey views outside through the fluid panes of ancient window glass.

How do you take leave of men who live comfortably in isolation yet who have so profoundly enriched you as to create a disparity in the exchange that you can never bring into balance? I worried that the silent brotherhood's inscrutable information network, by whatever means it operated, would fail to explain my absence to the Johns and to Wilf in tones of suitably grateful apology for skulking away.

Feeling humbled before the nameless eminences of the road, my thoughts of leaving came with a mingle of submission and sadness. I realized that my time there had simply to be taken as an interlude in a grander pageant, and I resolved to keep its lessons whole. But old doubts emerged, and the saddening likelihood that I would never see these good people again nibbled steadily away at my carefully tended, somewhat infantile serenity.

Partly because I was humbled by the interview, I shared with no one but the Abbot my intention to leave. I felt that I was being thrown out—politely to be sure, but effectually dismissed—and wished simply to slip quietly away at the first break in the weather. Besides, I didn't really have the words to express the fullness of my feelings to any of the men with whom I had formed such unexpected bonds. I felt as ignorant of how to take leave of their society as I had been of how to enter it. I was convinced that no one knew of the Abbot's gentle directive, though once or twice it seemed that a few men with whom I had but a nodding acquaintance smiled at me with needless solicitude when we passed.

When the third day dawned clear I returned to my room after lingering over breakfast and closed my little suitcase. I left notes for Wilf and both Johns on the table, knowing that they would all have been at their jobs on the back side of the ridge by first light, and with a final look around at the marvelous contraption of plumbing, closed the door for the last time on the tiny space for which I had grown such genuine affection. I passed quietly through the deserted foyer of the manor and pushed open the front door.

There, assembled in the close, were some 15 of the brothers, including all my friends. I was speechless. They gathered about, enclosing me with their arms and with their good wishes, some with cheeses and bread, which they pressed into my hands, wrapped for the journey. Others handed me personal prayers written on cards and folded bits of paper. Their eyes held looks of saddened caring, looks of inestimable fidelity. My throat caught, my lips parted like a dumb man's, but no sound would come out. I felt myself beginning to cry and tried hard to swallow down the growing pressure at the back of my throat.

John of the Hoary Fringe clapped me heavily on the back, his even rows of teeth joined like paving, while John of Nails shook me by the hand and grinned harshly. Young Colum was there, too, hopping about, chirpy and angular as a cricket, as openly excited as he doubtless would have been at the prospect of traveling himself. His toneless laughter rang forth like a cracked bell, his tiny hands clenched to grasp the vision that eludes us all.

The circle opened slightly and Wilf came forth, his naturally dark demeanor made grim by the cheerful surround of many bright countenances. He carried in his hands the most interesting walking cane I had ever seen. It was fashioned from a stand of twisted vine and fitted with one of his hand-wrought brass gremlins, mounted so that its back formed the handle. He held it forth to me, but my eyes so flooded with tears that I could hardly see it. I took it from him and turned it over and over in my hands.

I tried to thank him, but Wilf leaned in with his hungry aquiline smile and rasped, "Don't try t'express ye'r gratitude by sendin' flawers, laddie. They'll only cause rumor and dissension."

This made everybody laugh, including me. My gratitude was inexpressible. I could not summon the words to tell them how moved I was at this demonstration of affection, nor all they had come to mean to me. I hoped—I prayed—that they would somehow understand how I felt. Their send-off touched me as deeply as anything in my experience. Limping away with my new cane, my pockets bulging with their packages, I kept turning and waving for as long as I could see them.

Over the years since, I have often had reason to evoke the recollection of those smiles and to reflect upon the good will that provoked them, for it has the power to protect, to strengthen resolve, and to confer honor; it has the power to heal and to bring a man safely home after all other resources are exhausted.

I had left Vietnam without a backward glance, closing as well as I could a heavy door of memory upon it. Even though some of the terrors and muffled cries there still leak around the hinge pins, it is today the shared lamp glow of a small cadre of the Brothers Observant that lights my way.

As I walked down the long drive, away from that dwelling of sainted men, the trees overhead spread motionless against a flushed and brightening sky. Soon a wide dawning spread pink across all the taught bright morning like the exaggerated backdrop of an expensive opera. The mountains in the distance, which had appeared so blue from the ridge, were now verdant, smooth, bare and undulant, like folds in velvet. There was something sensuous about it, over-ripe and promising, as though all sorts of funny fruits might fall from it for my selection.

At the foot of the drive I encountered a small Morris automobile parked in the shade near the entrance columns, just off the main road. The car bore driving school license plates—a large red "L" mounted on the bumpers. Slouched against it was an indifferent-looking young man with full sideburns who was smoking a cigarette. He was dressed in a mid-length black leather coat over tight pegged slacks and a plain narrow tie.

"Morning," I said.

"Morning," he replied indifferently, the sight of a man in jeans limping off monastery property with his pockets full of bread and cheese apparently of no special interest.

"Nice day, huh?"

He took a drag on the cigarette and looked vacantly at the sky for a moment.

"Weather's been lettin' us doon," he said flatly.

It struck me as ironic that he would make such an observation on the first really clear day we'd had in some time. Then I thought, yes of course, the weather is not a neutral topic, even for passing strangers. We always impart to it a vibrant personification, involving struggle and conflict. It could be wayward and spiteful, as when people say, "It's been trying to rain all day." Or it could be toiling on your behalf: "The sun's been trying to come out." Or, as the man said, it could be lazy and selfish; it could let you down.

"Taking an early break?" I asked, smiling.

He glanced at his watch.

"Nah...I'm suppoosed t'teach th'moonkies oop theer t'drive." He gestured absently over his shoulder with a thumb. Then he pinched the cigarette stub between his thumb and middle finger and dropped it on the ground. He smeared it out with his shoe, nodded disinterestedly to me, and climbed into the car.

I felt a sharp resentment at his reference to "monkies." What could he possibly know of their lives, of the hopes and fears of virtuous men who drove themselves with daily devotion against the deeper currents of nature? I dismissed him as a fool and turned away onto the road.

Walking in the same direction I had been headed those uncounted weeks before, I resumed the journey to wherever the next town might be, not entirely aware yet of the many changes the long interlude had wrought upon the way I viewed the world.

I went forth, leaning on Wilf's cane somewhat more than necessary, enjoying the gift as much as the support it gave, my hopes trembling against despair. The weather was fine and cool. The road plunged through humped and grassy hillocks, past sheep, an occasional horse, and fields with breezes swimming through them where small cottages with sash windows built close to the ground snuggled into the green hills.

I remembered seeing steeples protruding from a fold in the earth and felt that a town must be near, for animals and cottages were things I had glimpsed only rarely on the northern stretches of the road. Eventually though, the valley broadened, and between its lateral heights went so far beyond sight that it seemed to be heading for open sea. It appeared endless, and I began to invest a bit of early despair again in finding a sheltered place to spend the night.

After some time, I heard a car approaching from behind and moved aside to let it pass. Instead, it slowed, and I turned just as the Morris with its "Learner" plates shuddered to a stop beside me. The engine quit, and with a plaintive squeak the car went silent. The plump and smiling face of Brother Royster greeted me from the driver's window, while beside him the young instructor looked at the ceiling of the car and threw lariats with his eyes.

"Care to join us for a wee lift, John?" asked Brother Royster.

"Why, yes, thank you," I said, "As long as it won't interfere..."

"We'll save ye some steps then," he replied cheerfully.

I got into the back seat with gratitude.

"So, you were elected, were you?" I asked.

"Yes..." said Brother Royster officiously, "...and I do no' understand this machine atall."

As he restarted the engine, and we bucked forward, it was clear that his relationship with machines was a new one. He was not finding it easy, the difficulties apparently being in large part conceptual and aesthetic.

"It seems to me," he said, "tha' if one is disengagin' the gears, one ought to have to let the clootch oot, instead of pushing it in. To me,`in' represents engagement, and `oot' represents disengagement."

"Och, come on noo, Broother Royster, baby," said the instructor, "Let's get the show on the rood, awright?"

After a harrowing ride of a mile or so, during which the good brother favored both sides of the road, they dropped me off at the intersection of a farm track, where bands of drying mud criss-crossed the tarmac and the shoulder provided room to turn the car around. I bid Brother Royster a fond good-bye, though he was preoccupied. With much over-revving and clashing of gears, they lurched back the way they had come, the sound of the tortured machine diminishing with distance and leaving me once again profoundly alone with the scuff of my shoes on the deserted road.

I walked on through most of the day feeling light and insubstantial as a handful of aurora, through empty and solemn hills which seemed inhabited suddenly with a great force of loneliness. Pastures heaped with silence rose at every turn, veined by the paths of unseen cows. There were fields that seemed held together by the very grip of a single ancient tree. I began to feel increasingly irrelevant, the way a ghost must, occupying the shape of its past to little effect. In the distance ahead more mountains lay humped against the sky, giving the landscape the blind and blunted look of a creature under blankets.

A few throaty crows and flocks of barking seagulls arrived overhead, and the smell of the sea returned. Then through their cries, I began to hear a faint rumbling sound, tinny, broken, and fetched on an unsteady breeze from the hills ahead. As it grew louder and more distinct, I realized that the noise was approaching around a turning in the road.

Presently two men appeared with a flatbed wagon on which an old upright piano was lashed to the stakes. One man sat the bench board while the other walked a tired-looking grey horse whose hooves made a hollow cupping sound on the road as its head bobbed in the wagon traces. Every time the unsprung wheels hit a bump the piano muttered an alarming and discordant tune of protest. I smiled and nodded.

"Evening," I said, slowing to watch them pass.

They stared back with wordless suspicion. The man on the road, the older of the two, passed at eye level, his red face contorted in a grimace of pain or effort, his mouth held slit to one side in a picture of private anguish. The younger man turned his head and peered down at me beneath the bill of his cap, eyes filled with mute and vacuous distrust. Both of them continued to stare as though I, a stranger, were unaware of being looked at, like a zoo animal. It angered me, and I stopped then and stared back hard as they rattled by, holding my gaze until they both turned away.

Eventually the road ahead crested a high, grassy bluff beyond which a faint grey haze portended a broad opening in the terrain, perhaps a loch or a steep valley. Here the mountains beyond stood in the dusk as pale and insubstantial as breath on glass. On reaching the top, at long last I looked down upon a small bayside hamlet. Its miniature houses seemed to spill onto a wide cut of water from a narrow footing at the bottom of a deep tuck in the upholstery of the earth.

Dozens of roof planes compressed on a small peninsula in jumbled profusion, like laundry spread over rocks at the side of a stream. Toy fishing boats nursed at its tiny wharf, while gulls turned above the sky-loaded water in a white marmoreal flock. Far out in the bay a lone trawler was heading home beneath a cloud of birds, its wide wake of endlessly renewed Vs spreading across the sparkling surface like the shadows of geese. Toward this secluded idyll the road curved sharply down through a tangle of green trees and speckled shade.

Instantly energized by this pastoral beauty and by a visible end to my hours of walking, I hastened down the long winding slope of road, my steps sounding crisp as straw and the leather handle of the suitcase squeaking softly in my grip. I noticed the sound of insects for the first time and looked up to see them dancing in a band of yellow air above the road bank with a luminous quiver of energy, while below, breezes blackened the waters of the firth in their passing like fingers closing slats.

From a distance the town's abrupt appearance at the bottom of this hidden slice in the earth appeared almost miraculous, complete with miracle's conjuration. However, the storybook scene soon gave way as I entered the village. I found it to be surprisingly dirty. The place looked as though it had been thrown out of the ground. Houses backed into the hillside were chiseled versions of the native stone they sat upon, just cut square and stacked—not brought in and built so much as carved out of the ground itself. The smell of low tide and stale fishnets came from the wharf, but the town seemed to have lost the habit of housekeeping that characterizes life on boats and the homes of seamen.

Odd bits of paper littered the gutters, and the cobbles of the square held fetid water along with the remains of what appeared to have been a large net-repairing effort. Lengths of knotted rope and barnacle-encrusted fragments of cork lay strewn about the open while bits of discarded sea life fermented between the stones. The place was clearly depressed, though a few buildings of timber and brick hinted at better days. Houses along the stony high street wore a pout of rejection, their shades drawn in what seemed an averted gaze.

I soon found a Bed `n Breakfast near the square. It proved to be cozy and warm, with a certain shabby gentility mixed with unobtrusive ruin. I learned from the robust and watchful proprietress that I could get a ferry across the firth in the morning.

I thanked her while her small blue eyes moved over my leather jacket and jeans, and to the strange brass-headed cane, assessing my potential for outrage. Her hands clasped at her throat, her mouth was small and uncertain, her eyes watchful. A rumpled cascade of reddish hair spilled in ringlets of disarray about her large rosy face, into the center of which her tiny features had fled to huddle in an attitude of guarded curiosity until summoned for further duty. It occurred to me that the quiet conditions of remote village life might, indeed, occasion the need for only a few emotions in a lifetime and that a living encounter with even a rare and transient foreigner might challenge their selection.

Her skin appeared fine and healthy, but very pale, and she had enormous, insistent breasts, over which her round face bobbed like a castaway in a lifejacket. She struck me as the perfect model for Earth Mother effigies made by native tribesmen.

I felt sure that she was pleased to have the business, but she seemed nonetheless a bit edgy about having a stranger in the house, and a foreign one at that. I wanted to put her at ease and prepared to comport myself with suitable modesty, by peering shyly about with conciliating discretion, as if my being there at all was a matter I could only hope she would regard as an excusable error. I paid her in advance, too. She relaxed a bit after that and showed me up creaking stairs to a crisp, clean room which overlooked the harbor through a tiny window.

I set the suitcase down with relief, the deadness springing up my arm again, carried on the appalling inhuman speed of blood. My legs were tired and a bit shaky. They felt swollen at the backs of my knees. I sat gratefully upon the narrow bed and looked around the room.

It was spare and pleasant enough, with a few homey touches meant for travelers, not the family. A primitive landscape, crudely framed, hung in a space of wall too big for it. The wallpaper depicted a trellis supporting some kind of creeping plant, along with some shapeless pink objects of a vaguely clinical nature. It was a room for in-laws, comfort and mild oppression blended. Satisfied that, for the present, I knew all I needed to about events in the morning, I lay back on the fresh pillows for a few minutes rest and promptly fell asleep.

It was dark outside the little window when I was awakened by the sound of a fog horn. It repeated, echoing around the harbor as though from a hundred holes in the night. Feeling refreshed and hungry, I got up and went downstairs to inquire about a place to have some supper.

The landlady suggested a pub called The Fish's Head near the wharf. Amused by the name, I stepped outside again, into a light drizzle and a fantastic coppery fog, charged with waterfront smells. It moved like an army of carnelian wraiths through the narrow streets and over the black water of the bay. It liquified the lights, giving them an oily dramatic gleam, and glistened on the roof slates and street stones. A few street lamps cast slanted ribbons of watery bronze across the cobbles, creating a fish scale of scalloped shadows on the ground that angled obscurely away to hide among the black silhouettes of the houses. The misty light was fun to walk through, making a small adventure of finding the entrance to the pub while serving to obscure the seedier things I had seen in daylight.

A short block away, beneath an amusing wooden fish head attached to its rack of bones, the front window of the pub sent a long rectangle of warm light vaulting into the mist, where it lay on the ground slurred and faintly peened in the fine rain. I stepped from the chill and into a cozy barroom lit by wall sconces and a cheerful fireplace.

A surprisingly pretty woman, probably in her thirties, was behind the bar, haloed in a crystalline ring of inverted glassware in which thousands of tiny orange flames shimmered. Long golden waves of hair, bronzed by the bar light, lounged upon her shoulders. She was resting languidly on her elbows and leafing through a magazine while she talked quietly with an elderly man who sat at the bar dressed in a suit of tweed with his trousers stuffed into high rubber Wellingtons.

The place was sumptuous of pipe tobacco and burning coal, mixed with smells from the kitchen. It exuded a quiet atmosphere of welcome. Just as I closed the door behind me, laughter erupted from a table of men in the adjoining dining room. It almost seemed like a greeting. The woman looked up, pulled a wisp of hair from her eyes, and smiled a white dazzle of cheer.

"Good evening," she said.

"Good evening. ...Am I too late for dinner?"

"Not here, sir."

She turned, reaching behind herself, and as I climbed onto the barstool near her, she slid the menu to me and said with a wry smile, "Ye look a bit the werse f'r wear. `Ave ye coom far then?"

I was unprepared for this very natural question and dreaded the remarks I might invite by announcing that I was fresh from a monastery.

"Um, yeah...Sterling," I replied, suddenly self-conscious in the surprising sparkle of her gaze, which fell upon me deep and dark as the earth itself. I tried to rake my hair into a semblance of respectability with my fingers.

"Sterling! Ooo...now there's a way then, aye Jock?"

She exchanged amused glances with the gentleman in Wellies and tweed. Her voice was half inquiry, half reprimand and full of precise ironies. It wasn't deep, but it was languid, with a maleness that trembled in it, making it sultry and attractive.

"...Yank?" she asked. Her directness surprised me.

"Yeah," I said, interested now in where this might be going. She regarded me speculatively beneath arched brows.

"...Reformed," I added, and a low, throaty chuckle rolled under her breath.

She had lovely eyes, almost black, but which shone with a mid-ocean blue luminescence, a straight narrow nose, and well-formed lips, which she had further refined with a pale, libidinous rouge. Reflections of the glassware speckled about her when she tilted her head, as though a fine net made of sunlight had been thrown over her hair. There was a kind of feline sumptuousness about her that compelled me to watch the way she moved. Afraid to appear obvious, though, I tried to dismiss her appeal as just an effect of my long isolation and sneaked a furtive glance at her while I looked around the room with feigned indifference.

There was something about her that struck me with a vague sadness, though, something familiar to me from the military: a sense of vested resolve, of compromise with life, which off-set somewhat her accessibility to a stranger and served to seal her within the context of the bar. Perhaps it was the matronly deportment of her clothing, or a flicker of cynicism in her eyes, like a fleeting pulse of light from the back of a cave, which told that she was resigned to this tiny village, that despite certain physical attributes which might have served her well in a larger context, she had come to terms with life in this deeply bisected gorge.

Sensing this gave me an unspoken connection with her and made her even more attractive. I tried to tell myself that such convergences are merely a conspiracy of the senses, and besides, her effortless sensuality had surely been whetted on the many pale bones of more adventurous men than I. But when I looked back her dark eyes were resting upon me with an amused inquisitiveness, and I felt the blood rush hot into my ears. I responded to her unvoiced query by asking for a whisky.

"What kind, Luv?"

At that moment I realized I had fallen so far from the ways of the world that I couldn't answer. In a moment of paralysis my mind went limp and irresponsive to the faintest call of memory. I had no idea what to ask for. She waited, breathing beneath her sweater, with her slender fingers spread upon the bar. I noted that her nails were manicured but unpainted, and fixed upon that detail, I fell into a small ecstasy of despair to remember even one brand name. I only hoped that she would misread my hesitation as reflective selection.

"Oh, um, something local..?" I offered at last hoping the request would make me sound discriminating, a sort of traveling connoisseur.

She continued to regard me with a kind of wistful mutability for a moment. Then she turned around and bent low at the hips. She opened a cabinet door but seemed to remain in that position a moment or two longer than was strictly necessary, her ankles crossed casually. I had time to wonder if she might be "presenting" to me—the rump show that means so much in baboon society. Was she symbolically submitting to the guest?

When she straightened up, turning smoothly as she rose like a dancer, she held an unlabeled brown bottle up to the light and squinted at its secrets. She reached down a glass as she approached, and her eyes narrowed slightly in the way the landlady had first looked at me. As she poured its amber yield, she asked teasingly, "Is it troo tha' all Americans are barbarians?...We read th' most awful things in th' papers."

The older gentleman looked over.

"...Yes," I said, smiling for their mutual benefit, "...they are."

She laughed then, the way a cat might, full-throated and with a little hiss of pleasure, stiffening her body. It was fun to watch her, and I enjoyed her attention though I found it slightly unnerving. I couldn't remember ever speaking with a woman this attractive, and I didn't really know what to do, so I concentrated on keeping my fingers laced around the glass. I told myself that all innkeepers had to maintain an engaging banter with the patrons; it was good for business. Besides, I knew that I had to watch what I said in order to keep dark my ineptitude at flirtation. I decided to let caution pass for wisdom and to retreat behind a screen of pleasantries.

"Well...in the New World, a barbarian is really nobody special," I added, and took a sip of the whisky. It had a fine, peat-smoked flavor, reminiscent of the stuff that Wilf had shared with me. It held a lingering after-taste of leather and other things brown and rich. It made me cough a little.

"Wow! That's good!"

"D'ye like it?" she asked with mock surprise.

"Mmmm. Its virtues plead like angels," I said, picking up the menu. The first sip re-awakened my hunger.

"Ya kinna' ge'it. It's no' exported."

"I don't blame you. Its secrets might get out. ...May I have a topper to take into dinner?"

"Surely," she purred, decanting into the half-filled glass a generously unmeasured addition. I thanked her, and she smiled her smile teasingly, touching the tip of her tongue to her teeth, enjoying her effect. I smiled back pretending hard not to notice, but knowing my face to be as red as it felt. She seemed so disarmingly open in the expression of her allure that for a moment I felt as though I were sitting with a cubist portrait of a woman by Picasso, with all her dimensions flashing at once.

I backed off the stool in a small torture of denial and retreated into the dining room feeling ambiguous and awkward—amused and grateful for the easy company, but sadly displaced, like a diver who has fingered fine pearls but not known how to bring them to the surface. I tried to reclaim my dignity by telling myself that a taste for the sublime is simply a greed like any other.

The adjoining room was narrow, with smoke-yellowed wallpaper and a threadbare woolen runner down the center of the long floor, but each table was set with silver and spread with clean white cloth. Wall sconces like those in the bar were spaced along the walls, but the room was lit instead by single candles on each table and by oil lamps that hung low from the ceiling, lending the space a dim and pleasing isinglass pearlescence. The light pooled soft and contained, meant only for the space in which it fell, with no excess. It seemed to symbolize the way of life itself in the monastery.

There were others present, so with an outsider's respectful attention to the contours of a settled community, I sought the shadows at the edge of the lamplight and selected a table in the corner at some remove from the others. I did not wish to encroach upon the space made intimate enough by its small size, and besides, the relative gloom was more suitable to my conflicted mood.

The only other patrons where a group of five men who sat together around a table near the front window, speaking in low tones, laughing now and again, their voices clear in the small room. Dark shadows cast by the lamplight collected unfavorably in the hollows of their cheeks and eyes, lending them a drawn and haunted look, while in the rain-streaked window glass behind them their reflections wavered, veiled and indistinct like the ghosts of drowned men, the image enhanced by coils of cigarette smoke drifting languorously in the air currents over their heads.

Unavoidably overhearing while looking over the menu, I soon learned that they were former North Sea oil workers, retired or laid off. They seemed to know each other well and conversed with a gruff familiarity. The flames of the hurricane lamps danced when a joke was made, and grew steady again when there was silence.

They talked of work overseas, opportunities that awaited those willing to leave hearth and home. I heard the name "Consolidated Mines" in Timmons, Ontario, where they said a man could make $60,000 Canadian in a single season by operating something called a rock drill. They seemed to agree that it was easy work to do, but that Canada was pretty far away, and besides, the mine itself was isolated. This was one of the reasons the work paid so well.

One of the men had an odd habit: when he addressed the group as a whole, he glanced around normally, but whenever he turned his attention to an individual, he closed his eyes, opening them again when he turned away.

The lamp over my table smoked, causing its feeble light to move across the surface of the tablecloth like shadows on the sand of a creek bottom. I sipped contentedly at the dark whisky and eavesdropped until the young waiter who attended the men turned his attention to me.

He approached with a shy smile and removed the empty chair opposite me. Oddly, I felt an immediate void. Somehow my need for loneliness was frustrated by the missing chair. It was a symbol, and its removal aroused my sociability. I ordered my dinner, then returned my attention back to the men and listened with renewed interest.

After more speculation about the economic woes of the local region, the name of the mining company came up again. There was more talk about leaving the area, and like men everywhere who brag to cover their misfortune, they eventually got up and shuffled past without resolve. They went outside, stepping into the fog with teasing jibes at the woman in the bar, whose bubbling bronchial laugh punctuated their departure, thus leaving me alone in the dining room, freighted with silences.

There was a small bookcase along the wall nearby. I went over to look through the selections and soon found a worn copy of Alfred, Lord Tennyson. He had been Queen Victoria's poet laureate, a man known for his mastery of rhythm and lyric, and though I feared myself deeply at variance with such elements of the harmonious, I brought it to the subdued arc of candlelight on the table.

It fell open to the poem, "Ulysses," which I remembered having to read in school, where under threat of enforced memorization, its actual meaning had escaped me. On this night, though, I came upon it in the way that we sometimes fall into those fleeting moments where the blind stumbling of our hearts cohere in a sure gesture of recognition.

> *"I am a part of all that I have met:*
> *Yet all experience is an arc wherethro'*
> *Gleams that untravel'd world, whose margin fades*
> *For ever and for ever when I move."*

Here was the same idea of experience that the abbot, in his strange parabolic speech, had of knowledge. Both were lessons discovered in the luggage of living—intuitive, yet hereto not so succinctly expressed—which came together in that moment with a silent click, fitting neatly a slot in one of the secret patterns which the world tries to keep from the unwary. There was an economical irony in the complement of these images that brought with it a neat retributive self-knowledge as a bonus, and it set my thoughts again on the brotherhood, dwelling high in their thurible of sanctity.

Already they seemed to be fading into a dream-like state that left me half believing that I had never been there. Just as in Vietnam when, having crossed a brief but brutal encounter with the enemy, I sometimes had difficulty seeing back through the curtain of new reality, of remembering events from only moments before, for they predated some new-born paradigm. But the influence of the brotherhood's reserved and elegant kindness upon me was profound, for they had honed off my despair to an edge so fine and thin that it was almost like vanishing, and it left me wondering again if I had not been brought to that place by some providential hand.

I began to wonder about the strange arithmetic of chance and if perhaps all of life was not an interconnected membrane, a weft of linkages like chain mail. If you could go far enough down through the multiple refinements of perception, might you not find what our sciences cannot locate or name—the substrate, the unseen ether which buoys the world—the force that holds a leaf together as well as our complex and inexplicable caring for each other; that which gives goodness and evil their power—the unified field, in which the protoplasm nudged nudges, thus passing the word throughout creation.

The next two lines of the poem, though, completed the stanza with a warning, and left me feeling that Tennyson, seeing our century but unable to reach it, had pointed his accusing finger through time:

"How dull it is to pause, to make an end.
To rust unburnished, not to shine in use!"

These words must have been a personal hosanna for him, but to me they scolded and warned of indirection. The eerie and fragile anarchy of being alone again pressed in upon me, and I wished hard for some conscious goal to congeal from out of the small chaos of resources within me. I had time, pocket money enough to get home, and prospects limited only by my own imagination, in which I vainly expected to find some gathering congregation of intent, some origin of purpose; yet my thoughts stirred only shadows and unformed glimmerings, wet seeds of hope in the cold blind earth.

Perhaps I was just suffering a momentary paralysis of will; it happens to everybody. But just then I couldn't shake the unknowable nature of the future and its indolent influence upon speculation and plans. Still numb with gratitude at having escaped destruction in the war and niggled with vague doubts about having been dismissed from the comforts of the brotherhood, tired from the long day's walk and mellowed by the whisky, I surrendered to the quiet of the room and the strange vacancy of all the chairs. The world takes its form hourly by a weighing of things at hand, but in the anguish of renewed transition I felt a stagnant powerlessness to puzzle it out.

I suddenly felt a great longing to be home, that life might not always be just tangle and drift. For not all freedoms put life aright. I had come to view those elements which comprise our romantic notions of the open road as belonging to an idealized and outmoded scholastic myth. In truth they are fraught with complexity, ambiguity, irony, and paradox.

When I thought about my friends at the monastery, I knew that my decision should stand, for what they had given would remain with me always; going back to that place someday would be like passing myself in the fog.

I thought about the oil workers in their forced retirement dreaming of goldmines, and found in the echo of their departure a shiver of recognition, a measure of mortality, while the blood of memory, legacy, death, and renewal coursed through me.

The line of hanging lamps flickered in the window glass, while outside, drops of water caught the door light as they fell from the eaves, and the numinous orange fog stole past like the flank of an enormous animal.

Part 2
Troglodyte

15
The Mine

Gold is interesting stuff. It is said to be the noblest of materials. With the possible exception of territory, it is the most killed-for commodity in history, and all because it's pretty. It doesn't tarnish. Well, mostly because it doesn't tarnish. It's pretty rare, too; and it likes to be left alone. It is one of the few metals which, as with platinum, resists combination with other elements. You might say that, like a captive bird, gold always yearns to be free. In cool crust rock, where I was about to encounter it, it generally is free. At very high temperatures, though, it will go into compounds, and the gold that is among the magmatic fluids in certain pockets of the earth's interior may combine, for example, with chlorine. Gold chloride is moderately soluble, and will dissolve in water that seeps down to circulate in or near the magma.

The water picks up many other elements along the way, too, like potassium, sodium, and silicon. Heated at frightening temperatures, the solution then rises and is forced into fissures in hard crust rock where the cooling gold breaks away from the chlorine and falls out of the water, where tumbled and ground, furrowed, fused and forced in the geologic blender of the ages, it can be found in flakes, in specks, sometimes in nuggets larger than the eggs of geese, and sometimes in imbedded veins as more or less pure metal.

Silicon precipitates, too, filling the fissures and enveloping the gold with veins of silicon dioxide, which we surface-dwellers know as common quartz. Quartz is therefore often an indicator of the proximity of gold, and so it was free chunks of this otherwise dull, cloudy rock that the old two-blanket burro prospectors were looking for on the surface back in 1849. A large quartz deposit on an exposed hillside could mean the discovery of a lifetime.

Gold is the only metal that is virtually indestructible. It does not rust, tarnish, or corrode, and it stands up to acids, alkalis, oxygen, water, and weather. Because of its indestructibility, all the gold ever poured in sixty centuries is still in existence — roughly enough to make a stack about 58 feet on a side. The gold in the ring on your finger may have crossed the Atlantic with Columbus or been used in one of King

Solomon's trading expeditions to Ophir; it might have been brought out of Persia by Alexander the Great in 334 BC, or been a nugget used to barter in a Mediterranean seaport in 4000 BC. Yet the market for gold remains closed, for the metal is still so rare that more steel is poured today in one hour than all the gold that has been poured since the beginning of time.

None of this was known to me, though, as I stood self-consciously among a large group of bearded miners in the dim, pre-dawn chill of the Ontario "out back," trying my best to look hard-bitten. Following a hurried interview two days earlier beneath the scrutiny of many grave countenances, I had been hired on as a rock drill operator, despite my complete lack of training or any relevant experience for the job. This happened for a combination of reasons, mostly because of the company's pressing need to fill the well-paid specialty, and fleetingly, because of my skill at reading upside-down on other people's desks the material requirements for the job.

That and a certain economy with the truth: they had asked me some pointed questions about my knowledge of the equipment. My mouth had opened, and out of it somehow came a ribbon of sunny upbeat cadences that wrapped itself around the possibility of dissent like insulating foam. With mouthfuls of the only terms I could remember that actually described the hand drills one uses for boring into wood, my veiling flummery worked to cast garlands of tender familiarity upon the ultimate purpose of all drills, which is simply to get holes. The committee must have shared an appreciation for theater.

That part had gone well enough, but now, as I stood in the darkness among the musty veterans and listened to the softly murmured patois which rattled in their throats like stones in a river, I wanted to run. Just prior to the interview, seated with what seemed to be a small company of outcasts on hard institutional furniture in the mining company personnel office, the prospect of getting this job had seemed vaguely glamorous, maybe even fun, but now the cold reality of going a thousand feet under the ground to do potentially dangerous work with equipment I knew nothing about, and in a language I could not speak, was releasing chilled rivulets of doubt everywhere within me. I might be unable to recognize directives or words of warning, and how would anyone be able to explain the equipment to me? Federico Fellini once said, "A different language is a different view of life." I used to think that he was just talking about the movies, but now his full meaning became clear, packed with worrisome implications.

I felt trapped and small in my newly-issued coveralls and gleaming plastic safety helmet. The un-scuffed equipment screamed out to the others, "Hey, over here, look at me; I'm brand new—untried, probably even untrustworthy..!" and as I fidgeted with the straps on my respirator, I felt again with excruciating intimacy the coward's unease, born anew of incoherent possibilities with every passing moment.

All the differences between the other men and myself seemed suddenly conspicuous and charged with danger, and I wished hard to avoid being noticed. I watched carefully their movements in the dark. They sucked their teeth and snuffled and stirred and picked at themselves like apes. Among them I was clasped in the tentacles of some living creature of unknown intent, afraid the beast might awaken to my presence and smell a boyhood fear of the unknown—the prehistoric fear of monsters.

I have always hated being the new kid, and here that adolescent feeling of displacement was compounded and greatly intensified by the knowledge that, on an impulse of naive adventurism, I had again entered into a situation where the stakes were unknowably high. My heart thudded dully and my temples began to throb.

Besides the fact that I had signed on with a U.S. passport and spoke no French, I had no beard. It seemed that all the other faces were fringed with bushy tangles of hair. Since I could see no practical reason for this, and in fact thought the beards might even reduce the seal of the respirators against their faces, I concluded that it was probably some kind of badge. The beards lent them a strange animalism too, darkening their collective aspect all the more and further deepened the gulf between us.

Then I noticed another thing: they all carried a simple piece of equipment that was conspicuously absent from my hand. Lunch canisters. I had given only passing notice to dim metallic starlight glinting dully from the concentric flutes of many food containers without registering their importance. Suddenly I knew of another discomforting fact about which I had not been told and that had not occurred to me. I had no lunch box. How could I have failed, even in my anxiety, to realize I'd have to eat during the day?

...And further, I wasn't named Pierre. Apparently, everybody else was:

"Alors, Pierre."

"Eh? Ah, como ca va, Pierre? Bon jour, bon jour, mon ami."

All the newness and the uncertainty nourished my anxiety. My bulky coveralls suddenly became too warm. They were heavily insulated against the cold temperatures I had been told to expect underground, and I noticed that all around me they gave off the curdled sour odor of dried sweat in oily fabric, the tart ammoniac pungency that fermented among the thronged men in woolen clothes. Cigarettes flared here and there, briefly illuminating part of a face, others moved in contained figure 8s, tracing gestures in the dark.

Crowded and silent, barely animated by the glow of smoking and soft, nasal muttering, the huddle of shapeless overalls made them look like a group of worn robots, abandoned to shuffle about in the open until all their servos had wound completely down. Perhaps in a few cases that wasn't far wrong.

I noticed that many of the men around me had their suits unbuttoned down to the waist, and the heavy fabric thus loosened enhanced the impression of their girth. I decided to undo mine, too, partly to camouflage my presence and partly in hopes that it would make me look bigger.

We stood in a graveled court that in the military would have been called the "company area", quietly muttering beneath the morning stars, not far from the headquarters shack, waiting for our shift to start. This would be signaled by an electric bell that announced arrival of the gang elevators at the surface. They would transport us, 50 at a time, down to our respective levels underground.

Not far away, looking as though it had been pounded into the hillside, was a large steel structure that rambled over the mine head in a haphazard amalgam of corrugated panels, where a few open seams and screw holes launched slender rods of dim orange light, as though from inner fires. Wisps of steam escaped noiselessly into the air from numerous standpipes, while beyond stood a silent chimney, leaning black against the stars. The place could have been Hell's exhaust on a ten-minute break.

We waited there in the vibrant stillness, each wrapped within an impenetrable version of anticipation. Gravel crunched softly beneath our shoes, its sound swallowed by the night. There was an occasional murmur and then again the stillness. The moments were un-breathing. A startled bird erupted from the grass and fluttered away with a faint cry. It was unnerving, but there was no escape. Each moment hung interminably. The blood pumped cold and sodden in my chest. I could hear it. I felt swallowed by circumstance beyond all ransom or reprieve.

While searching the sky for some familiar pattern on which to fix at least a momentary sense of belonging to the world, I noticed a dark bundle of electrical wires that sagged low over our heads. I followed them with my eyes from the shack to the operations building. There, in the sickly glare of a single work light, the cables gathered under the blackened helmet of a standing weather head that leaned forth and engorged them with its ominous overbite, then plunged abruptly underground. It seemed that everything around us was sloping into the earth. To what end? It was eerie, yet it pulled at me. It drew upon the hanging drops of time and made them fall, one by one. We were, all of us, inclining toward some complex force of unspecified magnitude that dwelt somewhere below us. Yet no hint of it reached the senses. Here on the surface all was quiet.

A few small prairie birds chirped tentatively on the morning air. Beyond our little compound the vast plains of central Canada stretched to a distant line of low hills on the rim of the dawn. For a moment I thought the earth trembled slightly as it rolled beneath the silent vaults of the sky, but I threw off the idea as a sign of nerves. A drop of time falling...fallen.

The sound of the bell shattered the air like a long burst of gunfire. I jumped, then instantly ashamed, looked around furtively to see if any of the others had noticed my alarm. It was a strange and disquieting moment. Nurtured by silence, the fears I had anticipated for this moment had grown and taken the formless and unreasonable shape of all things which thrive without light. I just wanted out of there, and like an old hound tethered to a post for the first time, my imagination ran from the alarm, got jerked into a flip, and landed scrabbling on its back thinking, "What the hell have I done this time."

After an odd moment of unanimous hesitation, the men around me began to stir. There seemed a consensual ignorance of the clangor. These were not men who were going to be ordered about by some damn bell like schoolboys. The glow of cigarettes arced to the ground to be snuffed underfoot. Trouser canvas shuffled. Then a quick, nervous tension seemed to scurry among us, as through a flock when the season of their migration is at hand.

The gates crashed open. A huge gang of impossibly dirty men burst from the elevator gantry and thronged toward us, teeth flashing white from their muddy beards, their clothing caked with pale, drying clay. Some hailed people in our group with rasping good-natured gibberish, but most simply shuffled wordlessly past, dark and reticent, black-eyed bedraggled men called forth from the earth, men who moved like the shadows of people they may once have been. They had about them a wary absorption, provisional, tired, and deeply suspect, as though observing some hazardous truce with the world. They seemed in a state of improvident and hopeless vigilance, like men committed to venture upon uncertain ice.

We moved forward in a unison of performance and took up the others' places in the steel lift cages, where the breath of their presence was still warm. The gates were drawn closed with a rolling clatter. I stood in unfamiliar shoes, my hands pocketed and head cupped between my shoulder blades, feeling in the earthy press about me the presence of a robed priesthood, seneschals of yet another god I did not know.

With my heart pounding, and the blood shrieking in my ears, I was vainly trying to tie together the familiar with the fearful aspects of this feeling when a sudden heavy electric whine shivered through the gantry, and the bottom fell out of the world. All my organs compacted upward in an instant, the blood bulged in my face, and with my eyeballs full of heartbeats, we dropped away into utter darkness.

As we descended, the rapidly cooling air took on the vaguely metallic odor of rock dust, tinged faintly with familiar hints of cordite. The smell itself was not altogether unpleasant, carrying as it did a mild association with boyhood experiments involving matches and little plastic cars, but it was pervasive and freighted with war memories, too, which brought with it an emotional overcast. There were engine exhaust fumes in it as well, and grease. Grease from the cables on which we rode and airborne lubricants from below that came up through the floor grating.

We plunged through this redolent breeze for several long moments before we began to pass fleeting points of light. Single incandescent bulbs flashed upwards, and the wink of their passing caught the men about me in the act of pulling on their respirators and adjusting their goggles in a flickering staccato of progressive poses. As I fumbled to adjust my own equipment, I felt a subtle change in the speed of the cage. The hum of the cables shifted down in pitch, and there was a slight buckle of noise in the air as we suddenly dropped past the first level of work.

In that glimpse, I began to grasp with a shock the size of the mine. An enormous opening containing trucks and tracked vehicles rose past us. There were dozens of men in motion against a haze of dust-laden yellow light, the ceiling a network of pipes and wires, and the racket of their work yelped as we passed. We dropped through several other levels without slowing, and each presented a similar picture, varying only in the smell of the strata at each depth and in the abrupt yawp of their thrashing as all sound fell upward.

These, I was soon to learn, were the actual tunnels or "runs" of the operation—the levels on which the digging and extraction of ore was done. We were riding in one of the shafts. Tunnels are horizontal; shafts are vertical. It was a far cry from the movie-myth "mineshaft"— a cramped crawl space, shored with timber and lit by helmet lamps— that I had once naively envisioned.

As we traveled downward, I began to sense that we were some-how turning slightly away from each platform. In the war, I had found the skill of the three-dimensional gaze, the rogue glimpse that could take in an object or scene and realign it, see all the false descants; and here, by the time I got my respirator adjusted in place, I had the feeling that the axis of each tunnel angled progressively to the north, like a spiral staircase. It was slightly disorienting, causing my sense of ver-ticality to tilt uncomfortably, and with the restricted peripheral vision imposed by the goggles, I began to feel nauseated.

Oh, great, I thought. Barfing in this crowd is all I need now. I jerked the goggles off my face and replaced them above the helmet visor, then sucked air deeply and noisily through the strange filters and stared hard at the framework of the falling elevator, trying to recap-ture some sense of stability against the upward blur. A helmeted mask fringed with beard turned toward me and, with the goggle lenses re-flecting dully the receding lights, stared blankly through the gloom be-fore turning away again. It could have been the face of a giant insect.

I tried to distract myself by thinking of the implications that off-set tunneling might have for the volume of earth and stone around us. Whether it was to follow the ore deposits, or to avoid subducting the level above, I could not tell and had no way to ask. I was still breathing hard when we slowed to a stop at level 10.

Here, the air was very cold and heavy with moisture. I turned my collar up, but the material was already damp. In the last seconds before the cage was opened, I stole a glance at the others. Each of us was surrounded by the vapor of our breathing, despite the masks. The headgear had now dehumanized each individual completely. With helmets on, ear muffs down, goggles over the upper part of each face and grotesquely disfiguring respirators clamped to the lower part, we looked like some beetle race moving through the filtered light of another world. Jets of mist snorted from the filters like hogs' breath, then hung about our heads in steady jets of renewal.

When the cage banged open and disgorged its contents, I felt as though I were stepping from an Earth ship onto some alien shore, utterly encompassed by variations of brown. As I moved, the chilled, musty air instantly entered my clothes. Everything around us turned wet. The rock walls glistened, dripping with cold sulfurous water, and the mud beneath our many feet sucked noisily at my shoes in grim warning that I had entered a strange land where even walking was governed by a separate set of laws.

I looked back once, but the cage had gone. As I turned to follow the others, I felt intensely fragile and very alone beneath the incalculable tons of pressure around us. I realized that my shoulders were hunched in a quaint posture of anticipation, the way people walk in early rain, and began to understand the claustrophobic's ordeal of relentless encroachment. I sucked air through the respirator and fought hard to suppress the fear which every shadow threatened to release upon me.

We slogged through a short, curving tunnel, along a twin set of four narrow-gauge rails, moving inexorably toward a crescendo of machinery sounds that rose from around the bend until it thundered upon me in a press of vibrations, shouting against my skin. At once, the narrow tunnel opened into an enormous excavation, brightly lit from above by amber lights that pulsed through the dust, casting their lurid glow over a puddled and trampled floor, littered with hoses and crisscrossed with the tracks of excavation equipment. The height of this space varied from about eight feet near the shaft to twenty or so toward the rock face, some forty yards away. The cavity was very broad and shored up in several places by steel columns, completing an image of the whole mine as a huge underground department building, carved out of the rock—a Petra Macy's—populated by dun-colored troglodytes who struggled against something intangible in a flame-lit sorcerer's workshop of stone.

Several large power stations on steel sledges roared, straining against their anchors in the middle of the space, their pressure gauges dancing and their umbilical cables snaking off in all directions, feeding out enough energy to vibrate the weighted air. It seemed that everything here but the people made noise. The ground lurched beneath me from the pound and jump of heavy machines.

At the face, a tiered scaffold attached to a Caterpillar tractor held the men who attacked the rock with long drills that screamed and chattered, squealing with friction and hammering away sixteen at a time, releasing clouds of steam, while tailings fell to the tunnel floor in cascades of chips and dust.

I noticed that a heavy steel roof had been mounted over the tractor to protect the operator and that it was distorted downward by many ominous dents. My mind filled with the mantra, "What the hell have I done this time?…What the hell have I…What the hell…!"

Electric generators fed power to the lights and to huge exhaust fans while the enormous compressors sent pressure to the drills through twitching hoses in a low and continuous vibrato. Everywhere men skulked through the dingy light, their muddy coveralls shellacked by the earth, their shadows curled beneath them.

Strapped to the overhead with giant staples, a maze of color-coded electrical conduit and air ducts ran between the light fixtures, humming with purpose. Steam pipes, joints, and valves hung among them, and through it all dripped the frigid water, lifeblood of the earth.

The new shift dispersed throughout the floor with few gestures. The chugging sound of work at the rock face seemed to pause as the new arrivals moved into position. Many of the men in place did not seem to know at first that we had come, that their long shift had ended. They hesitated, then turned, their masked faces seeming to gaze vacantly about, moles struggling toward to the light.

I had been told to report to Section 3 at the face. It wasn't hard to find, as most of the service hoses led in the direction of four adjoining sections of scaffolding where, with the sudden work stoppage for the shift change, the clouds of dust and steam were lanced through with swinging light beams as men moved about the drilling platforms.

Each dozer bore the painted number of the Section or drill team. On each end of the structure were curved davits, like those used on ocean ships to secure life boats. There were men standing on both decks of the scaffold, some of whom were handling what could only be rock drills. I suddenly realized that I really had no idea of what one looked like. They appeared to be much bigger and heavier than I had imagined, something like a cross between a rocket launcher and a jack hammer, only with a very long and narrow drill bit.

In mounting anxiety to get some idea of what to do, I tried to observe anything I could about the equipment as I approached the group whose tractor was marked with a large 3.

There were four teams of two men each on both levels of the mobile scaffold. One guy handled the drill itself, which was a high-pressure pneumatic device attached to two heavy air hoses that he also had to contend with. He had a pair of transverse handles with which to grip the drill housing, and from what I could tell, the thing looked pretty unwieldy. I was soon to learn that the second man in each pair, though he appeared to be a driller's assistant, was in fact the Blaster—the explosives guy—and the drill operator was in sole charge of the tool. In fact, I knew a few things about explosives but nothing about rock drill operation, or for that matter, about any other air-driven thing more sophisticated than a tea kettle.

I approached the number 3 tractor carefully, trying to appear sure-footed and to comport myself in an attitude designed to mask my timidity. The section foreman turned to greet me. He was several inches shorter than me, dark skinned at his neck and wrists, with shiny black hair, and as I was soon to learn, a deep and abiding dislike of anything which struck him as effete. He screeched at me through his filters in a version of French which even I could tell was heavily accented, and with a series of impulsive gestures, seemed to indicate that I was to mount the scaffold immediately and begin the work.

I did not expect to be thrown into the operation so quickly, and the nature of his order struck me like a threat. With my heart pounding, and wondering at my capacity to absorb unwelcome surprises, I crossed to the steel catwalk and climbed to the outside position on the right end of the upper level, where there was an idle drill with empty hose sockets. It lay there on the planks in ponderous stillness like some strange weapon abandoned by an alien race.

How natural, I thought, as though visiting the thing at an under-taker's reception. I nodded without response to the other insect-men on the scaffold who had stopped their work and whose expressionless goggles gazed toward me as blank as porcelain. The feeling returned that I was lost among machines, cast into Plato's cave to make my way among the Forms.

A pair of hoses was handed up to me, and a large pipe wrench was slid onto the planks at my feet. I stared at it, wondering what it was for and racing to remember which way the spindle turned to open it. What was I doing here? On some level, I had known this moment would come, but now I couldn't remember anything that had led up to it. Maybe this was how a mirage worked, and nobody knew I was the only one who could see it, the lone human abandoned in the Fata Morgana.

With this pallid substitute for any good idea, I stepped on the hose fittings to keep the dangling weight of the hoses from dragging them back off the deck, then knelt and tried to roll the drill to see how heavy it might be, while trying to sneak a look at how the other drills were hooked up. It looked as though the black hose attached to the right-hand fitting and the red India-rubber-looking one went on the left.

The drill resisted my pull. It was heavy alright and reluctant to shed its mysteries, but the bit itself was impressive. It was a fine piece of tapered hexagonal steel about five feet long and something over an inch thick. It shone dully in the gleam of brown light, its surface slightly damascened with fine striations. There was a slight flare at the outer tip, vaguely leaf-shaped, that appeared through a confection of rock dust to be little worn.

Grateful for the heavy gloves that hid the trembling in my hands, I pulled the hose couplings to the drill sockets and found with relief that they snapped easily into position. With a quarter turn to snug the steam fittings using the pipe wrench, the connection was complete as far as I could tell, and I stood up just as the other figures began to lift their drills. So far, so good. The tractor roared to life and lurched forward, throwing me against the safety rail, while the whole structure trundled toward the rock face about fifteen feet ahead.

The handgrips on the drill contained the trigger and safety switch-es to activate the bit, not unlike those on an industrial floor polish-er, though larger and clearly designed to be used while wearing the heavy insulated gauntlets we needed to keep our hands from freezing.

I thought I'd better try lifting it, especially since all the other men appeared to be ready with theirs, and in doing so, it almost pulled me off the scaffold. Not only was it heavy, it was very unwieldy, as its hoses tried to pull it backwards while the length of the bit itself served only slightly to counterweight it forward. This made it easier to hold than I feared at first it might be, but I realized immediately the inherent difficulty of placing the spade tip with any precision.

The moving scaffold came to an abrupt halt, pitching me forward. The hoses pulled me up short just before I would have fallen between the deck and the rock face, and as I stumbled around like a sailor in a storm, the other drills burst to life and began their attack on the rock. Dust leapt into the air, and rock fragments pattered around my feet, as I finally got the bit more or less positioned against what looked like a seam in the rock and pulled the trigger. Nothing. I gripped the other trigger. Still nothing.

Then, from out of nowhere, a large glove reached over and turned the pressure valve levers on the drill to the open position. Instantly, the pressure hit the hoses. They bucked, and the bolt rammed home, spitting jets of steam from both cheeks. The drill convulsed and began hammering at the rock face on its own. All I could do was hang on and try to keep it from jumping out of the dent it was trying to pound into the rock while it tried to throw me backwards.

My eyeballs began shuddering in the vibration, the muscles in my stomach seized, and I suddenly realized my helmet was too big. I had made the mistake of adjusting the headband for comfort rather than security. In addition, the helmet lamp was aimed high, and in trying to direct the dancing beam onto the drill point, I had to drop my chin, which brought the brim down too low to see anything but my hands. My feet weren't far enough apart, and the drill began to lean harder on me than I was on it. I was in trouble and knew it.

In the second before I could release the trigger, there was a loud clank, and the drill suddenly hove into the air, chugging without resistance. I fell back against the guard rail and onto the deck, and the drill fell across me. It lay there, suddenly silent, the remains of its bit, a shiny spike of fresh-broken metal, rising and falling with my heavy breathing. A little sigh of steam hissed forth.

All work seemed suddenly to have stopped. From below came the frenzied screaming of the little foreman, his voice like a whole village running into the street, tearing their sarongs. I pushed the heavy drill off and rolled to my knees in anticipation of facing the inevitable foreign music, which came on in a paroxysmal burst of epithet, in and back out of English, rich in color and pronouncement. It rose above the sounds of the machinery, which seemed to fade away in a kind of respectful wonder. He certainly had a gift for swearing, and though I could not understand much of it, I felt profoundly uncomfortable to be the focus of such tumultuous eloquence. Anyone who could be driven to such frantic excesses of rage was dangerously erratic and might prove to be a constant threat.

I thought to close the steam valves at least and lay the drill down, then got to my feet. I watched his leap onto the tractor carefully. My senses, still conditioned by combat, were habitually locating all the tiny choreography of objects within the killing radius of small arms fire around me, and I had no wish to add to the demands the drill was making on my limited talents any additional worry about some crazy Punjabi, or whatever he was, moving around behind me.

From all around, goggles were assembling. They stared at me like fish in a tank. All that was missing were the bubbles. I sensed instinctively that my very survival might depend upon what I could think of to do next. There was clearly no choice but try to bluff the challenge. I placed my hands on the rail and tried to sound calm.

"Anybody around here speak any English?" It came out unfamiliar, gravelly.

"Oui," said a filtered voice on my left. The figure standing there with apparent calm amid the storm, its weight on one leg, was thickset and taciturn. I realized that his was the glove that had opened my steam valves.

"Tell him we need a key and another bit up here whenever he's through."

The figure bent toward the rail and bellowed something down to the foreman, who hesitated, cut loose a renewed concatenation of syllables, then barked an order to someone on the floor. More language was spat up at me, which I treated without movement. I assumed he could not see my eyes behind the goggles, and I hoped the semblance of a steady gaze the lenses might impart would at least lend me a sort of substitute dignity under the circumstances.

A fresh bit was handed up, and one of the other drillers threw me the largest chuck key I'd ever seen. I saw where to insert it and set about opening the locking collar and freeing the broken fragment of the old bit. After tossing it down, I inserted the new bit. It fit well, seating with an audible snap. Then, jiggling the bit with one hand to find the center of the socket, as with any hand-size electric drill, I tightened the chuck evenly with the key. Then, calling for dramatic effect on my hard-won limited familiarity with the thing, I lifted the tool free of the deck and fired it for a two-second burst in the air to test the alignment. It seemed to vibrate a great deal at the throat, or chuck end, but I had no way of judging how it was supposed to look and signaled all around that I was ready to go again.

The other teams sorted themselves out and faced the rock once more. I heaved at the cumbersome drill and braced it against the slope of the face. As soon as the drills began to hammer, I took a better stance and leaned into the machine this time.

Handling it was a bit easier now that I had some idea of what to expect. I placed the flutes at the end of the new bit into the small dent I had started before and pulled the trigger. I began to feel more of what I assumed was some kind of control over the drill as the bit began to chatter into the rock.

When it had sunk in several inches there was a loud clank, the drill broke free to the right, and I pitched forward, almost stabbing myself on the split shank that protruded from the wall. Work stopped again.

I stayed on my knees for a moment wondering what went wrong and stared uncomprehendingly at the broken steel which was sticking out of the wall, pointing accusingly at my face. What could have happened? What had I done wrong this time?

All around me tools were being laid down. I reached over and worked the fragment out of its shallow hole and turned it in my hands. It had split like a chair leg, as though from twisting. It didn't make sense from anything I knew. I drew breath and looked around. The school of goggles had returned.

The obstreperous flow of language from below erupted again, and the foreman hit the scaffold running. The whole structure began to shake with his climbing, and as he reached the guard rail I grabbed the pipe wrench and stood up. I had seen a few men go berserk before, and I was afraid. The veins in his neck were distended, he trembled, and his tinny voice scratched out of the filters at me like the scrabbling of insects. He spread his fingers, and I knew in a second I had just one chance if he made a move toward me. A scurry of nerves passed through the back of my scalp. I could either stab him in the neck with the broken steel or swing the pipe wrench against the left side of his head. I brought the steel up, pointing it toward him in a manner that protected me but could be taken as a way of showing him the damage.

It worked. All he needed was something on which to spike his runaway rage. It didn't calm him, but it diverted his focus for a critical second, and I felt the momentary diffusion. After barking a bit longer, somewhat academically the way a dog backs away from a fight, he yelled at everybody for good measure, threatened me with his fist, then screamed down to someone near the tractor. I felt an effusion of relief when he turned and clambered back down to the floor.

He crossed to meet another man. This, as I soon found out, was the Section Chief, the overall boss of the whole level. I knew in a second that a broken drill bit was a rare thing.

The other men on the scaffold seemed to tighten the circle when the Chief climbed onto our deck. He paused, seeming to regard me evenly for a moment. This was it then. I knew that my fate was to be decided by this man. Whether I was to be fired summarily on the spot and take that long, lonely (perhaps grateful) ride back up to the world, or perhaps be physically attacked by the men, or maybe even thrown into some kind of detention chamber, I could not tell, but I thought of them all.

"Whad's de problem 'ere?" he asked calmly in slightly accented English.

"I don't know, Captain," I said; then quickly shifting the blame onto the equipment, "This drill keeps breakin' the bit." Then I remembered the vibration I had noticed at the chuck earlier, and in a serendipitous stroke of pure inspiration added, "...I think the chuck's out of alignment or something."

"...Huh," he grunted, kneeling over the drill. "Give me de key."

One of the men handed him a chuck key, and with a fluidity of movement that surprised me he freed the remnant of the new bit I had just broken. He examined the break briefly, then pitched the fragment off the deck. He stood and called down for another bit, which was quickly handed up to him.

Kneeling again, he seated the new steel as I watched every move. He tested the fit by hand to assure that his adjustments with the key were even. Then he hefted the drill onto his knee, checked that his air valves were in the open position, and fired a four-second burst through the jacket while he watched the throw of the bit along its entire length.

Then he stood and braced the steel against a seam near the hole I had started.

Tension gripped my entire body. Suddenly, keeping this job became very important. The specter of failure had been dancing in my mind for so long it had begun to look like truth. I knew I would never be able to live down my presumptuous ignorance, and that whatever the outcome of my posturing to these men, it was bound to involve some physical pain. I knew in a flash the private hell of the dilettante, and my verdict was about to be announced by an uninterrupted burst of power from that awful drill.

I added goldmines to foxholes on my list of places where no atheists are found, and then, trying to wangle an advance on my good intentions, began to pray: "Dear Lord, if you ever wanted a rock drill, please take this one. I'll always be especially good; I'll always—."

The chatter of the drill startled me. It ran cleanly with a clear voice, spewing steam. The bit chewed into the rock face ejecting a fine granular dust—for about five long seconds. Then there was a loud clank. The Chief lunged forward, then caught himself as the drill stopped. I could hardly believe it! He stepped back, and there, protruding from the wall, was a two-foot section of new drill bit, its bright wound a glittering vindication of all my worst fears.

The Chief reached out and pulled the shaft from the wall. He looked at the chuck, then turned and yelled something down at the foreman, who had become remarkably quiet. He put his hand on my shoulder as he stepped past and told me to unhook the drill. The foreman met him on the ground and started what I have to believe was a babble of self-justification, but before long the Chief began to indicate by a telling little glossary of head shakes and backward steps that social intercourse alone was detaining a busy man. The faulty drill was hurriedly replaced on a hand gesture from the Chief, and I set about hooking it up the way I had seen him do it.

Once I learned to balance the thing, the work took on a set of more or less expectable forces. During the next several hours, I gradually developed a workable counter-balance to the awkward tool and learned to time the heft and pull of its inertia. My forearms became overly tired too quickly, eventually cramping numerous times during the day, but there was no way to rest or knead the muscles. Steam exhaust from the drill condensed and froze on my sleeves, and large blisters formed on the palms of my hands, inside the gauntlets.

I soon learned the routine, which arose from the length of time it took to drill each phase. Each attack on the wall was affected by the type of rock we were working. Each attack by the drills required holes of differing depth and placement, and the rock presented varying degrees of resistance. The drillers would create the channels into which the Blaster placed explosives, and it was here that I learned one of those crucial, unspoken laws of living that is never in the brochures: there existed among the drillers an intense, but unspoken, competition to be the first man to complete a given phase—or at least to avoid being the last to finish. At some point that first day, I came to recognize that the game existed and that there was an ever-renewed machismo linked to withdrawing one's bit from the wall seconds before the others were finished. Conversely, waves of silent anathemas descended upon the last operator to stop. It had probably begun long ago as an outgrowth of the steady routine and the natural human tendency to compete, but it had taken on a life of its own among these men, who seemed at times captives of its impulses out of all proportion to their efficiency.

As soon as I understood it, I knew instinctively that not to cooperate would be to present myself as a product of unsteady masculinity, with numerous dark consequences. I soon learned to gauge my performance by sound and tried to avoid being last all day—with poor results.

As soon as the drilling was complete, the Blasters stepped in to pack and wire the charges, while the drillers stood by. Then the mobile scaffold was drawn back with all hands. On a klaxon signal that was pitched loud enough to be heard above the general roar, we climbed down from the framework and took shelter behind the heavy plates of several enormous shoring machines, while steel matting was raised on the davits, and the detonations were coordinated along the rock face.

The entire tunnel jolted with the explosions as the pressure wave slammed through us and back again. At first, it left me breathless, and I had to fight off thoughts of a cave-in. Though I knew about explosives and their use, being underground with them introduced a new level of dread, and I began to develop a wary eye for movement in the ceiling.

The rubble was then collected by a ground team using trucks and dozers, further broken up by other drillers when necessary, inspected and conveyed to the ravenous teeth of a huge grinder. From there it was transported to the surface, while we re-mounted the work platforms to begin the process again, a few feet farther into the wall.

Each cycle took between 40 minutes to an hour when everything ran smoothly, if there was no secondary drill work necessary after blasting. It was back-breaking work in any language. For hours on end, as my arms cramped with the ponderous mass of the equipment, my back remained clammy with sweat, while my feet and hands stayed numb in the constant cold.

As the work wore on, through periods of intense thirst and increasing waves of fatigue-induced dizziness, I gradually became familiar with the movements of the Blaster who worked with me. He had a casual way of standing with his weight shifted under one hip much of the time, with the thumbs of his large gloves hooked into his utility belt. I noticed an interesting detail present in his appearance. He had lost or removed the metal buckle from his utility belt, which he kept closed with a length of slip-knotted twine. There was something frugal about it that matched his conservation of gesture and stance.

Whenever I raised the drill for placement he would step in close beside me, though for a long time my concentration on the drill kept me from any but a vague awareness of his presence. He was shorter than I, solidly built, and moved with an almost graceful economy of effort. His thick shoulders rolled slightly with shifts in the placement of his feet, and he always stood facing the work. Obscured like the others beneath an anonymous veil of safety gear, he went silently about the job, his only signal to the outside being this eloquent containment of energy; and upon that singular characteristic I found myself building a tentative structure of conclusions about him. I don't know at what point his presence became a consciousness.

It was strange and discomforting to have only a stance and a few gross mannerisms on which to formulate a person's identity. With every helmeted face obscured, all impressions came through the unconscious telegraphy of posture, gesture, and the odd, lumbering morphology of heavy coveralls. Yet gradually I began to form a sense of connection with this man's dogged presence beside me on the platform. It may have been the cast of his shoulders or the devotion of his manner that gave me the idea that he had once been in the military, or perhaps been a prisoner, but I began to feel a certain comfort in his proximity without knowing why. He seemed to have long experience with the work, and he maintained an impenetrable solitude throughout the day, even when activity stopped briefly for lunch.

When we put down the tools for the mid-shift recess, I trudged away from the section in an advanced state of thirst exhaustion toward the communal water truck, partially to cover the fact that I had brought nothing to eat. I pulled my respirator down and was immediately struck by the smell of sulphur. It had been in the air all along but filtered down by the mask, and now it pressed into my nose with harsh acridity, like burning rubber.

I drank deeply and gratefully from the cold ground water in the tank and lingered by the truck, keeping some distance from the other men in the section and indulging in a decadence of leisure, alternately drinking and taking refuge in the mask. There was a container of salt tablets on a shelf above the spigots, and I fumbled two of them into my mouth, then drank some more.

A general lull settled throughout the tunnel. All movement seemed suddenly to have ceased. The noise level subsided, though the generators hummed steadily from their platform about 30 yards away. The rock we had been attacking relentlessly for so long seemed now to stare immutably inward, as though trying to understand what was happening. Glyphs of crimped and plaited light, reflected upward from the ceiling lights by many puddles, swung peacefully across the dark stone surface, imparting expression to its forlorn and broken face.

I looked around the tunnel, taking it in for the first time, and sensed a subtle shift in its dimensions, a realignment of proportion, engendered in part by my own participation in the process of its change. This rock had slept undisturbed for millions of years.

A tumble of thoughts charged through me as I remembered the American Indian belief that our connection with the land is forged by our attitude toward it, which is linked by touch. We are bound irrevocably to what we handle, and though we may eventually leave an object or a place behind, our mark remains upon it in the way, perhaps, that we can be said to surrender our image on film.

But the relationship is reciprocal, for the thing in turn reaches forth to touch us back and will continue to color the fabric of our lives, however dimly, if only by the shape of its impress on the weave of subsequent experience. If we choose not to grow by the connection, even the ignoring remains detectable within us nonetheless, like a gap in the plot, like plaster fallen away from a mural in the night. I wondered for a moment what residual effects of this rummaging in the earth might accrue to the tomorrows that lay in store.

Sated at last, I scanned the immediate area for any sign of an un-assuming place to sit out the rest of the lunch break. Even with their masks off, I could not tell one man from another at any distance. All were bearded, and most were huddled together in the heat of the main generator, sudden apparitions from another century. All but a few kept their goggles in place while they groped in their lunch cans. Some ate with knives, others with their hands, and wiped their fingers on their clothes.

I noticed that the man who worked beside me had selected a rock at the base of one wall and sat by himself, removed from the others. He was settled, seeking the company of no one, and ate very little. I decided to move over near him, if not to speak, then at least to sanc-tion our partnership by joining in his detachment.

Just as I was about to take a step, I saw the Foreman approach-ing, picking his steps carefully through the mud. Instantly, the phony peace was broken, and all my molecules jumped to the alert. I felt the blood assembling in my cheeks. The incident with the broken drill had changed the man's general body language toward me and had also served to contain his hysterics, at least for a while. Yet his goggles still followed me in silence, so I chose to watch back, feeling his resentful eyes upon me all day. I knew he didn't like anything about me, and now that he had been put down in front of the men, I feared the con-sequences of renewed conniption. I felt sure he meant to stage a con-frontation right here, with the entire section in attendance over their lunch, and was determined to stand my ground. To move away now would be seen as slithering. My arms trembling with fatigue, I braced myself on both legs and waited.

He stepped up to the adjoining spigot with elaborate nonchalance and began filling his water bottle. He pulled his respirator down, re-vealing a surprisingly handsome Asian face with a glossy black beard and straight white teeth. He took a long pull the water bottle, then turned and spat some onto the ground near my feet for effect. I won-dered fleetingly why a thirsty person would ever do that. He looked at me through his goggles for a long moment. Then he snorted derisively and muttered, "Farouche!"

I had no idea what the word meant, but the intention was unmis-takable, and I held his fixed gaze through the lenses until he simply turned away. I decided that he was the sort who embraced one crisis after another because they gave him significance, something like tragic stature, but I felt a profound relief to see him move off, picking his steps meticulously along the high places between the puddles. In the backwash of adrenalin I knew that I needed to sit down.

With the weight of the water swinging in my gut, I made my way over to the wall near where the Blaster sat and was surprised when he raised one arm heavily and waved me over. It was the first remotely friendly gesture I had seen since entering the mine some five hours earlier.

When I approached he tipped his goggles up courteously, the way a gentleman lifts his hat, revealing for a moment an older face than I expected. There were about his level grey eyes and slender lips the deep, tense lines often etched in the faces of zealots and of lonely men. There was a melancholy serenity about him that I felt had been put there by something more than just half a human lifetime. His look was mild, but it held me steadily while it seemed to assess the situation, run the odds, and make a decision all in the same moment. The combination lent his expression a certain dark wisdom. I could tell in a second that here was a man whose soul had struck a balance.

I lifted my goggles and pulled down the respirator to return the favor, and with a slight nod gave him what felt like a gritty smile. The seal of my mask was caked with sweat-soaked rock grit, which I'd failed to clean in my focus on drinking all the water I might have used to wipe it off.

"Beresina," he said simply, holding out a gloved hand.

"Moore," I said, shaking it. The name stirred a memory. "...Beresina. Like the Napoleonic battle?"

"Ah-hah, you know about zis?" He seemed pleased.

"Well, not so's to tell you anything about it."

"Don'worry. I know everyt'ing about it."

Smiling at the evident pedigree of the subject, I asked, "Your first name isn't Pierre, is it?"

He chuckled softly from deep within himself, releasing a dry shuffling sound, like nesting bats.

"Joaquin."

"John," I said, bending to sit beside him. My knees buckled, and I hit the rock in one movement. It was the first time all day that I had tried deliberately to sit down, and a wave of audible relief swept up from my legs in a tingling rush of tremulous exhaustion, which hissed out of my mouth in a hot mist that swirled in the air between us. He smiled again.

"Tired zo zoon?"

I rolled my head and looked at him, but the goggles were back in place on his face, making it impossible to read what he really meant when he added, "Well...you ain' dead yet."

That caught me. There was something in the inviolable solitude of this pronouncement which, uttered without eyes to lend it the cheerful irony that I could only guess was behind the lenses, left me to ramify uncomfortably among its implications. This was more than a casual expression. I began to fidget with the fingers of my gloves.

The very idea that I had been plunged anew into conditions which might give relevance to such words filled me again with dull alarm, their context sending out quick rootlets of despair to all corners of my mind. Images of the war flashed through my brain. It seemed for a moment that my journey since returning from Southeast Asia had somehow smacked up against the in-bound curve of space-time and that even as we spoke I was sliding down its wall like slung mud, back into harm's way. I could think of no response and just stared wordlessly at the vaporous morse of my steady breathing in the charged air between us.

"Zo," he said at length, nodding in the direction of the Foreman. "You don' like our Djeepah, eh?"

"Jee-pah? ...What's that, G.P.A.?...General Purpose Asshole?"

His mouth broke into one of those smiles that people reserve for small tragedies.

"Heh. ...Aah, he iz a squeek-pipe, but he knows hiz job, and he iz more loud zan ze machinery."

I had to admit the advantage of being able to make yourself heard in this place.

Like many people of broad experience, Beresina would in time reveal himself to be a harmony of contrasts. With wry humor, yet a hard-won fatalism, he was at once a loner and a ready member of the team, whose rare flashes of anger were invariably aimed at anyone who failed to pull his required weight. He lived within his own particular stratosphere of subtlety and protected himself against intrusion by the grotesque and wonderful perversity of comparing the rigors of any given situation with the prospect of immediate death.

A steady purpose, though, is a great tranquilizer, and over the next several months, I would come to associate his words "You ain't dead yet" inextricably with the measured and solitary nature of his comportment, as a pointed caption for his life, and as precautionary perspective for my own.

By the time the bell sounded announcing the end of lunch break, my legs had stiffened considerably, and I got to my feet in pain, the muscles shaking, refusing to cooperate for several steps. I knew immediately not to sit again, if I could only last through the rest of the day. My right hip, with an AK-47 bullet fragment riding against the bone, caused my thigh to cramp on the second step and I froze in dread of the pain and effort to take another. I took a long preparatory moment, risking the notice of the volatile Djeepah, before I could continue.

My hands hurt so much as I climbed the scaffold that I almost slipped off. I realized that they were sticky in the gloves. There was grit captured in the gloves, too, filling the blisters I knew were there with needles of insistent pain. As the work started again, and the men resumed the drilling competition, I was afraid that the pain in my hands would grow to become too much for me to continue. I could only guess at the effect such another provocation from me might have on Djeepah, but most importantly, I could not allow myself to fail. My hands would eventually recover, but I might not.

As I gripped the trigger handles again and hove the drill against the wall, the shock bolted from my palms deep into the muscles of my forearms. They cramped immediately. I cried out in the deafening racket of the drill and swore that I would ride the damn thing until I dropped if that was required to salvage my sense of worth. Each blow against the wall jarred up my arms and into my shoulders as if my body was being repeatedly hit.

Gradually, though, the heavy vibration actually served to ease the cramping and, over time, sent the level of pain in my hands to a kind of pulsing numbness. I guessed that blisters must have limits in their capacity to inflict agony and kept wondering if I had reached it. Each time the drilling stopped for placement of the charges, the blood surged back into my hands the instant I released the handles, sending up renewed walls of pain. I took to keeping my fingers curled into fists during these breaks in an effort to maintain pressure on the sores.

As we worked on in the permanent rain of condensation for another four hours or so, the air around us roiled in its dirty light while the burn of the helmet lamps spilled against the wet earth releasing strange shadows that moved alongside us like a platoon of giants. Beresina and I slowly improved our wordless co-operation, and with it my speed crept up, and though I was never the first drill to stop, I was no longer always the last. I learned to read the rock and to judge its resistance. Thanks to an occasional indication from Beresina, I began to find the likely placement points on the new face long before we remounted the scaffold, as each phase changed the wall.

Back on the scaffold I tried to imagine the structure of the dark rock before me, its internal shape, its possible fissures, as the contours danced before my gaze in the bleaching eye of the lamp. The face took on a hundred expressions an hour, revealing in its darker bands a grim determination while squinting back with cold eyes to hide the vulnerability at its seams. Here it would try to fool me with an impression of tetchiness or vanity, and there, the glint of crystal in shadow could beckon like the wink of a whore, full of dark and illusory promise.

Gradually over the dim incalculable hours, the drill assumed an intelligence of its own. Feeding on momentum, it seemed to swing from invisible tethers, carrying a separate intention to the rock along an intangible bridge of wills. The ground rose and fell before me, and things took on a strange color. My awareness of time dissolved into hazy irrelevancy, and I worked with numbed obsession, drifting through the routine on ragged strands of energy that seemed to emanate from outside myself. Conscious decision-making gave way to a painful metronome in my chest, as all movement of the drill bit became the locus of points along which dragged the remnants of my full attention.

The Japanese have a word for the moment when the mind is free of thought, when you become one with your actions: "*Satori.*" It occurs when you are abandoned to the fullness of the moment. I must have remained suspended in a limited form of this state for some time, for when at last we struck a fahlband, and the drilling was stopped for a geological inspection of the metallic sulfides in it, my brain had to struggle for long moments, as though arriving from a distance, to grasp the idea that work was over for the day.

I turned to see several dozen men in clean coveralls approaching across the tunnel, as most of those around me scattered to retrieve lunch cans or use the portable toilets. With my legs trembling in the effort to hold me up, I shuffled into line with the dirty ones. The men around me seemed far away, as in a fog. There was nothing real but the pain. We assembled in the shaft for the ride to the surface.

It was pitch dark outside when we stepped from the cages into a warm evening breeze. I pulled down the respirator and sucked at the ocean of air like a man rescued from a near-drowning. The night smelled of grass and sage and carried with it the faint perfume of wildflowers, just for decoration. My lungs filled as though for the first time, sending a twinge of pain up my spine and a warm effusion across the skin on my back. I wondered if this was what returning astronauts felt upon first stepping from decompression chambers. All around us the land was an ample, viscously glistening space with only a membrane of moonlight stretched tight across its surface, embraced by a vast silence which had come from across the universe to press upon my ears and reveal the hum of my own small being.

I stood among the others awaiting the company bus with no thought of who I was or why I was there. I had no history and no future. I was just a consciousness in the darkness in the middle of the world. I eased my hands tenderly from the heavy gloves, but it was too dark to examine them. I could tell only that they were wet and pulpy. It hurt to wiggle my fingers and they throbbed when I let them hang at my sides, but the fresh air curled between them and bore away the fuggy smell.

The bus swung out of the darkness, the strenuous rattle of its diesel hammering against the night air, and drew up to our group with a wheeze, as a cloud of bitter blue smoke drifted past the headlights. I clambered on board in a daze, allowing myself to be carried by the acumen of the crowd. I slid in next to an open window and leaned out. As we lunged to a start the welcome prairie breeze rose and brushed my face like fur. I watched as the featureless starlit countryside, wide and vacant of event, came on and passed by, as on a moving backdrop. I wondered idly if any of the men sitting around me were in Section 3 and had been just a few feet away for the past 14 hours. Now, jouncing in their seats with faces unveiled and beards pressed by the wind, they were magically transformed into bus passengers, familiar yet remote.

16
The Man Behind
The Mask

The Chinese devise the ideograms of their place names with striking simplicity, frequently elegant lyricism, and occasional farce. The tarnished magnificence of the Dragon Joy Hotel afforded amusing confirmation of this tradition, with its carved wooden sign, showing two dragons in apparent retreat from each other. (Perhaps a dragon's joy is to avoid another one.)

It was a tall shiplap building strongly reminiscent of the hotels in photographs of the old American West, an impression strengthened by the colorless residue of long-faded paint on its exterior boards. It bore a long palisaded front porch beneath a roof supported by a march of slender posts on which the paint lay open in long fents, like slashed paper. It even had an old-fashioned two-way louvered door at the front for summer use.

The company had contracted with its irascible owner, Mr. something Loo ("Loo the Shoe," for his willingness to physically kick drunken miners, some of whom outweighed him by 100 pounds or more) to engage the hotel for use as bachelor quarters. As part of the agreement, they had attached a large laundry and medical facility behind the main structure. The building stood virtually alone, accompanied by a few tawdry little shops and shanties, nursing hopefully at an underground spring and trying hard to be a town, surrounded by miles and miles of whispering grass.

The welcome light of the hotel's main saloon vaulted across the porch and out onto the rutted ground, where its broken geometry moved toward us in the windshield until it lurched to rest beside us as the bus squeaked to a halt and let the breath out of its brakes with a dramatic sigh. Most of the men in my section were apparently staying here, for I stepped down with all but a few of the passengers, and we trudged toward the laundry annex to shed their coveralls.

Outside in the lemon-colored glare of the doorway were several logs set horizontally upon stanchions, like hitching posts. Before heading into the hotel, the men began to step out of their coveralls and to flail them against the logs, swinging them over their heads in the manner of firefighters, until the mud cracked free, pattering onto the ground in fragments of clay.

Rolling my palms toward the light, I was alarmed to see how bloody and filthy they were. Suddenly, they seemed to hurt more now that my tired brain was confronted with a visual aid. I got out of the coveralls with fingertip precision and threw them onto the counter inside, where the attendants were busily dragging them into hampers and exchanging insults with the men. Instead of following the others back outside, I stepped into the dazzle of the adjoining clinic.

The duty nurse was a plump young man with nervous hands, whose tiny face swam in a pool of mottled pink skin. He had deep-set black eyes that stared nervously out from the shadow of a single connected eyebrow like a den of trapped foxes. His miniature smile of welcome was frozen in place, slow to catch up with my mood and out of synch with the apprehension that began to settle over the rest of his face as soon as I rolled my hands over. He regarded them with gentle contempt. He probably thought correctly that only an ignoramus would have allowed this to happen, while I thought that his cheeks were admirably suited for the storage of acorns.

Yet his pudgy fingers fluttered about my hands with the gentleness of moths. He had obviously seen this kind of thing many times and quickly set about bathing them in a soothing solution which fizzed on contact, like Ginger Ale. He removed most of the grit with a small pick, then applying a silvery lotion, he bandaged them and told me to shower and to come back in the morning before work. I thanked him, then stepped back into the night and went around to the front door of the hotel.

The swinging doors opened into a wide barroom made entirely of varnished pine freckled throughout with dark brown knots. Along the left side wall, a row of sconces, busy with clouds of moths, emitted a feeble wash of dusky light that spilled along the paneling in consecutive elliptical pools.

The main floor was crowded with round tables at which many still-dirty miners were sitting with drinks, some beginning to play cards, their feet shuffling on a nap of sawdust and broken peanut shells that crackled beneath the sound of their movements and the general din of voices. Tobacco smoke already curled languorously among them, eventually to settle above their heads in a blue stratus throughout the room.

Along the right side wall was a long bar, behind which was stacked tier upon tier of liquor bottles, a wall of glass and earth-colored liquids displayed under dust-clouded light bulbs in a large chicken wire cage. The place had a rough frontier character, held in suspension by the surround of scarred wood and its spare utilitarian furnishing.

The sounds of a noisy kitchen came through the wall behind the bar, and the voluptuous smell that wafted from a grill was already running its seductive fingers over my nose. I moved over and sat at the bar where there were several vacant stools. A sallow Asian barkeep stepped over. There was a large black mole on the left side of his chin from which half a dozen extraordinarily long whiskers played in the air. He pinched a paper napkin from a stack and dropped it in front of me.

"Wha' habba?" he asked blankly.

"Scotch, please. Neat. No water, no ice."

He stared at me without moving, his eyes as empty of expression as the buttons on a teddy bear. I wondered if he understood English or needed more information.

"...Just straight," I added. "Like cough medicine."

He turned away without acknowledgement, leaving me wondering if I had failed some secret requirement. I surveyed the counter. It was well-worn and had evidently been subjected to harsh treatment for a long time. It looked as though it had been repaired with unfinished flooring planks in several places and smeared with filler here and there. The close grain of the darker wood drew in tight upon itself, while even its patches held old stains of impenetrable origin. Above the coolers the wire screen that protected the display of bottles was dented inward in many places, its upper mesh a lacy fabric of fly nets hanging like dusty vines.

Looking back across the tables I began to glimpse signs of damage to the furniture among the patrons' many legs. The glint of metal reinforcing straps appeared on a few table joints, and many chair rungs were banded.

The wooden smell of the building, richly mixed with beer, stale sweat, tobacco and sagebrush, skulked restlessly around the room carrying roast beef smoke from the kitchen. With throbbing beneath the bandages on my hands and the rattle of conversation on my eardrums, punctuated with bursts of laughter throughout the room, I was indulging in a selection of the senses when the glass of whisky was placed at my elbow.

"Eat?" the barkeep asked, staring vacantly past my ear.

"Yeah!"

He produced a dingy menu encased in yellowed plastic and then waited, staring blankly. I made a quick pretense of looking at it but, as a complete captive of the essences coming from the kitchen, said, "Steak. Medium rare. Large." I spread my arms in what I hoped would be an amusing gesture and added, "With everything."

I smiled good-naturedly with all the hopeful expectation of a child on Santa's lap. He shifted his gaze wordlessly from the space beside me and turned away. I wondered if some white man had beaten his grandfather to death on the railroads.

I lifted the glass with anticipation. The smell of the liquor was full and peaty. It tasted sweet, faintly nauseating, and instantly spread its gratifying warmth through me, mournful as a drizzle at dusk. Then from behind me:

"If you hef a problem an' you trink, you hef two problems."

Beresina hove onto the bar stool next to me with a grin. I turned, instantly glad for his company.

"No problem. Celebration. Want one?"

He turned and said something gruffly to the bartender, who responded with noticeably more animation than he had chosen to show me. In a few moments, he was back with a Schnapps and beer for Beresina and another whisky for me.

"Well, thank you," I said, surprised on two counts. "You have a way with him, I see."

"Yez, zat iz true. He knowz I vill beat ze shit out from him."

He seemed to enjoy my amusement at this truth, and we slipped into easy conversation. He stayed to order dinner, too, and as the sea of voices rose and fell behind us, we talked of war and of abstract philosophy. He had been a bit player on the world's stage for so long that he thought in global terms. The things that concerned him were ageless, and I listened with the feeling at times that my own travels had been made in deafness to a world that shouted its lessons.

Austrian by birth, he had been in the German U-boat service in WW II—one of the small percentage of men to survive it, thanks to having been forced to the surface and captured by an American destroyer off the coast of New Jersey in the winter of 1944. He had learned English in a prison camp in Mississippi, which he pronounced with voluptuously caressed Zs in a lazy and amused sibilance. He seemed to enjoy saying it.

As a teenager, he and three friends had run away to join the French Foreign Legion, carrying only food and a sack of clothes. They had jumped a train bound for Athens. He had developed a fever along the way, and delirious in the smoky compartments, had climbed outside to ride much of the way on the roof. One of his friends had joined him up there, and having fallen asleep, rolled off in the night. They never saw him again.

In Greece, they bribed the captain of a stock carrier to give them passage to Trieste. By then all three had fevers, and an Italian they met on board showed them how to drink blood in the animal pens to keep strong, but another of them died on the crossing anyway. Beresina and his last companion slept most of a week in the basement of an abandoned sewing machine factory somewhere on the North African coast, unaware of the world outside, embracing each other much of the time to keep warm until they were well enough to approach the Legion.

There he had learned camel wrangling and been among the last to see service along the old line of colonial forts in the North African desert—just like in *Beau Geste*. Eventually rising to the rank of Sergeant, he was transferred to Alpine training, back in the mountains not far from his home, where he had learned to ski off cliffs, then to deploy American-made parachutes above the lower slopes, finishing their descent into the villages on skis.

The Nazi annexation of Austria had caught him up in its glittering promise of world-class opportunity, so with all the wide-angled hope and the sanguine guesswork of youth, he and a friend whom he never saw again had gone north, to be led astray with an entire nation. He told me with contained emotion of the early days, when they dispersed, breaking across frontiers, spreading out over the map of Europe, following the unfurled banner of madness and drunk with early success, over the valleys and through the forests, across the fields and seas; and in this inhuman effort, the nation itself ground to scrap, pulverized.

By the end, he was in America and glad of it, but the effects of his disillusionment were profound and colored still his view of the world. Some of his friends who had survived the war in Europe believing airily in Dr. Goebbels' wishful propaganda even as their cities burned, had killed themselves after it all rather than confront the collapse of the dream, even amid its wreckage.

I was to learn that Beresina was a man of opulent contradiction. Sometimes absurdly outrageous in his remarks, his robust self-assurance and gruff rejection of sentimentality served as a permanent vote of confidence in human nature. He, like virtually everyone the world over who has direct experience of war, rejected it on both moral and practical grounds, seeing it as a political, social, and profoundly psychological disaster as well as a perceptual and rhetorical scandal from which total recovery is unlikely. Yet his eyes glowed when he asked me about fighting the unseen enemy in the jungles of Southeast Asia. I couldn't help but like him.

For the first time since returning from that baleful kingdom of pain and despair, I felt in his company the grip of my reticence loosening enough to tell him some of my experiences of running deep-penetration reconnaissance and interdiction missions across the borders into North Vietnam, Cambodia, and Laos with a small team of Chinese mercenaries against an unsuspecting enemy who nonetheless sometimes managed to find us. As he listened the grays of his iris pulsed and turned inward, adding to his store.

He was a voracious consumer of a subject that for hidden reasons lived close to his heart. He was the product of a terrible hegemony, made the more sinister and perhaps more protracted even in his now self-imposed isolation, by the lights of perverted science. Yet like many other veterans of the Second World War on all sides, the issue of who won or lost remains secondary to the intensity of their personal experiences. Right or wrong, front line or support, Beresina was part of a generation that had played out the most exciting years of their lives on a global stage, and the gradually diminishing force of it had not yet let him go.

He talked with veiled nostalgia of blowing up American ships as they moved in clear outline against the well-lit Carolina coast at night, sometimes within sight of the beaches. His crew could not understand why a nation at war would leave its shore towns ablaze with lights each night. He told how they had hidden in the open just behind the curvature of the earth, rolling gently on the surface of the dark sea, smoking cigarettes while airing their mattresses and watching the lower stars disappear in the lume of our coastal lights beyond the western horizon.

It became common knowledge at Donitz's Admiralty in Germany that the lights of Coney Island could often be seen directly in the vapor which lay upon the horizon from over thirty miles out. Beresina described how they had even surfaced in New York harbor one night and had, by turns at the heavy periscope lenses, marveled in excited whispers at the buildings, the electric advertising, and the traffic in the streets.

I thought of all the American lives lost to this very man and to others like him, yet had to join in his wry disdain for our leadership, both then and now. His eyes twinkling with minor malice, he pointed out that everywhere, throughout history, the greatest mass murderers have always been people's own governments.

Warming to his subject, he drew for me on a cocktail napkin a map of the Atlantic Ocean and the coastlines of its continental boundaries. Then with precision he showed me the exact codified subdivisions the Nazis used to plot every hundred meters of it. It was an ingeniously simple and thorough code, easy to transmit in open Morse if necessary, and made it possible to arrange un-compromised rendezvous at any place in the whole ocean with the transmission of a simple five-digit code. I stared with fascination at the provocative grid while its global implications converged in my brain. In the next instant, as the ceiling fans turned quietly in the spoons on the counter top between us, I realized that Beresina had been no ordinary seaman. He knew too much.

He talked of their months at sea in the stifling little boat and how the stale, musty air mixed with diesel fumes inside had often made them sick. Fungus would begin to grow on the overhead after a few weeks, eventually covering the light bulbs, and their bedding became soggy with mildew. They lived within their own fetid emanations for weeks at a time, surfacing whenever they could, and only at night in the western Atlantic, but they were doing the work of the New Germany.

I was to learn that his experience with explosives had intriguingly sinister origins, deepening my conviction that he had been at least cross-trained in a specialty not strictly necessary for service on submarines. Perhaps he opened up to me just because I was a combat veteran too; perhaps simply because I showed an interest. It may only have been because he wanted to practice his English, but the profound implications that lay in his response to a simple question based on what I soon came to realize was the merely rudimentary demolition training I'd had in the Army, might have put him at some risk of investigation had we been overheard in some public metropolitan restaurant.

He explained casually that the ingredients to make a bomb could be obtained easily over the counter at any good British hardware store or pharmacy. (British? I wondered.) He listed potassium nitrate, a fertilizer, potassium chlorate, a common chemical for killing garden slugs, and potassium permanganate, a throat gargle. The British, he said (the British again) used ferric oxide as a floor stain and ground aluminum as a silver paint powder. When he drew a diagram showing how to connect a series of linked explosives with dynamite wire and detonating fuse, I thought at first that he was explaining how the blasters planned their attack on the rock face, but it turned into the formula for calculating how much high explosive would be needed to bring down a bridge: length times breadth times depth times 2 equals one half the number of grams of explosive required.

He went on to explain that an effective fuse could easily be made by filling an ink bottle with sulfuric acid and placing a strip of thin cardboard between the glass and the lid. The acid would slowly eat away the cardboard, finally making contact with a fuse screwed into the lid, where the heat of the reaction would detonate the attached explosive charge. The process leaves plenty of time for the "artist" to be well away.

As he spoke with slowly metered caution on a subject that I realized was being released with the unspoken understanding that it was strictly proprietary, I learned, at least in theory, how to delay an explosion for up to fourteen hours by linking the detonator to the winding spring of an ordinary bedside alarm clock.

He told how one could sabotage (there, he said it) a ship by drilling a hole in a lump of coal, packing it with explosives and a detonator, then disguising it with plasticine, shoe polish, and coal dust. Placed in the coal bunkers of a ship or locomotive, the device would be invisible and inert until shoveled into the furnace where the heat would set it off.

One of my favorites was a booby trapped package that detonated when the string around the parcel was cut. Two tiny strands of wire, insulated from one another, were wrapped inside the string, so when cut with scissors, an electrical circuit was completed, setting off the explosion.

Thus, over time and many subsequent conversations, my amorphous companion of that first day underground turned into a most interesting character. I came to notice that Beresina kept very few friends, spoke little with others, and generally comported himself as a man who kept within a store of accrued inertia, yet held in check by all the necessary resources to make of his life no more than he chose. There were times when, as much as I wanted to know the answer to the question of who he really was, I held back for fear of unintentionally cutting the string on the package.

The noise from the tables behind us gradually rose to a level which made it necessary for us to lean together and speak loudly. It became an irritation, especially as I could tell that he meted out his own past with caution. I did not want anything to compromise my evident privilege at this wellspring, so we took the first outbreak of temper at one of the card games across the room as an excuse to retire. We signed our chits at the bar, and as we left, I pushed them over to the stony barman, who muttered grudgingly like a child who has been forced to express gratitude for something it neither wishes nor enjoys.

Behind the dining room bar area, the main floor led to a broad staircase with a curving banister rail that swept with worn grace to the second floor. Here there was a large lounge area containing ponderous leather-covered furniture that squatted in grudging communion on the border of a threadbare oriental carpet. From there on up for two more stories, the building was open in the center, surmounted by a winding stairway with the most extraordinary continuous wooden banister I have ever seen. I thought it must be listed somewhere in the rail carvers' record book.

My assigned room was on the top floor. It was clean and well-maintained by the hotel staff, and being high, it often caught a breath or two of breeze during the airless summer nights. It contained a small writing table and a spoke-backed chair in addition to a narrow bed with an incongruously high mahogany headboard upon which artful carvings twisted and turned in fixed and sculptured ambiguity.

My evenings soon became as ritualistic as the days were strenuous and routine. After dinner at the bar downstairs, often with Beresina or one of the other men, I would trudge up the many flights of stairs to the room, open the window and prop it with a chair rail, kick my filthy clothes into the corner, and take a shower.

The water pressure left something to be desired, depending upon how soon in the evening one used it. All too often, once I was in the shower and well soaped up, the water would go from a warm, forceful flow to something like a kid pissing on my head. This produced a certain economy of procedure for a time, while I experimented with cleaning first those parts of the anatomy which I would least like to be stuck with afterwards should the water supply disappear altogether. The decision to begin soaping each subsequent part then carried all the pre-game excitement of a race against time.

There was a small refrigerator in the room, too. It was old, but still trustworthy enough, though the freezer was shot and always seemed to wince when I opened it. It took two days to make ice cubes. I kept a few bottles of beer and fruit juices in the main compartment, though I avoided storing any food. Fish, in particular, might have been risky fare.

After the shower, I would often take something from the fridge to sip while reading in bed one of the two dozen books I had brought with me. Propped against the headboard, I would stare at the words, while the shower dripped endlessly, mocking my efforts with a repetitious banging sound in the bottom of the hollow tub. I would soon turn off the light to sleep while the ruckus of distant fighting filtered up through the building from downstairs on drifts of faint-heard din and tumult.

On this night, though, I fell upon the bed with wet bandages on my hands, in the very last stage of exhaustion, slipping into unconsciousness on a succession of such low biological events that they escaped all notice. My leg twitched once.

17
Second Day

At around 3:30 AM the second day the buzzer hummed in my room to wake me for work. I woke with a start, and with head swimming in a mire of sleep, swung my legs out of bed. Instantly, I was locked in a muscle seizure so severe that it jack-knifed me forward as though I were trying to sit in my own lap. The muscles in my back cramped as soon as I tried to straighten out of it. The fibers of my body began pulling together with a will of their own. It took my breath away. I gasped at the pain.

I had been mildly muscle-bound often in the past from hard workouts but nothing approaching this. I was taken over by it, completely inhabited, as with growing concern I strained to unfold. They continued to tighten in spasms of constriction with every movement while I strained against their rebellion. I rolled onto my side and slipped backwards off the mattress onto my knees, and in that prayerful attitude, at last felt my abdominals begin to loosen their grip in twitches of resistance. I reeled with the excruciating effort to push up from the bedding and to balance on trembling legs.

After a few lurching steps and a pause to catch my breath and assess if any of my extremities would respond, I bent carefully forward to reach for my clean clothes, trying not to use my stomach. I realized that my arms would not straighten out. The flexors in my forearms, too, had stiffened during the night, clinching them at acute angles. They were frozen in place and laced with a purple tracery of bruises where the muscles had torn. My legs shook with the effort to remain standing. Wavering over the clothes, I groped at them mantis-like, and with temples pounding, consciously forced my limbs through the cumbrous and painful process of dressing as though donning heavy armor.

Dressed at last, I pivot-walked toward the head of the stairs, gulping at the still air of the hallway. The floorboards seemed to mock each of my steps, chuckling softly in their joists. Leaning for a moment to steady myself on the newel post at the top of the staircase, I breathed deeply the morning essences of the building. Furniture wax and desiccated woolens, mixed alluringly with coffee, bacon, and a hint of mothballs, made a heady argument for staying in. Breakfast and then a change of bandages at the clinic seemed impossibly distant goals to achieve before the bus came.

During the long and punishing journey down the stairs, I acquired an intimate appreciation for banister joinery, every foot of it observed close at hand. Arriving at last at the bottom, I rested against the newel and surveyed the room to which Beresina and I had our backs turned for most of the evening before.

By appearances, it had somehow been all but wrecked during the night. The sullen staff was righting chairs and tables, sweeping spills out the front door, and scattering sawdust. A few of the miners sat with helmets on in isolated readiness at the tables, ignoring the cleanup efforts around them, and clutching mugs of coffee. From the kitchen the clang of large pots mixed with the voices of the cooks, whose wan, expressionless faces appeared in the amber light of the service window. In the mysterious recesses behind the opening they screeched at each other with speech like cats.

Just as I achieved a bar stool, the sound of broken glass crashed into a metal bucket in the corner of the room where one of the Loo family was collecting the night's debris with a hand broom and muttering to himself. I began to appreciate the family's surly attitude toward their tenants.

I could not swing my leg over the stool, so I backed onto it and pivoted my knees into the bar. Thus parked at the counter, where I could manage feeding myself with arms bent by bobbing at the fork like a duck, I quickly bolted down an excellent breakfast and then feeling somewhat improved, carried a mug of coffee out to the clinic.

I stepped into the harsh light and saw that the duty nurse that morning was a woman. I held up my hands, presenting the stained bandages, not knowing if she spoke English and trusting that the evidence would communicate my needs.

She looked up from a table in the back of the room, then approached the service counter moving in a frail agony of grace, her heels scuffing softly on the concrete floor. She was a humorless, taciturn woman of indeterminate age with pale lips and an explosion of tiny moles on her neck—the first woman I had seen since arriving. She had smudged black eyes, like those of silent movie sirens found starving in hotel rooms, found dying by gas, eyes dark with the moral mascara of defeated beauty. Her high smooth pompadour gleamed yellow, like glue, and the heavy fugitive odor of her perfume filled the air, lingering in little waves as she moved.

She was careful and gentle, treating my hands again with salve and rewrapping them with kindly attention. Yet she bore a sadness which tipped the lightly balanced mechanism of my sentiments such that when she finished I turned to face my day with an odd sense of loss.

Afterwards, there was just enough time to struggle painfully back up to my room for a few minutes to swallow two aspirin, brush my teeth, and run water through the filters of my respirator; then, back down to draw clean coveralls and a lunch box. By then the bar was crowded with men and the smell of hot coffee.

Steam rose from the tanks of two large urns that had been set up on tables, and the men were arranging themselves in a line to fill their thermos bottles. My arms had begun to straighten a little with use, though two round trips on the staircase had my legs quivering so badly I had to rest for a moment at the nearest table. I soon joined a group that was shuffling past enormous stacks of sandwiches wrapped in butcher's paper on the bar. I took two packets which bore a completely illegible scribble in crayon, then, clutching my newly-issued lunch can like a cask of found money, hobbled out into the morning dark to join the throng awaiting the bus.

Day number two might have been a carbon copy of the first, except that it presented a number of surprises of its own. Building on the previous day's experience, though, I learned rapidly and found that the routine would follow the same relentless pace of the day before.

It was still pitch dark when we assembled for the elevators, and even though I now knew something of what lay beyond the eerie, pervasive silence, I felt again my foreignness preceding me when I stepped from the bus and was left alone in the crowd. I felt caught in the open. A chill raced through me, despite the balmy night, and I hugged myself against it. Having survived one full day in the strange, airless underworld of violent sound, dangerous currents, and relentless disassembly of the earth had heightened my anticipation of being flung again into the pit. Fear of the unknown is nothing to the fear of what is known, and a day's worth of familiarity made me acutely conscious of my own frailties. I looked about hopefully for Beresina but quickly realized that I would be unlikely to recognize even a far closer friend in the silent milling crowd of anonymous overalls.

I knew that later I would be unable to raise my arms above my head, would stagger for balance on the scaffold, swimming with the weight of the drill case. I now knew also that as soon as I went underground the humidity would fall back into my clothes quick as rain, and I shivered in anticipation. My hands began to hurt again. There was a falling of sounds. Behind us a tree full of darkness spread itself high over the southern end of the company area beyond the shack, and out of it fell tiny bird notes like drops of water.

Many of the men around me had disappeared again inside their equipment and now stood about in crowded silence as profoundly de-personalized as they had been the morning before. Their clothing smelled of the angel they wrestled each day deep in the shifting and treacherous opera of stone. Even those faces still exposed were closed, turned inward, downward. The few whose eyes traveled in my direction looked back from a wordless black distance I would eventually have to cross.

Once I thought I recognized one of the men from the hotel and prepared myself with an expectant expression to speak. He shuffled past vacantly with his hands in his armpits, like a fugitive in a madman's overcoat, leaving my smile of greeting to fade in the dark. The limited camaraderie I sensed the evening before had fled the alien assembly like a wraith at dawn. A cold claw raked up through my chest. Who were these people who would choose the claustrophobic uncertainty of this work? Who indeed, I thought, assessing my gear and adjusting my respirator with painful hands and wishing for a friendly face.

The seam we had broken into just before the end of our shift the previous night had been well worked through by the section that came on after us, and there was anticipation of an ore strike most of the morning. By noon, though, we knew that the sill was bending away, and only a few traces of yellow metal had been broken out of the occluded quartzites. Nonetheless, even these tiny nuggets were a good sign. The excitement they engendered among the assayers provoked a shift of activity among the drillers, and I was borne along as in a river by the acumen of their pace throughout the morning.

As I learned to use the momentum of the drill, I found myself adopting the characteristic stance of the others: feet spread wide apart for balance, a lean into the rock with the upper torso for leverage; then rocking back over the hindmost leg to extract the bit. There was a rhythm to the process, dictated by the weight of the drill and the recurring movements necessary to work it into the stone. I had begun to feel it the day before, but now it began again to evade the best efforts of my reduced capacity. If I directed the bit at just the right angle, it backed out effortlessly, but if it was canted in the hole however slightly—the result of trying to reduce pressure on my hands at the wrong moment or of misjudging any one of numerous balancing acts—it would bind in the rock, and my delays in extracting it were never overlooked by the others.

After the first few hours of struggling to learn the dance, the pain in my hands subsided to a dull, throbbing presence at the base of my consciousness. Gradually, my muscle stiffness eased with use but left me feeling weak and unsteady. I abandoned myself to the process with numb resolve, concentrating on the swing of the drill and hoping not to fall down, while the wordless Beresina kept the steam hoses free of obstruction and bent to his charges in each of the holes we made with practiced and seemingly effortless caution.

All morning, as the sweat moved between my aching body and the damp clothing, we repeated the strenuous choreography in a mindless, tilted ballet of lunges, lifts, turns and rests. We swung onto the structure for the work, then clambered back down to take shelter behind the shoring machines, leaving the rock face bristling with a grid of blasting wires. After each series of detonations we rose together with the all-clear bells to repeat the ritual and again swarmed the structure like some many-legged creature of single purpose.

I learned not to cringe at each round of seriated blasting and to clench my teeth to keep them from chipping when the shockwave came. I learned to watch the dirt and chips spill from overhead cracks in the tunnel with the same benign resolve as one might regard the sift of dust from attic floorboards.

Working the opposite end of number 3 gantry was a tall Bantu tribesman who had learned his trade in the diamond mines of South Africa. He had blue-black skin, large muscles that moved in his forearms like wet cables, and a bloodline that must have stretched far back along the stems of Darwin's logic, down past strange haunted places, and all the way to the roots of Eden. As soon as Beresina introduced us on the mid-shift break, I knew from his stance, from the slightly stooped set of his body, that his was the tireless rhythm that was setting the drillers' pace. The maddening competition at the rock face was not only to finish first but to conform to the relentless grace of this man's pitch and sway.

I had just settled myself on a coil of rope among some large stone fragments and opened my lunch can when Beresina strolled over with the big man towering behind him. He stepped aside in a comic "reveal." Then, with a short sweeping gesture, as though ushering something invisible between us, muttered our respective names and sat down.

The black man politely removed his helmet and goggles, exposing a large mat of woolly hair, tied back with a strip of faded red cloth. His long face was striped with mysterious ceremonial scars, and his large protruding eyes were the hard marbles of a man transfixed in permanent fascination. As he leaned forward, he rolled them along my arm and out to the point where the gray bandages on my tiny hand disappeared into his fist. He snapped my arm once in greeting and then opened his fingers as though releasing a bird.

He was called "Levi," which didn't sound very African to me, and when I said so he smiled broadly, revealing formal rows of gleaming white teeth, like a parade of Chicklets, but offered no explanation. I decided that his tribal name was probably unpronounceable, and in any case was a part of the enigma which enshrouded every man on the shift and to which each was entitled by unspoken agreement.

The three of us sat among the slabs with our sandwiches and watched Djeepah perform one of his periodic inspections of the tractor and gantry. He moved effortlessly around the equipment with a supple grace. I was struck by the ironic contrast his movements presented to the hard purpose of the machinery. As I watched his silken progress through the splintered shadows of the scaffolding, I felt a grudging admiration for his strength and expertise, the way you feel free to admire a panther from a safe distance. He paused for a moment among the cross braces, making an observation, then stepped back, dissolving in a pattern of dim reflections.

Here was a man I had actually been willing to stab with the broken rock bit in self-defense just the day before. Yet the significance of the incident had already blurred in the filter of subsequent events. I felt oddly unclear about it, as the thing seemed both near at hand and far at the same time. I knew, though, that to sustain my bluff against his dark mania, he would always have to be kept in the periphery of my awareness. It was a tiresome prospect. Oh, well, I thought, he'll just have to be a watched pot; and then, remembering an old sailor's expression, muttered, "The price of good navigation is constant vigilance."

"What?" said Beresina.

"Huh? Oh...uuh...Djeepah..." I responded, surprised to realize I'd said my thought out loud. I tried to think of something courteous to say about him, but what came out was, "He moves in there like a monkey."

"...Hah...," Beresina grunted after a pause, speed-reading signals I was yet to learn. He turned to Levi, who was engaged in lighting a carved wooden pipe that he clenched upside down in his teeth, and said something which made both men smile. Their mouths sent forth plumes.

Levi puffed vigorously on the inverted pipe, working his large lips like a bellows around the stem until he had a good burn. He then rolled his moist eyeballs at me through a rising cloud of blue smoke and stared with a strange, amused intensity at my bandages. After a moment he suddenly barked,

"Bleesta?"

It startled me a bit, and I nodded with one of those oblique head gestures that idiots and children use to convey a certain vague accountability.

"Peezon dem."

"What?"

"Peezon dem," he repeated flatly, shifting his gaze back across to the tractor, apparently dismissing the issue, a genie of smoke hurrying to catch up with his pipe.

"...Oh, yeah," I said, believing that I was being told to tough it out. I had intended to rewrap the dirty bandage cloth before pushing my hands back into the heavy gloves, but in view of Levi's evident distain for indulging injury, I stopped fooling with them.

"No. Piz on dem," added Beresina, touching my arm. I looked at him and saw that he was serious. He made a swizzle gesture with his fist and thumb.

I couldn't tell, though, if he was advising me or simply trying to encourage me to accept some kind of test, so I chose the only sensible course—to play along. At the very least, it might amuse the placid few who were near enough to behold my initiation.

I adjusted my respirator and goggles, unwrapped the stained gauzes, and took a deep breath. I rose and stepped behind the rock pile which served as our dining area to begin the long process of unfastening the coveralls.

The hot stream stabbed into the open jellied sores in my palm like heated nails. I jerked back, sucked in my breath and held it against the burning as though a lung full of air would somehow keep the pain at bay. It was all I could do to keep from pulling my hands away. I heard myself, as though from a distance, slowly exhaling in a long seep of voice.

The wounds I had received in Vietnam had of course been deeper and, compared to this, profoundly consequential, but somehow the mind seems to adjust to the magnitude of such events, and I had been able at the time to put those injuries in perspective by the realization that I was at least alive. Yet here, the intensity of this surface pain was fed by the knowledge that it was being self-inflicted and perhaps for no other reason than to prove some point of endurance or some gamely social objective.

By the time it was done, my eyes were stinging with the pressure of tears, and my vision pulsed in fields of green with the heartbeats that continued to fill my head. I stood for a while afterwards trying to clear my eyes and wondered if, for the sake of a tease, I had just given myself blood poisoning.

Crossing self-consciously back to the rock, shaking out my fingers, I was grateful for the equipment that hid my face. I sat heavily and slowly began to rewrap my hands, preparatory to the gloves. It no longer mattered if anyone had been amused. The open blisters continued to sting, and my hands trembled. Now on top of everything else, they stank, too.

As I fumbled with the worn gauzes, I stole a glance across at the men who sat against the generator, then to the two beside me, searching for the knowing grins and the snickers. No one showed the slightest interest in my tortured little world.

I got the gloves back on in time for the bell. As we began to move back toward the rock face, Beresina nudged me and gestured with his chin as if to say, "You okay?" I leaned over and yelled through the masks, "If that's the treatment, at least there are no blisters on my back!" I could not see his face through the reflection off his goggles, but his shoulders rose, and the muffled sounds that came from deep within his respirator were like the ruffling pages of a heavy book.

My hands were better within a half hour. Levi's advice had been surprisingly helpful. Something, perhaps the uric acid, had served to harden the raw skin quickly, and they ceased to hurt as much. As the pain subsided, I was able to handle the drill with more control. The slight increase in my speed that resulted may have been a marginal gain for the shift, but it was a great boost to me.

A general work stoppage was called a few hours later for the purpose of shaping the tunnel. With the morning's gold fever, our progress forward had produced a dangerously low overhang of rock. This was making for pockets of confined headspace, where a few teams had moved ahead of the gantry, working on their knees, gradually shaping the rock face into a tiered stope and then faired into a wedge. Djeepah and the other section bosses discussed the best procedure while we took a welcome break. This was when I became the last person ever to meet Geoffrey Lemmon.

There was an odd quality about Lemmon. I have long had an instinctive affection for the English. I don't know where it comes from, but England and the ancient, rousing history of her people have always been of great personal interest to me. So it has been a disappointing surprise at times to encounter one of them who fails to satisfy my singular predispositions. There was none of the inherent humanity of island people in Lemmon.

Muttering curses, he approached the water wagon where I stood at the end of the line with my own preoccupations. He nudged me. I turned. He was slightly taller than I and stood with his respirator down and blaster's helmet pushed back on his ginger hair. His beard parted, revealing long, stained, horse-like teeth and an amount of gray gums. He lifted his goggles, nudged his heavy eye glasses up on the bridge of his nose, and tilted his head back so that he could observe me in the optical center of the lenses.

"You the Yank?" he asked flatly, leaving his mouth open in an odd grimace at the end of the phrase.

"Yeah. John Moore," I said extending my gloved hand. He ignored it, still staring, his large eyes, rounded in the lenses, at once direct and elusive. My hand occupied the space between us like something presented for validation, and I withdrew it. He gave a small, moist laugh that exploded through his nose.

"Don' like yanks; never did." He stood almost casually staring down at me. He had large, heavy hands with thick tendoned fingers and dirty black fingernails. There was a look of power to him, a coiled, tight set to the way he stood—balanced, ugly, contemptuous, and at least momentarily, watchful.

Then he shifted his gaze over my head for effect. That gave him away. I had been around enough genuinely dangerous men to recognize the contrast in that flicker of focus for what it was: some momentary intrusion of doubt upon an unsteady pulse of will.

"Can't say as I blame you," I said. "I've met a bunch I don't care for myself," and I turned back in line.

Lemmon evidently disliked having his performance ignored. He nudged me again, harder.

"Lemmon's moy name. Wi' two ems." Then in a voice heavy with hauteur, "Don' chew forget it."

I turned back to face him.

"I shall do battle with my natural awe," I said as evenly as possible and stepped to the spigots. I could feel his anger on my back long moments before he came up beside me.

"Well, now, ain't you the cute one, though..."

I cut him off:

"Look, Lemmon-with-two-ems, I don't know what your game is, but if you're lookin' to get your balls kicked up into your throat, you just keep at it."

I was tempted to throw the water in his face, but was afraid it might provoke something I might not be able to finish, so I turned and walked away, giving him my back, the way I'd seen bullfighters do to great applause. He didn't follow, leaving me to assume that at least for the present, I had won a round of some kind.

During the lull, I ran a check on my steam hoses as I saw others do, all the way back to the generator couplings. We handed the drills down from the platforms so that the tractors could maneuver the structures back, and as the hoses were gathered and coiled, I wiped down the drill housing and inspected the bit carefully. The whole time I told myself that I was doing it for safety and out of respect accorded any important piece of equipment, but secretly, I was beginning to feel a certain attachment to the thing I had ridden, and been ridden by, for almost two full days now. It had taken on a kind of surly infantile consciousness.

This was a time for first echelon maintenance and the replacement of fuel and supplies for both men and machines. Beresina and several other blasters departed in a group to ride the elevators down to the explosives room, while the drillers and "mechanicians" attended to their equipment in preparation for excavating the overhead—the ceiling—of the tunnel. Electricians were called down from other levels to plan the extension of the lighting system, and large stocks of ducting, lumber, bearing plates, pre-formed pad stones, steel beams, and cement began to arrive on the elevators.

I was feeling much improved from the extended break and the reduced pain in my hands by the time the blasters returned. As alterations to the gantry were nearing completion, Beresina approached with a case of dynamite and a coil of orange fuse, along with some electrical connectors piled on top of the box. I went over and took the ancillary stuff off the crate so that he could set the box down without spilling anything, and we quickly began sorting the caps and wires.

Behind us, closer to the shoring equipment, the other teams were beginning to separate themselves out as the blasters came in and to reorganize for the resumption of work. There was a burst of laughter, and I turned just in time to see Lemmon turn sideways. He giggled and said something to one of the men nearby. Then he took a peculiar sidelong half-step, moving from shadow, though a band of yellow light, and the nitroglycerine canister he was holding exploded in a bright concussive ball. It flashed on the wet rocks. Men with expressions of amusement were momentarily frozen in its light. Some stood like trees with their leaves turned against bad weather.

Most of Lemmon was blown up into the rocks, leaving only his legs, which tottered for a second in the silence that contained the last echoes of the explosion before toppling over. Pieces dangled from the rocks.

There was a long, still moment accompanied by the ringing in my ears before the scene began to move. Men began to pick themselves up and to glance dazedly around in the dust-flecked smoke as though searching for someone to tell about it. Two guys were ordered up to peel him off. I remember a whitish bone in a piece of sleeve and a sherd of helmet spinning down. There were large, greasy folds of skin and pulpy viscera and something wet and pale that slipped off a ledge. The gore was horrible, especially as several men had been blown down, lacerated, burned, or cut by bits of flying bone, and lay writhing upon the ground. What remains suspended in singular clarity, though, is Levi singing "Lemon Tree" as they threw down the parts:

"Lemon tree very pretty, an' de lemon flower is sweet,
but de fruit of de poor lemon is eempossible to eat..."

At the end of the day when we arrived back at the surface, we stepped in silence onto a world soaked with recent rain, the air heavy with the smell of wet prairie grass; a strange silent place where the men's voices echoed flatly against the dead machinery in the lift shed. There were a number of empty seats on the bus, and no one said much. Alone by the open window, with granite dust in my hair and a taste like iodine still in the roof of my mouth, I watched as lightning all along the horizon provoked from the seamless dark a distant mountain range in a soundless flickering of muted light.

The bus splashed up to the front of the hotel and decanted its spent energy. Shuffling wordlessly, the men crowded the aisle. With clay hardening on their clothing and whitening their arms and hair, they pressed toward the door in subdued urgency before the coming rain, which could be heard sweeping in from the darkness behind us like some phantom migration. I waited until the bus was all but empty before stepping down.

Shrouded in black thunderheads ahead of the storm, the distant lightning glowed mutely, like welding seen through foundry smoke, as if repairs were under way at some flawed place in the iron dark of the world. Just as I stepped onto the hotel porch, the blackness all around erupted with the noise of rain. In a flash, the soft night buckled under a fist of downpour. The porch roof shuttered beneath the weight of the astonishing cascade, and as I peered out, water fell through the wan light of the open doorway like a solid object. Dust that had lain upon everything for months was bounced off the ground, and the smell of it rose to sweep over me in waves of intimate, fervent emotion. I stared out at it, thankful to be alive, delighted with nature's determined intervention, my eyes resting on the curtain of movement, and I breathed in the tactile smell of wetness, the earth, and oxygen being pounded so hard into the ground that it soon became difficult to inhale.

Sitting again at the counter inside, amid the dank, vinegar reek of the damp and the bathless, I surrendered comprehension to the sound of the rain. I rolled my skull against a fresh snifter of whisky, contemplating in the trade-worn wood of the bar its memory of a day's harsh traffic in glass while we were away. Spills and the wiping cloth. Confessional. *Tabula Rasa.*

The place and its inhabitants spoke a language of stringent event. It blended with the day's experience to blur my criteria and worked to funnel down my alternatives toward unity with some intangible thing that claimed possession. It left me with a strange longing, like a courtship performed in absence.

The explosion and its violent disassembly of Geoffrey Lemmon had left upon me a baleful shadow and enforced a selective amnesia by which I consciously strove to forget such first-hand events. It caused moments of increasingly familiar lapses when I could not remember how I had got here from the places I had been that year. Yet it forced me to connect the dots, to again force-fit the new and the unprecedented into the scheme of things.

Why had I come to this hazardous juncture? I knew nothing about gold. I sensed that a dramatic shift in my courses of need, engendered perhaps by long months under threat the year before, had left me with an inarticulate restlessness, as though I had been stumbling around the edge of some immensely important universal concept, but then unable to formulate it, had just moved on. I wondered if somewhere along the way I might have picked up the Rosetta Stone and simply skipped it into a pond without ever knowing what I had held in my hands. Perhaps, after all, we are simply drawn to the company of strangers by the same pleasurable force that pulls zoo-goers to the gorilla cage: a desire for the connectedness that comes from recognizing parts of oneself in the lives of others.

Beresina's voice startled me from reverie:

"Don'worry—"

I jumped, sloshing the glass, instantly aware of whose voice it was. The second half of an incomplete catchphrase is like a blind man's shadow—only there for those who know it's missing—and it fell into place, completing the expression, as his heavy hand came down on my shoulder: "—You ain' dead yet."

"...True," I said, "True," wiping the spill from my face. "Have a seat...Let us drink to the dark background that sets off the richer colors of life."

He swung a leg over the stool beside me, and signaled the bar-gnome, who stood with half-lidded eyes, his back against the bottle rack, smoking precisely, moving his hand with the cigarette fully away from his face when he blew the smoke out. The little man gave a barely perceptible nod, then prepared two drinks, which he placed before us with melancholy serenity.

The hall was far from full this night so we took our drinks to one of the empty tables. I stated a preference for the corner, and we moved along the periphery of chairs to settle at a table against the wall, be-neath a metal sconce. Its wan light spilled reluctantly through a dusty glass lamp containing a deep accumulation of moth wings, like desic-cated flower petals. A horde of night insects bore about its chimney in frenzied colliding orbits.

"I am hungry."

"Me, too."

"You like ze bifsteak, eh?"

"Yeah!"

"I vill tell Loo to put more champignons." He got up and went back over to the bar, while I studied the vile-looking concretions in the gouges on the tabletop. I took a gulp of the warm whisky and sur-veyed the surrounding space, sensing its vaguely settled atmosphere of compression, a bit like the air before an explosion.

A few tables were surrounded by card players who spoke careful-ly, spending words like coins. Here and there about the room men sat alone or in pairs, drinking and speaking in subdued tones, their con-versation all but drowned by the sounds of downpour outside. Nearby, a man—already drunk or simply exhausted—was asleep, with his head resting on one arm stretched out, the callused palm turned up-ward as though awaiting donations.

Beresina shambled back across the room, smiling to himself, and I was struck by how casually I had learned important things from him in a short time, the way children learn by watching how adults angle a hat or approach a strange dog. I noticed that he wore no metal, neither watch, buckle, nor buttons—a precaution of long habit for a man who assembled explosives rapidly in bad light on a daily basis. I remem-bered suddenly with a smile how, as a boy familiar with firecrackers but conditioned by movies, I used to think that mining fuses were all loose powder that zigzagged like a hound's nose across the ground.

We sat for a few minutes feeling the soft spread of the alcohol and listening to the rain. I thought again without remorse about Lemmon.

"You know," I said, thinking out loud, "When Ethan Allen was dying, people around his bed said to him, `Ethan, the angels are expecting you', and he said, `God damn them; let them wait'. ...Then he died."

Beresina gave a soft, moist chuckle that gurgled into a brief spasm of coughing. He started to say something, then he looked across the room, hesitated, and said, "Well, look who iz here."

I looked up and followed his stare across the room to where a handsome dark-skinned man with a well-trimmed black beard and glossy hair was moving slowly through the cigarette smoke along the bar. His wet clothing was of good quality and fit his stocky frame well, though his boots were caked with clay and there were streaks of dust in his beard. He walked carefully, as though out of place, or stalking. He looked vaguely familiar.

"Who's that?" I asked.

"Djeepah."

At the sound of the name, little waves of apprehension sprang along my shoulders, and I felt a tingling at the back of my neck. I drew breath and held it when Beresina waved him over. With a nod he changed direction and began coming toward us between the chairs, occasionally nudging one aside with his thick forearms. I had never seen him without his headgear, and as he came on, the sleek black hair flowing back with his momentum lent him for a moment the appearance of some ancient warlord charging out of the steppes. The shadows that hid his eyes were the shape of slits left by knives in a wall.

I moved my feet beneath the table to position them flat on the floor. Djeepah's eyes darted about the room as he approached, and when he stepped up to our table, he rested them upon me for only a moment. They were dark but contained pale amber crescents, as though preserving tiny cuticles of forgotten daylight, and were deep the way cold seas are deep. I felt an uneasy respect for the force of his presence. I didn't enjoy finding admirable qualities in people I disliked.

He couldn't have recognized me, but he must have known who I was. I believed it entirely possible for him to take any public opportunity to avenge the incident of the bits, and I braced myself, acutely aware of his every move. There was something coiled about him, and I hoped that Beresina would not introduce us.

As the two of them exchanged sentences in grossly accented French, Djeepah's eyes hooked to objects all around us: the edge of our table, a strip of molding, the sconce. He appeared distracted, but I could see that he listened carefully. His eyes rarely flicked across either of our faces as they talked, as though his comprehension required hearing nakedly, without seeing a face around the words. I couldn't decide if his restlessness betrayed a nervous condition or was the habit of long watchfulness.

At length they finished talking, and he turned away without any response or the customary words of leave-taking. The words ended, and he left. As he withdrew I noticed that he wore an eight-inch blaster's knife on a belt in the middle of his back, as though to hide it; except that it wasn't a blaster's knife at all. It was a well-made clip-point skinning blade in a custom sheath. He sat alone at a table so close by as to beg an invitation. I relaxed a little and looked at Beresina, who was watching him askance.

I had understood nothing of what they said to each other but saw that their conversation had lacked any notably friendly or companionable intonation. I had the feeling that the two men were somehow bound to each other by a fulfilled recognition within which they had to live and to think, so that their apprehension of one another could not be so distinct and separated as to include admiration for the other's fairness or merit. A grudging consensus enforced by an interdependency in hazardous work was something they nursed between them, and it called for an exaggerated indifference.

Then in a hoarse whisper Beresina rasped, "Don' ever kill no vimmen."

He breathed cryptically into the hollow of his glass just before tossing his head back and draining the contents. When his face came back down it had hardened into a stare at Djeepah's back. His glare was chilling. So was his admonition, delivered as casually as a warning about spiders, and it left me wondering what it might have to do with Djeepah. Then he abruptly changed the subject and began to talk as though the other man had never been there.

Yet as Beresina began telling me about his experiences on a prison train in 1944—in transition from submarines to farm work in rural Mississippi—I was gripped by a conflict of attention, keeping a wary eye on the solitary feeding habits of the man nearby. When Djeepah's dinner came I watched him begin it, and it gave me the feeling again of observing a captive predator. He ate without looking at his food, watching instead the card players, or the barman, or the open door. He drank water from a green bottle, which he stoppered after each swig, as though he mistrusted the intervals, while his eyes gathered information from several yards away. His posture was casual enough, but he was not relaxed. He may have been listening to every sound in the room.

He was a vault of secrets and memories, revealing nothing of his past, and trapped in the cross currents of disparate cultures while remaining separate, without certain nationality, like those other men of his lands whose wrapped heads contain such mystery. Some inner force of nerve seemed to be straining to make the muscles in his back tighten. He sat like a steel spring that has been freed of its function in a machine and allowed now to use all its strength centripetally. Free at last of its pull against stronger forces, it was striving to attain the shape of its original coil.

Beresina's voice came through this musing about Djeepah. He was saying he had never seen Pullman cars before. Neither had any of the other German prisoners, and most were delighted to be in America and out of the war, even as POWs. He talked about how luxurious the prison issue clothing had felt to the men who had been captured in ground action and shipped to the States after living for years in the only uniform they'd been issued by the *Wermacht*. They had been deloused, cleaned and fed, in many cases with better food than they had ever tasted before.

He remembered how quiet and smooth the train had been, how many had fallen asleep like children almost immediately, lulled by the sway of the coach and the rhythm of the railroad joints, and how surprised most of them were to find themselves well-treated by the guards, some of whom were German trusties. He had been appalled at how large the country was.

There were a few exceptions, though. Soon after departure southbound from Newark, New Jersey, a few dyed-in-the-lederhosen Nazis got into the aisles and began telling the other prisoners that they were now in an excellent position to work the Fuhrer's plan from inside the enemy's own camp; that here they were being handed an opportunity to strike a blow for the historic imperative of Nazism.

These fanatics were ignored for the most part, but still, they had been a disruptive influence on the trip—that is, until the train was sided just outside Pittsburgh for a few hours to let a priority train through. While waiting they had crowded the windows along one side of the car and looked out at the mills along the smoke-filled Allegheny River valley to stare in wonder at more steel production than had existed in the entire Ruhr even before the war. Those who understood its implications, which apparently included the agitators, were stunned into silence.

Beresina chuckled as he remembered their arrival, a day or two later, in Mississippi: "By ze time ve vas discharged from ze train, nobody could remember who vas ze Nazis. Haw!"

I smiled to myself as he told his story, thinking what an unexpected subject he must have been for his de-briefers, and wondered at the circuitous route philosophical inspiration often takes to sneak itself across the generations.

I knew the instant the legs of Djeepah's chair rubbed the floor and watched carefully as he pushed away his plate, rising straight up. As though wishing to leave no imprint of his presence, he gathered up the plate, bottle, and utensils and took them to the bar without a backward glance, leaving on the table a single odd trace: a solitary wet ring from the bottle, which he had evidently divided into quarters by drawing the moisture into a cross with his finger. I looked at the strange mark as the wood took it in and for some reason suddenly remembered once seeing a dog's footprints in the snow on a garage roof.

Later, in my room high at the back of the building, I was drawn to the window by the mute erratic glare of lightning. Thunder moved up from the southwest and electricity lit the desert all about, blue and barren, with great rumbling reaches charging out of the absolute dark. Sheet lightning quaked sourceless beyond the dark night thunderheads, making a bluish day of the distant desert, and in its flickering glare I was startled to see odd white objects sprunt about on the prairie below. They were grave markers in rambling disarray among the grasses—planks, crosses, weeping angels, weather-beaten busts, and other lonely outbursts of petrified grief, leaping into light and out again. The far mountains on the sudden skyline were stark, black and livid, like a land from some other order out there, whose true geology was not stone but uncertainty.

I lowered the window in retreat from the eerie sight, showered anxiously, then fell upon the bed, while the room pulsed with ineffable gaudiness along with the sound of warm rain.

18
Caveman

Over the next several weeks, each day blended into the next in accordance with the company's relentless circadian imperative, beginning before sunup with our huddled and wordless descent into the anthropophagous dark gullet of the earth. There, bottomed in the void, we worked, each closed off to the other, yet bound by a terrible intelligence common to all but of which none would speak. I came to understand what they all knew, that something invisible was pursuing us. I needed only the limited peripheral view we had of one another provided by the goggles, from the dingy insectoid figures moving through dust-clouded air, to the broken walls, to the dripping ceiling, back to the men, to realize how tenuous and insignificant each of us was.

Tunneling together into the bedrock beneath the largest prehistoric seabed in North America for twelve to fourteen hours a day, each man, locked in the complex architecture of his own past, tended to ignore the others, and thus demanding by tacit implication a similar kind of indulgence, slogged in private at the torn earth as the poisonous breath of fresh explosions skulked around us all, clinging to the wet clay and filling the cavity with dark smoke through which lamp light swung crazily against the rock face.

Strange shadows leaped across the ceiling as men moved about in the shattered light of steel crossbeams and timber decks to set their grids of wire against the seductive veins of quartzite which marbled our world of mud and glistening grey schist. Formed eons before the molecular birth of oxygen in the dim, gaseous infancy of the Earth, the ancient rock slowly martyred itself to our shrill hammering, yet kept its enormous secrets dark, and the promise of treasure just beyond reach.

Like all people at all times we were confronted each day by the hard, ambiguous present, which always arrived in a deafening promiscuous rush, with the dangerous, the trivial, the profound, and the fatuous all tangled together. It molded us like beaten metal, for the longer we prevailed, striving in our muted fury against the furnishings of darkness, the more oppressive became the weight of its thwarted capacities. Our efforts seemed scarcely to be contained in the space allotted them, even as the rock gave way before us.

Yet I began to feel the deep and secret history of the Earth itself congealing around us and to fear it. Sometimes, just after a detonation, as shadows of the men began to move again within the dizzying swirls of smoke and falling dust, I imagined that I saw among them strange humped beings rising to some dark and ancient purpose. When the shifting pale eyes of the lamplights winked and swayed in the black clouds, their chilling semaphore sent a scurry through my scalp, as though the invisible acolytes of death had crept a step nearer.

At the end of each shift, unknown replacements took our positions on the scaffolds with hardly a letup in the drilling. The men about me removed themselves from the wall like specters, dark with mud, anonymous in the steamy cold, or standing in the corrugating heat of machinery exhaust. Sometimes they appeared primal, provisional and without order, like beings provoked out of the absolute rock and set nameless at one with their own loomings to shuffle doomed and without purpose in the brutal wastes of an age before there were names for things. It always frightened me a little and set me at odds with myself at these times when my perspective would shift involuntarily, casting up such dreadful primordial images, for I knew that I was trapped in the idea.

Brief nods were exchanged through the goggles as the new figures moved into position. We trudged in laborious convergence toward the shaft to take our places at last upon the elevator platform, thereon to rise compacted in a delirium of fatigue toward the surface. The column of air in which we rose shed the chill of its depths, until we finally tumbled back onto a warm starlit world, there to breathe in the fresh, salvational validity of another night.

I gradually hardened to the work, steadily sharpening my instinct for the rock, and in the process, lost track of the fact that the world above ground was sunlit in our absence. To this day, my memory of the hotel is as it appeared at night, riding like a galleon upon an ocean of grass, when the prairie wind, swollen with insects, pollen, and distant smells leaned against it, breathing mournfully through the eaves. Tiers of pale yellow beams, fanning from its high windows onto the restless waves in dust-laden courses of lamplight, undulated at times in the passing chaff like the movement of oars.

Caveman

I began to look forward each night to dinner with Beresina in its warm-lit bar, or with one of the other men I came to know, as the day's only respite. Afterwards, I would trudge the long stairway back to my room in hopes of beating the water pressure drop to my little shower. Most nights I read myself to sleep while the stars soaked with wet light my tangled clothes upon the floor, and the muffled sounds of fighting filtered distantly up through the timbers and joists.

19
Claudine

The first time we were paid came after I had been on the job about three weeks. We emerged from the earth with a cloud of steam into a hot, dry night like a helmeted Wagnerian chorus, rising on a stage trap to the mighty *Te Deum* of distant thunder.

The men were more talkative than usual as we stepped from the platform. They gabbled in anticipation like schoolboys. There was some good-natured teasing, dust rose as shoulders were slapped, and our feet moved loudly on the gravel, freed of the drudging suction of clay and animated by a sense of rewarding destination. The humidity of the mine fell away, and I felt the skin on my face tighten in the desert air.

While the bus waited quietly with lights out, we shuffled into a semblance of order, a ragged assembly of filthy men that looped across the yard to a breezeway that made a gap in the operations shack. There the men near the front of the line passed through a wash of dim and greasy light. The muddy figures straggled forth before me, pieced out of the darkness by the intermittent blink of dry lightning to the south, a swaying progression of bulky coveralls spanceled to their shadows on the ground, and in each flare of the advancing storm, their forms reared in clay-white redundancy like some third aspect of their presence, flickering black and white upon the gravel.

The air flashed again with ominous quiet, and after a pause, the low grumble that followed released a flock of small birds from an old tree behind the shack. They burst forth, rose up, and passed back overhead with thin calls. An early crescent moon hung in the east, while the long flat shapes of night clouds passed before it like a phantom fleet running before the storm.

Soon the sky cleared its throat much nearer to the southwest. The sound imparted a heightened urgency to those of us toward the back of the line who stood in the open. The men began to joke nervously about our slow progress, not wanting to get wet, of all things. Helmets tipped upward and turned, as eyes searched the blackness overhead. We pressed forward, involuntarily closing ranks, and the dank smell that rose from the clothing of the men around me began to hold the fresh prairie breeze at bay.

Suddenly the sky exploded with a monstrous rolling crackle, and the sound fell upon us in solid waves. In a blinding flash of pearl blue light the muddy line staggered, and the figures declined into their shadows with a quick collective cry. Within that instant I was on the ground, my face burrowing the gravel, finger bones rattling my skull, the horrifying warble of incoming artillery still too fresh in my mind to suppress the impulse. My helmet rocked inverted nearby, its light somehow switched on, the beam rolling crazily across the yard, as the heavy rumble echoed down the canyons of the sky.

I quickly realized my mistake and sprang to my feet as it passed, silly with relief. Breathing with heavy pulmonary gasps the burnt smell of broken flint, I looked sheepishly about, the blood roaring through my temples. I was met with nervous laughter and loud, unintelligible teasing.

By the time my section of the line shuffled into the shelter of the shack, the storm was drawing its breath across the territory, the air smelled of the coming rain, and the wind that fled before it chuffed at the corners of the breezeway, causing papers on the notice boards to flutter.

The office was a plain clapboard affair which, like the hotel, had a frontier quality that seemed cozy enough by lamplight, but which must have been sparse and drafty on a harsh winter day and held heat and dust to the limits of endurance in the summer. On this night its wooden panels reflected a sepia-tinted era in which the whole place might have been plunged into the grainy monochrome of the mid-1800s.

I noticed a tremendous amount of ruined insects on the floorboards and swept into the corners. Coils of flypaper hung from the ceiling and lamp fixtures caked with black lumps, and I counted three flyswatters in various places around the little office just from where I stood in line. The windows held drifts of dead flies between the double screens, piled there in the frames like wind-driven soot. It occurred to me that working conditions above ground during Blackfly season probably lost some of their edge over our own.

Claudine, the Paymistress, sat at an open table on a raised platform with her ankles crossed demurely, the bones and hollows of her face flattened in the harsh glare of an articulated desk lamp which squatted over her books like a vulture. We filed into the room, first passing her assistant, who sat at a small table by the door with his knees pressed together like a spinster's.

He was a balding young man with a permanently intense expression and a sudden, mirthless laugh, who checked our identities against the company list as we stepped in. On the floor beside him was a large steel suitcase to which he was attached at the ankle by a chain. We referred to him as *"Le Chien,"* the dog, because he was always chained, and at her heels.

Claudine maintained a steady repartee with the men, pretending to be embarrassed by their teasing as she processed each payment, enjoying their ooh-la-las of unconfined delight. Almost everyone seemed compelled to impress her, and she repaid each for his compliment by smiling in a peculiar, secret way, running her tongue over her lips. It was one of her most characteristic gestures and very effective. It seemed to promise all sorts of undefined intimacies, yet it was really just as simple and automatic as the word thanks. She used it to reward anyone for anything, no matter how unimportant.

As we approached her table the men exchanged glances of anticipation with lustrous, red-rimmed eyes that stared as though from cages at feeding time. I noticed that several could not sign their names. When one of these arrived at her table, instantly shedding his bravado in a muddle of priorities, he would bend over the roster, his whole body a rictus of frustrated will, grasp the pen in the manner of one unaccustomed to light-weight tools, and carefully draw his mark, then hurry his escape into the night holding a certificate he could not read.

Each man left the table clutching his slip of paper like the prize that it was. Some kissed it theatrically in the manner of old French comedies, then stepped away laughing and shouting to the others, waving it like a toy banner; some simply slipped it into a pocket as casually as scraps and stepped from the room with elaborate nonchalance; while others folded and refolded it into tiny squares, as though securing it beneath ever-deepening layers.

"Soooo...," she said in her charcoal-filtered voice as I stepped up. The generous use of mascara gave her eyes the appearance of bottle caps, which she flicked at me in combination with her invitational half grin. "...you`av many girlfren', Monsieur L'Americain?" she coo'd.

"...Legions," I replied, trying to recall the year I had last been out on a date.

She paid us every month, and the procedure seldom varied, except that about every other time she did not like to be teased. I found her ways inappropriately flippant for dealing with men who stood before her enlightened by the divine portent of their own survival. Her virtue seemed to be that she said what she thought, and her vice was that what she thought didn't amount to much. She was likable, though. We certainly liked what she represented, and most of the men seemed to think her looks striking.

She had wide-spaced eyes of a frank, frightened blue with dark radial points in the iris, which pulsed in time with her enthusiasms. The interval between her thick black eyebrows was always shiny, and so were the fleshy volutes of her nostrils. The somewhat course texture of her skin, after some thirty years of exposure to the dry winds of the region, looked almost masculine, and in the stark lamplight at her desk her pores fairly gaped at you, like something in an aquarium.

She used cosmetics with zest but with an additional slovenliness around the eyes and mouth that resulted in her lashes getting caked and her large front teeth becoming rouged. She was attractively dark, and she had what I thought was a good figure; but all of her was a bit frowsy, which made me think of a farm girl striving to affect modish banalities in fashion, gathered from magazines. Her fingernails were gaudily painted, but somewhat bitten, and her fingers were never particularly clean. This was no doubt due to her work, but it contrasted oddly with her other efforts.

As the season progressed, the temperature eased above ground, and the flies died back. The vicious attrition rate among the miners meant that our periodic visits to the pay office often presented her with some new faces on which to practice her allure, so that every pay day promised a show, and I began to look forward to it. She flashed once a month like a beacon in the night for the men below ground, yet she bore in many small ways the indelible signs of a saddening, spurious elegance.

One night I realized with a start that *"Le Chien"* was in love with her. While I stood next in line, she suddenly became incensed at something in her books and released an impassioned tirade at no one in particular, though her words seemed to fall hard upon him. At first he just stared at the floor the way a despairing man might regard the dark and melancholy water running before his last leap. When he looked up at her, it was with a lingering expression of mingled hope and sadness, his eyes glistening with reflected light, like the eyes of a man trapped in an agony of suppressed emotion. As their voices counterpoised, his right hand stole down to one corner of the steel suitcase which he began to fondle absently but with unutterable sensuality, his voice modulated and conciliatory, while she railed.

I wondered afterwards at his taste whenever I glimpsed with a secret shudder the higgledy-piggledy striation of black hairs that showed all along her pale shins through the nylon of her stockings with the scientific distinctness of a preparation flattened under glass; or when I sensed in passing her desk the stale, not particularly conspicuous, but still pervasive emanation that her unbathed flesh breathed from under weary perfumes and cream.

On this, my first pay day, I took the chit gratefully from her hand and stepped down into the breezeway. The rain had broken free at last of the locked heat clouds, and large drops began falling out of the wild darkness with heavy plops. It looked as though the center of the storm would pass well to the south of us, its grumbling now low again, as though to warn us, insolent in retreat: ...just wait 'til next time...next time. Distant thunderheads reared quivering against the electric sky then were sucked away in the blackness again. I enjoyed the quiet pulses of uncertain light and felt in the compression of air surrounding them a mounting sense of excitement mixed with the promise of change.

A brief rain fell steadily for ten minutes when we arrived back at the Dragon Joy. I stepped down from the bus and stood in the open, feeling in the folded paper fragment in my pocket all the tangible promise of immediate delights, free for the moment of any practical sense, and with no ambition to make more money and no qualms about my future means of subsistence.

With the chit rolled tightly in my fist to keep it dry, I took off my helmet and felt the raindrops pelting my dusty hair. Soon the taste of mud ran into my mouth. The water came down my back on a wide front, crowded into a narrow channel across my rear end, then divided into two branches and emptied into my socks.

20
Redistribution

"Well, Yank, dere's a dollar ye did not haf yestiddy."

I turned at the rasping voice to find "Ivan," the Latvian coal miner, leering up at me with his perpetual squint as we stumped into the bar, our wet boots sounding on the floorboards like dogs lapping at gruel. He was small and wiry, aged like a leather whip, with grey whiskers, three fingers on his right hand, and about as many teeth. He wore a faded woolen watch cap and a ragged flannel shirt with homemade buttons whose cuffs looked blown off, or tailored by watchdogs.

It was said that he had lost an eye to a Russian bayonet during the investment of his country by the Soviets in June of 1940, and I saw no reason to doubt the rumor that he had stitched the wound himself, which gathered a part of his gnarled face into an aspect of strange and baleful leering, that may at one time — before the rigors of his subsequent life had added their signatures to the composition — have resembled a smile.

"You're right," I said. "And I feel guilty being paid for sitting around all day the way we do."

"Ah, yaz. Perhaps you should buy us a trink, to rid you-salf off dis undezerfed bounty, yaz?"

His eye shifted focus for a moment, and he tossed his chin, a small gesture darkened with a certain ambiguity, then swung onto one of the bar stools and sat very erect, his face moving over the tiered wares with predacious curiosity.

He was hard to read. Despite the generally upbeat mood of the place on this pay night, his one good eye, black as a gun bore, shifted beneath its tangled brow like a probe from the galactic void, absorbing light. It kept him distant, and I couldn't tell if his oddly lyric manner of speech was something performed for my benefit, or if his real view of the world was simply a continuing blend of observations decocted from out of the secret tunnels of the earth and then neatly conjoined with a kind of humorous austerity into abstract metaphor. He soon revealed a gift for summary, his words like strings drawn together through the eye of a ring.

The tables were crowded with diners and card players whose stakes were pinioned to the tabletops with knives, and a standing audience had formed around a few of the games. The smoky air was filled with loud voices and argumentative laughter. As they drank the noise level rose, and it became more difficult to hear Ivan's words. His speech began to wax poetic, so I leaned in to hear him better through the ambient racket:

"...avery man iz tabernacled in avery odder, and he in exchange, and zo on in andless complaxity off being and vitness, to de uddermozt edge off de vorld."

He was sitting backwards with his elbows on the bar, the crag of his face turned out to the room. The collar of his shirt had separated, and in the smoky light the shredded facing stood about his neck like some tawdry sort of lace, lending him the improbable look of a ruined dandy. He gestured toward the card players with his glass.

"Dey will zoon be fighting."

"Fighting? ..Yeah, they do. A lot...Why? That big hole in the ground is about enough for me everyday."

"Aah..." He shrugged dismissively. "Dey always fight when dey are paid. It iz a form of re-diztribution."

He was right of course, though I had not thought of it in that way. Night after night I had fallen asleep to the distant sounds of their fighting with fists and feet, with bottles and knives. All races, all breeds. Men whose speech sounded like the grunting of apes. Redistribution.

I learned that his name was not Ivan. That was a nickname given him by the other men, knowing his hatred of the Russians. His real name was Brotol, and I determined to call him that. His world was reconciled, and he existed truly apart, insulated from the intrusion of all he judged to be petty by a resolute and amused determinism which he applied with a tender impatience to practically everything he didn't like. Yet the world had taught him caution, and his every move was careful, like a man listening hard behind himself.

As a philosopher he was surprisingly tolerant of ignorance. It was not necessary in his view that individuals know anything of the world, for the facts would ultimately accommodate history willy-nilly, with or without their understanding. He sketched with gestures as he spoke, his hands drafting with a marvelous dexterity the shapes of his ideas, tracing the varied paths of his logic, alighting here and there upon his salient points.

With a broad sweep of his good hand in a pontiff's gesture toward the room, he explained in his emphatic, italic way of speaking that even deliberate slights to the individual are but a secondary consideration when compared to the grand mosaic of all events, in which the tiny transpirations of our individual lives are but a part. He was proving to be a man completely our of sinc with the initial impression he presented, the tiers of his thinking layered away in dark recess.

"Hiztory," he said, "iz not a random sequence of unrelated events, you know. Oh no...Avery`ting affects avery`ting else." He paused. "... Diz iz zeldom clear in de prasent. Only time sorts `tings out, and it iz den, in perzpactive, dat patterns emerge...eh?"

He turned his ruddy, crimped face around to me far enough to clear a field of vision for his unremitting eye, which poured forth across the bridge of his nose a dusky obsidian stare. I liked the rhythm and abstract tone of his musings and had a smile waiting for him. It was clear that he was enjoying his audience of one.

"Yes, but what about the role of consciousness?" I asked. "Do we simply have a need to read order into chaos, or do patterns represent the formal agenda of a universal will, a kind of divine intent?"

After a few moments of ashy speculation he turned with a dry wheeze to his glass, which he lifted in the remnant of his right hand. As he drank the whisky his slack throat pumped, and his face tightened again. He crossed his legs and drew a long, speculative breath.

"Wall...," he began. "Reality iz but de dream of God. De larger protocol of a univ—"

There was a sudden eruption at one of the tables. Men shouted and chairs fell backward as a round of card players sprang to their feet, cursing. Several people stumbled back in noisy retreat from the circle of light as one of the players swept cards from the table with a high wild cry that carried flat and barren across the room, hushing other sounds. My heart caught at such a cry from a grown man, and I backed against the bar in the wash of dark energy that spread from their conflict, instinctively alarmed and confused.

A large bald man with an expansive belly, his domed pate shiny in the swing of the lamp, pulled a knife from the table and shouted across at another whose shaggy hair and broad back loomed from the crowd in a heavy woolen shirt bearing a dark cross-hatched pattern. At this challenge there was a general gasp from the room as more people shuffled away from the light.

The shirt dropped a shoulder, and in a single movement punctuated with a faint hollow clack, produced a blade of its own that flashed momentarily in the lamplight. A compressed stillness settled over the room for several long seconds before the bald man shifted a step to the side. He regarded his foe with bright lidded eyes as the other man, too, eased to one side. I was reminded of the way wild animals fight. There was a certain casual, languid grace in their movements, a slow and formal pavane of assessment in which death was a third dancer.

As the two men pivoted carefully around the table that separated them I realized with a shock, as he swung into the light, that I knew the man whose back had been to me. It invested the conflict with a quick and terrible thrill. Pierre was not a small man, yet as he circled, trading places with the fat man, he seemed thin, almost frail, lost in his clothes. He watched his opponent through sunken eyes with an expression of almost melancholy serenity, as though what he saw had somehow been made disappointing by what he knew of it elsewhere.

I had never witnessed a knife fight before, and as I waited with the others, caught in the throb of violent intent, I could not help but watch with lurid fascination, at once both repelled and captivated. Each man lunged and feinted while the voices of the crowd rose or fell with a mixture of amusement, awe, and dismay. No one made a move to stop them but instead shrank away, some retreating farther and peering across their shoulders with dark, uncertain eyes.

In the compacted silence of their circle the fat man taunted, his eyes glistening, his words, individually forged, dropped into the galvanized air between them as he flipped his knife from one hand to the other in a practiced road agent's pass of such alarming fluidity it was done before I could follow it. Light went in a long bright wink upon its blade.

Suddenly Pierre lunged across the table, his sleeve darting through the lamplight. There was a whisper of sound containing a tiny metallic click—thwip—and a tug at the fat man's shirt front, and for one fleeting, amused moment I thought Pierre had sliced at the man's belt to cause his pants to fall. A nervous chuckle rose in my throat, then caught when the rubbery gray convolutions of the big man's intestines began to spill from beneath his shirtfront and to slither out upon the table.

There was an intake of air in the room. At first stunned into immobility, the cut man's face began to collapse into a terrible wreckage of conflicting emotions. Disbelief, fear, regret and surprise all passed about the raddled features as his fingers began to grope and tangle his clothes. Then, as he stared at the steaming wet things before him, he laughed.

It was a frightening haunted-castle laugh that began with a sharp metallic cackle like burning sticks, then gradually increased in volume to a rapid bark, then fell away to an obscene chuckle. After a short pause, it climbed higher until it became the nicker of a horse, then higher still, like the howl of some chimeric soul, building until I thought I might lose my own mind in its repetitive and lunatic screeching. Then abruptly it stopped. With eyes still staring, the man collapsed to his knees. With a faint moist popping noise in his throat he toppled from view below the rim of the table, drawing his guts stuck with playing cards, money, and cigarette ashes with him.

Pierre stood over the slimy table with the rack of his chest bones rising and falling, his knife hand still outstretched, and gazing with a sort of terrified insolence at the space where the fat man had been.

There was an instant of stunned silence. I glanced at Brotol who sat perfectly still, his face hung in a mask of morbid tranquility. Suddenly the crowd rushed at the table. I bolted for the front door, my eyes carrying into the night the afterimage of Pierre, his knife held aloft, while dozens of arms reached to pull it down, in a fleeting tableau of the Marine Corps Memorial.

Outside, I ran far beyond the band of orange light that spilled from the door and stood trembling in the muddy road, sucking hard at the fresh air, trying to swallow down the upward pressure in my throat. Wet moonlight lay like cold slag in the ruts, and behind me, bent into its silver wash from the porch, a man was being sick. His retchings echoed the calls of some wild animal out in the darkness. Knowing I had company out there did nothing to calm me. My gorge rose anew at the sound, and I hurried farther out onto the prairie to escape it.

There, beyond the shouts and the lights of humans, with the grass slapping my trousers, I walked into the dark night where the wind rubbed against me and the clear sky seemed to bear me up into the swarming stars. At length I sat down on the ground and listened to the emptiness and watched the great turning bowl of distant worlds falling down the long black slope of the sky.

With the insistent images of events in the bar crowding my brain I thought about the irony in Brotol's sermon: "...every man is tabernacled in every other..." I wondered at the haphazard convergence of men's lives and by what hand of cynical fate I had been conducted to so lethal a congruence with these others. Perhaps the wise high God, in his dismay at the proliferation of violent intent upon the earth, simply wetted his thumb, leaned down out of the abyss, and pinched a moment of it into hissing extinction, and then amused himself by posting us others as witnesses—for what can be said to occur unobserved?

There was a dull thump far to the southeast, where the retreating cloud banks, limbed in moonglow, rose above distant crenelated mountains like the dark warp of the firmament itself. I lay down beneath the star-strewn reaches while the smell of the ground seeped out around me and listened to the sand creep past in the dark like an army of insects on the move. The grass dipped and clashed as if fled through by something unseen.

A pale green meteor came up the sky behind me and passed overhead, then vanished silently in the void.

21
Cynosure

Late in the summer, when the nights on the surface were turning cold, fire barrels made of 55-gallon oil drums were set up for us near the mud rails outside the laundry, and they became brief gathering points for men with frozen hands and faces. The fires introduced a change in routine that percolated subtly down through the rest of the day, manifesting their importance in many small ways, though no one spoke of it.

With the knowledge that the barrels awaited us at the end of the day, a slight edginess crept into some of the men's behavior, as though the furniture of our lives had been rearranged in our absence. Certain meridians of power had been realigned, and now it became a matter of some personal importance to determine what claim each of us might have upon this new development.

Men accustomed to routine accept change cautiously, as though mistrusting of its threat to a settled predictability. Therefore, when the introduction of the fires proved irresistible, there was a manifest urgency to incorporate them within the realm of the familiar. Thus the barrels were quickly invested with their own routine: the same faces that gathered around them the first night they appeared were to be seen around the same barrels each night thereafter, even though there were plenty of barrels to go around. I saw at least one fistfight to regain a particular place at one of the barrels—a position which had been chosen in the first place entirely at random.

Most of the men were infected with a sullen discontent anyway, a suppressed surliness at our subjugation to the dictates of that harsh subterranean world. Within the ultimate authority of that alien place, it was only through an esoteric construct of behavior as related to familiar things that we could draw a sense of individualism. The tools, the character of the rock face, break times, and how you were feeling, all took on an importance that left an indelible signature on the character of each day. Even the daily disappearance of one's acquaintances into the dehumanizing anonymity of their bulky equipment fed this inveterate sense of isolation and nourished a need to fix upon the familiar. Thus when something new was introduced, our patterns of behavior underwent a subtle shift toward an initially tentative form of acceptance, expressed in tiny increments, as though everyone could see something desirable but harbored a secret fear of some existential gap which had to be crossed in order to embrace it. In this way, as a small change was introduced, our ultimate enthusiasm for it was coaxed forth and redirected to the marginal realm of possible things. In this way any innovation—even a beneficial one like the fire barrels—was clumsily embraced while we remained in a state of grudging fidelity to our old situation, sunk in the ever-renewed inertia of protracted custom.

The barrels gave us something besides a sodomy of hazards in the hotel bar to look forward to each day. Thus they sweetened our anticipation while underground, where an almost comical preoccupation with claims upon them served to quicken the drillers' competition, as though there were some prescriptive correlation between the two events.

In addition to this development we had a modest gold strike in early September, which further heightened the level of activity in the lower strata of the mine. We knew we were close for several days in advance. The tunnel above us, working slightly in advance of our position to the north, had broken into a sizable downward-trending vein of quartzites containing numerous splays of good quality gold. We worked fast, advancing the run a good five to ten meters a day. Everyone left the section at the end of each day hoping that the replacement shift would not be the ones to make the strike.

Shortly before the middle of the day that we at last began to expose the plaits of ore, Section One, working to our right, broke into a gaseous cavity in the rock which contained a breathtaking agglomeration of enormous quartz crystals. Fortunately, work was halted for the mid-shift break, and those of us who were interested crowded around to peer into the opening.

To say that its interior was beautiful is to say almost nothing of the place. It gleamed from its most inner recesses in the play of our lamps with rainbows of refracted light that leapt from hundreds of slanted surfaces in a busy scintillant array of colors that sparkled about within it like living things.

Transparent prismatic columns, growing in geometric congruence, crowded forth from the rock in a crystalline festival to form an

enchanted garden of enormous faceted jewels in whose organic striations it seemed one could read news of the earth's very origins. They
winked and flashed with inner fire, as though to show us the birthplace
of stars. I stood enthralled, speckled all over in the glitter, unable to
look away, and stared without speaking, while the jumbled precision
of their obelized planes mirrored a thousand lamps.

During the lunch break I took the opportunity to crawl deep inside
the opening, back where the noise of the mine receded to the white
hiss of distant surf, and I curled up among the giant polyhedronal
lobes. There, encaved in a quiet symphony of color from the play of
the lamp, I knew for once and always that the earth is a living thing.
As I looked in wonder about me I was overcome with the sensation of
belonging somehow to its secrets and of my own small part in the dust
of primal matter that drifts continually down the millennia.

A lump rose to my throat in an ache I could not swallow. Inhabited by something obscure yet powerful, I felt an odd, inexpressible
longing. There was a powerful ghostly energy lent by the place, and I
strove to erect images, like ramparts, about the feeling in an effort to
grasp it—at least to capture it in a snare of metaphor. But no words
would come. All experience remained a voiceless echo in the back of
my head. The event enfeebled all language.

After a short while one of the geologists, pausing in his inspection,
climbed in, too. He crept adroitly along the points like a spider on a
broken mirror and joined me at the back of the cavity. We spoke softly,
with involuntary reverence, our voices echoing in resonant baritone
amid the crystals, which rang with sounds as musically as colors. He
removed his goggles and showed me with a hand-held magnifying
glass the thousands of tiny compacted striae—growth layers—that
constituted the identical structure of each node.

"How much time does each line represent?" I asked quietly, my
voice deep in hollow reverberation.

"About fifty thousand years each," he replied softly, "...More or
less."

When he looked up, his dark eyes freighted with constraint, I realized in an instant that, of course, this magical little grotto, sprung from
the depths of an eternal darkness by the accident of its proximity to
some gold and water, was to be destroyed, probably within an hour.
Growing with excruciating slowness through all the unrecorded eons,
hidden in a weight of silence beyond our imagining since the very

beginning of time, it was to have one brief moment to dance in the light, one leap of joy, before its careful and delicate structures were ground to fragments in the jaws of our machinery. The mine was going to push through, and this wondrous fairy hoard was of no account in the scheme of the enterprise. Even as I had these thoughts, I knew I was indulging a purely human need to personify it, yet the place had touched me profoundly, binding me in a lasting connection with the event.

"May I have one?" I asked.

"Of course," he said and immediately set about looking for a representative sample.

"Here's a nice one," he said from under his arm. With a few judicious swipes of his rock hammer, he dislodged a beautiful hexagonal column about 4" across and 7" high, its history marked in delicate pink striations, and rising clear as Waterford to a singular point. I have it to this day.

When at last we climbed back out, I thanked him and shook his hand. He smiled, but as he turned to look back again at the glittering hollow, his face took on a morose and bitter set, as if he had been insulted while someone held him back. I moved away, clutching the crystal with its high plangent meaning that I could not quite formulate in a thought, even as it pled to me with a vague and secret pathos.

That afternoon we broke through several mofetts from whose fissures noxious emanations of chlorine breathed more excitement into our work, and the pace picked up despite the late hour. When the final line of detonations at last revealed the elusive gleam of pure gold amid the smoke, there was another stoppage, followed by a general shift to close-in work as the steam drills were pressured down, and we scrambled to set upon the seams with picks and hand tools.

It shone yellow in the lamplight, already polished, even brighter in the tool marks, and when I saw it my heart jumped in spite of myself with the same thrill that must have gripped the ancients. Compelled by a child-like curiosity to reach out and touch it, I pulled off a glove and extended my index finger into the recess, as though the answers to questions lodged deeply in its elusive nature could be found in the cold press of its surface. It was surprisingly soft.

By long exposure to Beresina's encyclopedic knowledge of geology, I had learned something of its unusual properties but still did not expect such high malleability. I gouged it with my fingernail, thinking that, as far as the properties of durability and surface tension were concerned, gold was pretty lousy metal.

I dug carefully amid a contagion of enthusiasm to free every possible speck from the crumbly silicon dioxide in which it had been captured in dollops like egg yolks and in shining tangential runnels. Its bright contrast with all the dullish and durable rock that held it was so dramatic that I could not help but wonder at its prehistoric origins, bubbling among the magmatic fluids at temperatures that sound like annual salaries.

Forced gradually upward during centuries of slow violence as molten regions of the earth gradually contracted, it had slowed and coagulated here in the depths of this place, eons before primates like us emerged upon the world from our own origins in the primordial ooze, and where I, the first human being ever to touch it, would work it free with my fingers. As I picked at it, I realized with a start that after uncountable millennia have worn the very mountains down, it is only the tiny deposits of this yellow metal that remain largely intact. Gold is the one element that persists through all geologic processes, and it is this singular durability that has drawn all the world's economies to it.

Is the ultimate definition of wealth, then, simply that which endures? Durability engages confidence, yet there is certainly no lasting value in the paper that governments have circulated as a substitute for the metal. Although paper certificates are a convenient representation of value, much easier to store and more comfortable to carry around than any metal, they are nothing more than symbols—marks on bits of paper. They are readily destructible by a single match or a trip through the washing machine.

With each generation our medium of exchange has become increasingly conceptual, with a corresponding retreat from any product of nature. The checkbook as a substitute for money, and now the plastic credit card as a substitute for checks, has brought us to the point where convenience is worth more to us than durability. We are now in the process of giving up the use of cash to place our trust in the silent binary frenzy of electronic credit transfers, creating a society in which there is a dramatically decreased need for money itself. Our willingness to exchange goods and services for value is, after all then, simply a matter of perception, all but irrespective of anything that endures.

The gold we took from the ground would ultimately be formed into ingots, stacked in a Canadian vault somewhere, to be accounted for in the assets of the world's banks, then traded upon as a commodity, like pork bellies. What a comedown for the "noblest of metals."

In the orgy of security measures that accompanied a shift change in these circumstances, we were later than usual leaving the tunnel. As we shuffled into the elevator the men joked in an ironic mix of pride and dark humor that our discovery would not improve our circumstances in the least.

Exhausted and preoccupied in the ebb of the day, I stepped into the cage and stood next to Levi, grateful for his taciturn nature. The gates clashed to and were latched in a clatter of finality. In the silence of anticipation before the lifting tackle began to whine, I felt a darkened ambiguity settling upon the weight of crystal in my pocket. What spirits might rage at my agency in bringing it to the surface?

The cage lurched, jostling us against one other, paused, then accelerated noisily upward, the inertia pulling at my eyes and tugging the equipment down on the skin of my face. Staring past the shaft lights as they flashed downward, I felt somehow compromised by the day's events. My mind crowded with questions as we sped past the higher tunnels, the opening to each level sucking at the air pressure on my eardrums like a passing train.

I began to muse uneasily about the irony that some of the greatest truths fraught with vagueness and contradiction are hard-forged in the black-and-white arenas where people are placed in the way of hazard and travail. It is in conflict that we learn there are no absolutes, that all, all is compromise. The vast complex of the world's systems, both natural and contrived, is maintained in giddy balance by trade-offs in what is ultimately just a great muddling harmony of imperfection. It was a saddening exercise, but it made me smile, too.

I wondered at the elusive meaning of the little cave and what I had experienced there. Was the piece that weighed heavily in my pocket and the images of its surreal discovery that trembled in my mind to be the only legacy of that magical place? I tried to think noble thoughts, to make myself worthy of whatever its message might be. I was glad to have rescued it and knew I would not forget the magical place of its discovery.

As for the gold itself, we had been slogging at the tunnel like draft animals for so long I had at some point stopped thinking about the metal altogether. Now, the importance of actually finding it did not seem to fairly balance the effort, and I felt robbed of achievement. Despite its vaunted nobility, gold in its natural unalloyed state was clearly too soft to be useful, even for jewelry, yet I had held enough in my bare hands to be worth ten times my own life.

There was a sudden grinding sound among the cables. It snatched me from reverie. The cage decelerated abruptly to a trembling stop in the dark shaft. All went profoundly quiet. We huddled suddenly, blind and unmoving in the stillness, while upward momentum continued to reel behind my eyes in a diminishing replay. I felt in the soles of my feet the long emptiness below us and heard the distant hum of machinery through the faint husking, husking of the cables. No voice broke the silence.

Goggles turned to one another. Some tilted up. I looked up, too, and guessed the gantry was still a few hundred feet above us. Then, just as suddenly, the equipment sprang to life again, dropped a foot, jounced, and began to rise. I exhaled, and only then realized I had been holding my breath.

At the top there was a wordless push to vacate the platform. With my own anxiety adding to the acumen of the crowd, I pressed, profoundly relieved, toward the night sky, the lump of crystal tugging at my coveralls with a sudden impatience. From a dim incandescent bulb mounted somewhere in the structure overhead, a wan braided light fell among us through gaps in the timbers as we crowded off the ramp. Our passage through its narrow bands made us seem to be moving even more urgently than we were.

I felt fragile and oddly diminished by the contrary nature of the day's events and thought with envy about old Brotol's amusing confidence in the arbitrary nature of destiny, especially for the corollary it inspired: that the aims and purposes with which people imagine their movements to be invested are in reality but a means to describe them. All our actions in fact are merely the subject of larger movements in patterns unknown to us, and these in turn, the consequence of other causes yet.

Surely, I concluded, there is no will-o'-the-wisp so elusive as the absolute cause of any event; no amount of information exists such that we can see in it so clearly as never to question in particular the cause of a single human act. For every act, every choice, soon eludes the grasp of its propagator to be swept away in a clamorous tide of unforeseen consequence far removed from any original intent. Therefore, it would seem that you must be certain that your intention is large enough to contain all wrong outcomes. Is this possible? Not everything has such value. On the scales of choice, then, one pan lies ever empty while the entire weight of reason always tips the other down. I wondered what dark forces might Brotol name to effect counterbalance?

We stepped into the cold wind-torn purity of a clear autumn night and crossed toward the busses under a nacreous demi-moon that shuffled hesitant light through high scudding clouds. I was glad to be above ground again, especially after the odd stoppage of the lift, but I couldn't shake the implications of Brotol's philosophy.

"What you `tinkin'?" asked Levi as our shoes crunched together on the frosted mud. "You ‹tinkin abot de leeft motor?"

"...Causation is never more than an inference..." I thought out loud by way of answer, pulled by his question from the mire of philosophical speculation. "...and any conclusion necessarily involves a leap from what we can see to an infinitude if things we cannot see."

I could feel him looking at me. Unsure of how long I may have been muttering out loud, I reached out and touched his sleeve and asked, "...Do you think "Ivan" is a little crazy?"

His face was turned toward me against the sky. "...I `tink you are *all* crazy," he replied, his teeth forming a disembodied grin in the darkness beside me.

We walked a few more yards chuckling together, when, despite Levi's cheerful company, an involuntary spasm of fear scuttled up my back. Perhaps it was the sudden chilled breeze, but I sensed a presence stalking us from somewhere out there on the prairie beyond our vision. I knew it was just the product of my imagination, like the demonic figures I sometimes thought I saw in the dust and smoke following the detonations down below, but I also knew that it awaited only my cognition to name it, to give it form and function, and it made me shiver with a discomfort not entirely due to the cold.

Our clothes snapped and luffed in the wind as we shuffled into line, hunched against the chilly air. The breath streaked from our mouths as my hair and Levi's head cloth blew sideways, as if drawn by some vortex out beyond the dark, some unnamed consciousness waiting beyond the black mountains.

Back at the fire barrels, the men were slow to shed their coveralls in the biting wind and jostled themselves to fast claim their places around the tubs. Light from the laundry spilled through the eaves along the upper walls and carried the shadows of the interior rafters out into the yard. The illumination from inside seemed to bow the entrance outward, and in the apron of light before the open doors the shadows of figures inside reeled and fell away.

Beresina, always meticulous and thoughtful, his caution born of long experience, liked to wash his own shirt each evening, just in case there were remnants, little seeds of explosive, caught in the fabric. Some thought this obsession amusing, and he often came in for some harsh teasing about it.

On this night I stood at one of the barrels, my open palms tingling near the hot steel while the cold night air seeped up my trouser legs from the ground behind, and the wind moved sand against my shoes in a constant migratory seething. I was still unable to shake off the gnawing unease the events of the day had produced and stayed by the barrel more for the company of the men than for the warmth.

About the fire were men whose eyes gave back light like coals socketed hot in their skulls. Once clear of the barrel top, the fire leaned downwind in the darkness and chains of red sparks raced off into the night. The ragged flames flapped and sucked for their lives in the gusts like a thing alive.

I shook myself from its hypnotic draw just as Beresina passed close by on his way to the laundry, where there was now a hot water trough placed just inside the entrance. Several men called out to him laughing, addressing him teasingly as "Poof", and raising their arms in elaborate gestures of protection, feigning shelter from his imminent detonation.

He said nothing, stopped, looked down at his shirt, then grasping the fabric with both fists, ripped it from his body in a single motion and tossed it onto the fire. The cloth fizzed and sprayed sparks over us all. Without a word he continued slowly on, unmindful of the cold.

The next night I noticed several other blasters had joined him at the trough.

22
Slag

Our progress underground by the Fall had pushed the tunnel some 70 meters northward, through laminar bands of colored rock and into a region of deep subterranean water courses. These were not streams of the kind found at the surface, rather areas of such broad saturation that they produced permanent falls of leach water in the runs and general flooding to a depth of several inches at the face, where a shallow pond transformed the lower end of the tunnel into a luminous, curving plane whose surface reflected in busy concert with the uncertain light upon the wet and scalloped rocks. We began using grease and wax compounds on the explosive charges and worried some about electrical shorting.

Giant centrifugal pumps with their shell-shaped impellers, more valuable than any man's life, were trolleyed into place just in case, with Levi, who enjoyed large tractors, riding erect with hands on the roof of the cab, as though he were some newfound evangelical being conveyed out of the very mountain bearing news of divine retribution upon a fantastic and wondrous float. Most of the heavy equipment was moved forward to conserve energy, hoses, and conduit, leaving behind stands of shoring piles, a forest of steel and concrete columns, spaced to support the ceiling.

Structural engineers were always busy behind us during this time, as we worked to extend the tunnel. They performed seismic tests on the rock overhead, and where loose structure, called "slag," was detected or suspected in sufficient depth, they erected supports in clusters. These were built of steel beams, usually encased in concrete. After the steel was raised into place, shells of lumber were built around them into which cement was poured, and then the wood removed, like hardened bandages, to reveal the piers.

Others were temporary, the naked beams erected upon solid cut pad stones and shimmed at the top with heavy steel bearing plates. These moveable braces were sometimes rigged with crown pins to allow their plates to adopt the pressure of uneven surfaces. Others were made with slip joints, like those used in bridge construction, to accommodate limited side loads. However effective under tremendous weight as long as pressure remained at the vertex, this system had limited sheer strength and a trifling tolerance for lateral impact. It usually worked where areas of potential slag were identified, though the ceiling was not uniformly supported.

One of the engineers, called "*Poisson*," because of his distinct resemblance to a grouper, but whose real name was considerably more elegant—Beaumarchais—was a former oil worker who had spent the better part of his life either in, or thinking about, the earth and its structure. He had a broad, fleshy face with prominent eyeballs, which swam back and forth between heavy, florid jowls. When I first met him I thought that his wide mouth, thick lips, and inflated visage gave him less the air of a fish than of a mad trumpeter.

He was a man cast against type, alright. Heavyset, with a cant to his body, as though one leg were slightly shorter than the other, he walked with a peculiarly awkward sway, which gave the impression that the rest of his movements were clumsy, too, but that was deceptive. He lurched about adroitly enough to run his section well and was respected by his men. Educated, and always ready with a wry sarcasm which he could deliver fluently in three languages, he was invariably open and friendly, and he took the time to instruct me in the tell-tale signs by which rock will often reveal its intention to move.

Once, in a discussion about stress, he led me over to a slender steel beam which stood alone in a section excavated some months before and asked me to feel it. Not knowing what to expect, I placed my palm flat against the cold steel and was horrified to feel it trembling with the strain it bore.

To his great amusement, I jumped back instinctively, as though it had been hot to the touch.

"But eet iz hold up ze hole' world, n'est-ce-pas?" he said with a grin as long and wet as an eel.

I got the impression that he enjoyed demonstrating the arcana of his expertise this way. It bred gratitude for his work while enforcing respect for its risks. It worked. I realized as I stared more closely at the beam that its vibrations were actually visible, and though there were no stress cracks to be seen in the rock overhead, the experience instantly impacted the ceiling with the same brooding sense of perilous intent that had haunted my first days in the mine when all the rock had borne in upon me with tyrannical imminence.

I thought anew about the constant noise and vibration in the tunnel, the wrack of our machinery, and the effects of our sequential detonations. This triggered the same strange sensation of unspecified threat I had felt with Levi the night the lift had stalled.

Months of concentration upon the details of my own job at the stope had all but supplanted my concerns about the shoring system behind us, and I, like the others, had walked daily among the pillars with no concern for their science and little thought about the relative integrities of steel and rock. Yet with the sudden insistence of inanimate things, the touch of that single vibrant beam seemed to set into motion a sequence of dramatic events which worked to undermine my carefully husbanded confidence.

Over the following few weeks the very rock itself took on an uncanny spookiness as I began gradually to slip into a dangerous and cloying fear of everything about me. Each day became an increasingly perilous journey in which, as in war, growing skill brought greater hazard, as though knowledge itself were dangerous. An unfamiliar tension rose into the back of my neck, and I would often catch myself with shoulders hunched, as though anticipating the tap of a stranger.

One morning we arrived on the shift to discover a coincidence so extravagant that, had it been unwitnessed or happened in some other place, I might hesitate to record it. A large pile of boulders, the main one about the size of a Cadillac, had come down without warning on the south side of the tunnel during the previous shift. It must have been instantaneous, as indeed they said it was, for it caught a man full-on as he walked alone from the latrine. The lack of residual slag fall showed the man and his fate had converged at exactly the moment the imbedded rock had given way.

There had been no point in interrupting the work to clear it. A hand, bloated and purple, wearing a buttoned sleeve, protruded from beneath the stone in silent supplication. All day it beckoned, asking from each of us the answer to the saddest question of all—Why?

Later I was instructed to go with another driller to break up the fall. When the rubble was at last cleared from the depression, we found that the flattened sleeve disappeared into a dark, fibrous smear dusted with gravel and rock powder, a dirty fruit compote in which a few bright splinters of yellow helmet plastic lay pressed into the confection like bits of candy in a baker's mix.

It was a shattering sight. I thought Vietnam had shown me just about every way in which a human could be disassembled, but this small death at the hands of the rock itself somehow broke the seal on my resistance and brought forth a crushing and inescapable mistrust of everything about us. I knew at once what it was that had been growing within me for weeks, but at that moment, the integrity of all the glistening, broken surfaces which crowded in around us vanished forever, leaving me naked and small.

As I stood staring into the shallow pit, I felt the rock behind me creep nearer. I spun around and, for an instant, glimpsed its fleeting expression of malevolent intent before the rattled features could settle. I stared and heard myself breathing in the mask, heavy and deliberate, like an animal. I was still watching when the wall released an insolent trickle of pebbles. A small sound came from my throat, and I jumped back instinctively to retreat through the crowd, glad to get away, but knowing that there was no escape and that some kind of end was approaching.

I lost whatever sense of purpose, of mission, had once underlain our drilling and clearing and began to see our progress as serving merely to increase our exposure to a brittle perimeter of lethal possibilities. Even in periods of relative quiet, during breaks and at the end of the day, the mine spoke softly beneath the systolic rumble of blood in my ears: "Get out. Leave. Whatever your purpose, it is served."

It happened again not many days later. This time it got three men from Section 2. Two escaped with sustainable injuries, but the other was crushed so completely from his waist down that he said he felt no pain. He was given a cigarette, which he smoked casually while a few of the men discussed with him what to do.

By the time the doctor got there, another driller and I had bored holes into both sides of the rock and were screwing heavy pintles into the holes in order to secure a cable harness to their lifting rings. The victim was on his second smoke and joking quietly with the men when the doctor, a man who knew not to waste time on false sentiment, said to him,

"Well, Pierre, we can leave it in place, and you'll live maybe an hour or so. That'll give you time to dictate a will or talk to a priest. We'll keep you company, and I'll give you something for the pain if you want. Or, we can lift it off, and you'll drown. It'll go pretty quick...What'll it be?"

Pierre took the cigarette between his left thumb and middle finger and moved it aside. Staring at the ceiling, he released a slow coil of grey smoke, and then, with a quick dismissive gesture of his hand, gave the unmistakeable answer, chilling in its clarity: "Lift'er off."

A crane was brought up, and we rigged the drift tackle. We each shook hands with him in turn. He exchanged a few insults with his friends as we took up the slack in the cables. There was a quick growl from the crane engine, and the cable pulled taut with a vibrant "thun-ggg." The rock came up and swung free a few inches above the dark crater in which Pierre's seemingly empty coveralls were pressed into the ground, lost in the black crescent of its shadow.

It happened the way the doctor said it would. Pierre's eyes bulged wide for a moment, then dimmed just as his mouth brimmed over with black blood. He coughed once, as his exploding heart stopped him still, sending up a dark spume which splashed back down over his unseeing face.

In that moment, that pause, when the soul undoes its buttons and the world falls away, it is said that those who stand at the shoreline can sometimes feel the breath of its flight. It was as though someone blew lightly on my face for a second, and it startled me despite the faintness of the sensation. I looked around at the others, my scan arrested by the staring eyes of a gaunt-faced miner with his goggles pushed up who must have felt it too, for his hand was slowly retreating from his face on which an odd expression of wasted cognizance was likewise fading. He may have simply been reacting to what we all had witnessed, but in that moment his hollow gaze left me profoundly uncomfortable, its dark promise settling in my brain like a group of buzzards in a tree.

Here underground, beyond the judgments of civilization, all covenants with men and nature were fragile. One had just been broken, yet in the following instant I was bound forever to another by an eerie stare, perhaps compelled to some fraudulent destiny by the accident of standing in a particular place at that moment in time.

What a terrible place to die, I thought sadly, especially if you feared that you might be doing it for nothing. On the other hand, it was a perfect place for concluding that you had nothing to lose. Well, perfect in the sense that Euler called zero the perfect number.

As the men began to leave the scene, I had to retrieve a steel pry bar near where the staring man had stood, and I stepped toward it just as he came forth to pass behind me. Our sleeves brushed, and thus we divided, each passing back the way the other had come, pursuing as all travelers must, inversions without end upon other men's journeys.

"Come on," said Beresina. "You ain' dead yet."

23
Not Dead Yet

Parallel to the main elevator shaft was a much smaller, vertical ventilation shaft which ran from the surface all the way down to the very bottom of the mine. In addition to providing a strong convective draft at each level, it was intended to serve as an emergency escape route also, and contained some 2200 feet of more-or-less continuous steel ladder that ran its entire length, accessible from each level and terminating at the bottom in an ample excavation where explosives were stored.

Blasters working in the lower tiers often tried to impress each other on their visits to the explosives room by swinging onto this ladder and making their re-supply runs hand-over-hand, rather than by ringing for the lift and doing it the far safer way. The company left them alone about it because of the savings in time and electrical power.

I had accompanied Beresina down this ladder a number of times, at first just for the experience, but afterwards, out of an aversion to the consequences of not doing it. Thus I had been drawn by precedent into the competition surrounding the ladder and its attendant heroic myth. After years of ineluctable marriage to fatality on a basis far surpassing anything imaginable in ordinary life, most of the blasters could tell fear no matter how softly it walked, and I had no wish to inspire questions about my own clay within the dangerous parameters of their game.

The "hole" was always dark, and the air in it, dank from constant leaching run-off and smelling of silicates and mud, moaned like restless spirits. The narrow rungs were always wet and often slick with deposits left by the last man's boots. One hundred feet of clambering down against its constant wind, then back up with whatever I had been given to carry, was an elemental contest of strength and balance without a net. It was usually exhausting and sometimes dizzying. All of which contributed to the reasons we did it of course.

Thus, by late November, when the ladder was sprung with icicles that stood upright on the rungs and super-cooled air charged up the shaft, freezing on contact with all clothing and skin, I knew that if

Beresina needed a favor, my choice of passage would be duly noted and any hesitations judged.

Beresina was busy with Djeepah and some others, planning a series of timed detonations, when we realized that he would need more dynamite. I had not been down the hole for awhile and had no desire to enter that freezing black bore this late in the year, but it was clear that we had a time problem. I told him I would go, and with secret heartfelt reluctance, began tying off my cuffs and sleeves to keep out the wind.

As I approached the opening, I could hear the rush of air in it and shivered involuntarily. The sound was created just as it is by the fipple hole in a toy whistle, but here it moaned impatiently in an ominous low register as though it was late to a ghost story.

Standing in the draft at the opening, I reached into the living darkness, and as I groped for the ladder, the frigid air tried to lift my arm. It tore at my helmet. The chin strap bucked at my throat, and I realized too late that I had forgotten to tighten it. The wind immediately found places to get its icy fingers up under my coveralls, and I was soon working my way down, a single rung at a time, with all my clothes fluttering, helmet buffeting my skull, and my jaw clamped shut against the needling cold while the air howled upward about me like the cries of outraged farm dogs.

Finally, after a long and careful descent, I stood breathless and alone in the stillness at the bottom, below the deepest work level of the mine. I turned stiffly from the platform, brushed the frost from my arms and legs, and felt in the gloom for the wall switch. It snapped on loudly in the silence, and a frail light fell from fixtures on the ceiling, shaping the room and its contents from the shadows. The chamber smelled musty. Most of the equipment was carefully wrapped in plastic or waxed paper, but a musty smell meant moisture—not good for the dependability of explosives, and I decided to report it to Beresina.

Here was a repository of destruction. Tiers of wooden explosives crates were stacked upon each other on the floor and along shelves made of rough-sawn lumber. White coils of detonation cord were stacked high beneath the oily light, and dark spools of fuse in green, orange, and yellow—color coded to burn rates—rested upon wooden pallets, while cases of electrical ignition equipment lined the shelves in open bins. A layer of straw lay scattered upon the floor. It crackled under my feet as I stepped into the hollow, the loom of my shadow rising to bend across the boxes like another presence in the room.

The room itself was simply an arched cave chipped from the sparkling gray schist, but the air it contained was stagnant. It smelled of wax and tar, and it lay heavy with foreboding—a sense of terrible power barely contained, as though some medieval monster in fitful sleep might rise from the shadows at the slightest sound. Here were tremendous forces held in suspension, awaiting a single spark.

I wondered suddenly about the metal I wore—buckles, zippers and snaps, nails in my boots. Thus haunted by my own clothes, I turned carefully about. Close on my right lay an odd collection of leaf springs piled together in a dim alcove. I wondered what they went to and why they were being stored down there. They resembled an ancient armory, like a clutter of bows in the shadows, as though in some nearby hall, warriors were singing and drinking by torchlight. Far above, the wind hummed with their song.

A large first-aid kit, bearing a heraldic green cross with lions rampant on a field of white, was fixed to one end of the shelving with metal straps, a shield in the night. Its quaint reassurance struck me with amusing irony as I tried to imagine what would happen if the place were touched off, if the dragon were to wake? Its prominent placement was purely symbolic. Safety regulations, I thought, decreed no doubt by some bureaucrat in the quiet sanctity of a conference room, far from influence and drafts.

With an effort, I shook off the leering phantasms which lurked in the angular dark places. I selected a crate of dynamite and placed it gently on the straw. Taking a hand spike from its holster at my belt, I pried up the top. Then, in spite of all my training and knowledge of the potential consequences, I selected a box of caps from the cabinet where they were stored and nestled them into the layer of straw on top of the cakes of explosive, then pressed the lid gently back down.

The blasters enjoyed out-scaring each other with this kind of stunt, in which they indulged calculatedly just up to the point of outright stupidity. I was confident that, upon arrival back at the face, delivering the caps and explosives thus packed together would assure my reputation for an admirable degree of reckless indifference. I hefted the crate onto my shoulder, snapped off the light, and started back up the ladder.

About 50 or 60 feet up, climbing one-handed, my hands and arms stiff with the cold, I began to lose my grip on the box. I felt it slipping off my shoulder. With a quick gasp, I hunched myself into the ladder

off my shoulder. With a quick gasp, I hunched myself into the ladder in an effort to tilt the load forward enough to rest an edge against the steel. When I tried to adjust my grasp the box slid a little farther down onto my back. I had a slim finger grip on the frame of the box, but it wasn't enough, and in rising desperation, I groped with one leg in an effort to get a foot against the wall of the shaft behind me. If I could contort myself into a two-point brace between the ladder and the rock, I might be able to take my other hand off the ladder and scrabble a better grip on the frosted box lid. But there was nothing behind me but empty space a long way down, and for a few awful moments, I stood in this absurd position, trembling against the ladder, unable to move and afraid to breathe, with the box in precarious creep upon the curve of my back. It was no use. The crate inched down until it pulled from my fingers and fell away, tumbling into the darkness below.

Instantly I hugged the steel uprights in a convulsion of fear and listened to the diminishing sounds of the box as it struck the ladder and the walls of the shaft. I stared far up the sinuous track to the tiny pinpoints of light which leaked into the opening a half mile above. My mind raced in horror of what was about to happen, willing me upward yet powerless to move. I was frozen in place, rigid with terror. I heard whimpering. I cried out a word, but it struggled up in a hollow echo to be lost in the higher air of the empty shaft. Aching in rapid spasms of recoiling blood, I realized that this was The End, that I had actually, incredibly, arrived at the final moment of life—survived everything in Southeast Asia only to be blown up through this chimney in a particle vapor of calcium and iodine. And, even worse, it was all my own fault. I had a fleeting awareness that I was a child.

Then I heard the box crash distantly against something. It hit again, then nothing. I stood trembling among the rungs, waiting, utterly alone and frail, clinging with excruciating fragility to the rails, straining to hear through the wind and the shallow repetitive wheeze of my breathing in the respirator. Nothing.

I began to shake. Really shake; not just shiver as from the cold. I realized in the spasms that I could not hold on. If I did not try to get off the ladder, I would soon have to fall.

Knowing that dynamite sometimes cooks off, I decided the only salvation lay in getting back down to the room as fast as possible. I might make it in time to separate the blocks of explosive. I scrambled back down the ladder in seconds, slipping, missing rungs, banging my shins, once painfully striking my chin, hanging, and finally dropped in dizzy relief to the floor.

Wheezing in the new-risen dust at the bottom, I found the shattered box in the darkness. It had hit right side up, and though it had broken open, the caps had been cushioned by the straw. The contents were scattered about like a child's blocks.

Almost faint with a heady mix of trembling relief and driven by anxiety, I moved the wreckage of the box to one side and replaced the first set of caps in their cupboard. Moving quickly, I took a fresh package of caps and placed it gingerly in my pocket. Then, when I lifted a new box of dynamite, I suddenly felt in it all the tangible evidence for the message that the mine had been whispering to me for weeks.

With the air all about filled with the cackles of retribution from unseen harbingers, I carefully made my way up to the first work level, and there I stepped unsteadily off the ladder. Trembling all over in the ebb of adrenaline, I shuffled over to the main shaft and rang for the elevator. My knees gave out before it came, and I sat abruptly in place on the ground by the gate.

When the lift eventually came, I took it up one level. I carried the box over to Beresina, handed him the caps separately, and said with measured calm, "See ya later."

He regarded me evenly for a long moment, shot a quick glance at the elevator gate, and said nothing. I knew he had seen the way I had left and noted the method of return, but he guarded his thoughts as he did most of the facts of his life, and after an almost imperceptible nod, receded without comment into the anonymity of his respiration gear, turning his broad back to me as he bent over the box in preoccupied silence.

I wanted to tell him what had happened and to let him know my decision, but he was busy, I was weak, and without a word of explanation to my friend, the ex-Nazi submariner who had helped and befriended me from the first day, perhaps even saved my life, I turned away feeling in the blackness of my heart a gaunt centrifugal conflict of will and the humbling harness of thwarted exoneration.

I trudged back to the shaft in savage silence and re-boarded the lift. I rode it all the way to the surface, where I stepped out alone into the late afternoon glare of the first daylight I had seen in five months. I pulled the respirator down from my face and gulped gratefully at the crisp, farraginous air. Its smell was a mix of dried flowers and the dust from my clothes, with a hint of distant snow, and it burned as it curled into my lungs.

Although the day was well advanced, the sunlight dazzled my dark-sprung vision, and I tottered to the operations shack with eyeballs aching in their sockets, and squinting hard against some conjectural collision.

In the office I announced my departure and arranged for final payment to be forwarded. The clerk warned me that there would be no bus. I assured him that it didn't matter and, glad to be alone, began the long walk to the hotel in the cold purity of the early evening air with a profound sense of release.

All the skills I had accumulated in the ground had worked to secure a tenuous survival. In the process they had demanded such exhaustive vigilance that the effort had supplanted my awareness of the outside world, and now, all alone in the abrupt stillness and bathed in the angled and unfamiliar light, I was struck by the contrast between the landscape's unchanging tranquility and the mortal struggle which only I knew raged unseen beneath it. Here was a wondrous expanse of quiet living things, sunlight, and the humble cry of birds.

The world about me shimmered with a luminous intensity, as from all directions the long grasses rushed in, waving their hats like the monochrome masses in old German newsreels. As though under consignment to some other destiny, these ecstatic patrons of recurrent light thronged to witness my alien trespass, yet in blind celebration of something apart, something remote and intangible, to which I was held a stranger.

Once I stopped in the road and turned slowly about, letting my eyes rest on distant objects for the first time in months. Laminar bands of color to the west were bleeding out beneath the hammered clouds in a moving violet-colored hooding of the earth. Far back the way I had come, the ramshackle metal structure at the mine head glinted dully in the distance, while all about me a boundless sea of stiffened grass whispered in a voice too old and vast for human comprehension.

I became acutely conscious of my own insignificance in the midst of that enormous, silent panorama. I had been spared one particular fate only to be loosed upon a larger world whose rules of conduct I couldn't clearly remember.

Random strands of exhaustion, the legacy of terror, laced through me in waves leaving me light-headed. I feared my knee joints would relax without warning, and I would have to sit again, this time in the road. I felt oddly suspended, as though something was falling away from me instead of directing events as it had, and in that momentous passing, I faced an empty and windswept horizon of my own.

What had I been seeking here in the first place? Perhaps on one level I had hoped to find something permanent on which to rebuild a coherent system of values after the experiences of the war. Maybe by scratching into the ground, I was attempting to reaffirm my own tiny role in the great system of living things after my time in the monastery, seeking in the ultimate authority of the earth another kind of confirmation of my own species. Yet on another level I knew it had been simply because I had overheard a small group of North Sea oil workers as they rumored that the pay would be good. I knew that it had never been a quest for gold.

Yet all things luminous have a will to deceive, and I had often seen that it can manifest likewise in retrospect, and thus by sleight of some fixed part of a journey already accomplished, may lead a man to wrong conclusions about himself. That much I knew, but as I began to walk again the abstract nature of my efforts to frame a conclusive thought about the meaning of it all bore in heavily upon me, and I feared to be setting forth along a road that might wander forever through a world closed to whatever searches it might inspire.

Well, to live at all is to be gradually born, I thought by way of dismissing further speculation, as I trudged along the frozen road with a mounting sense of the cold, my shoes crunching on the hardened earth. I pulled my collar up, and its chill against my neck scurried down the dry skin of my back, as with fists in my pockets, I tried to hug the cloth about me. The restless prairie grasses nodded their heads respectfully as I passed, and gradually, thoughts about the impenetrable nature of the world gave way to my rhythmic treading.

I soon became aware of another sound beneath each footfall, remote, yet insistent, intimate, and bringing with it a sense of forgotten warmth: the dry noise made by breakfast cereal. Shredded Wheat being rasped in a bowl some winter morning long ago as bright sunlight fell through a latticed window and laid upon the spotless cloth a pale and bent mandala. Suddenly borrowing an enlarged privacy from this boyhood moment, the sound of each crisp step upon the road became intensified on the evening air, and through it I began reaching back for a source of the confidence I had felt in the life of my former innocence.

I saw then for the first time that I was the living future of that little boy at the breakfast table. For better or for worse I was the man he must once have dreamed of becoming, and even though I could not remember how I had got here from there, I thrilled at the tender resonance of those hopes and expectations. All the flavors, smells, colors, and motion in endless variations of circumstance and event that formed my connection with that singular vivid memory flashed through the crowded arena of my experience in a bright, epiphanous bridge of enlightenment. There, in the very parade of events themselves, lay endorsement enough of my presence at this place and time, and I saw, even in the terrible midst of darkness, the consecration of my life, to which mortal danger itself had lent a formed and substantive grace. We are all products, directly and otherwise, of all that happens to us.

The early evening sunlight lay long upon the prairie, and across the shallow swales where the land dipped in pockets of darkness, the ancient ground about me was shaped by the rose and canted light. The shadows of the smallest stones lay on the road like pencil lines across the ruts, while my own shape advanced elongate before them like strands of the night from which I had come, like tentacles trying to bind me to the darkness. The tracks of the company busses lay interlaced in the frozen mire with channels of milky grey ice that stove under my shoes like trodden isinglass.

Far to the south across the plains the distant mountains lay folded in their shadows. Drifting in and out of an uncertain cloud cover, a lone pale ridge rose among them like the back of some sea beast surfaced among dark archipelagos. The last shadows were running over the land before the wind, and the sun to the west lay blood red now among the distant shelving clouds, where the far terrain ranged down the terminals of the sky to fade from violet to misty blue and then to nothing at all.

When at last I approached the Dragon Joy, the rude innocence of its west-facing wall rising dim-lit like a cut-out in the fading purple twilight, I was surprised to hear the faint tinkling of piano keys. They rode delicately on the evening air like bird notes. From a high window there came the sound of a child practicing scales on the family piano. Do, re, mi, fa, ploink. Fa, fa, sol, la, ti, ploink, do. Plaintive and poignant. I was struck by the quintessential appropriateness of the sound and had to chuckle at the sheer magnitude of the connection it carried with the outside world.

It had never occurred to me that the Loo family had any young children, indeed, had any normal family life at all. The very idea of raising a child amid the nightly violence in the place had not borne a moment's speculation in all my grim and rousing weeks here. I had only seen a few members of the family, always men, and then only in positions of grudging servitude or as their dark faces glared over damaged property.

Well, they would be glad to see the end of one more infidel. I decided to seek out Mr. Loo to say goodbye, just to give him the satisfaction as he turns away of wringing his hands and banishing me to the outer temple of something-or-other under his breath.

— — — — — — — — — — — — — — — — — —

I often think about the men I knew there, and how things they set into motion within me have angled across the years. They seemed for a time to have come from some legendary world, and they left behind a strange tainture, like an afterimage on the eye. The air they once disturbed was altered, electric. There was a fury about them, today long reduced by time and distance to the sad remove of existing only through some third party description: he was an operator of tractors, or a tarrer of roads; he washed elephants for a circus; he was a blaster. Such summary labels convey nothing of the experience that shapes entire lives—nor can they express the lasting residual effects of exposure to even those who are touched merely in passing.

I wonder if they got out in time, before the earth took her revenge, and where the few still living might be. In my memory they remain suspended in time at the height of their powers, and it is sad to imagine them as they must be now, leaning into the last rays of sunlight on some provincial stoop, profoundly deaf, with knobby hands on sticks, ignored for their age and irrelevance, and all but invisible to the passersby. Little gray men who have left no imprint of their skill, whose message remains locked behind them, like letters frozen in a mailbox, yet whose quiet legacy lies hidden in the ornamental yellow metal that, from ring fingers to spacecraft, is indelibly woven into the fabric of human values.

I used to question the way I left and was long troubled by a sense of something incomplete, a niggling sense of failure which lived beneath my recollections. After all, I was thrown out of the monastery, too. But it eventually became less important, until it has come to bother me only now and then, as on rare occasions when my mind and body are idle; like an old injury that still hurts in wet weather.

Still, unlike physical wounds, a past injustice is not improved by age, nor is an injury to self-worth dignified by the fact that it happened long ago. Brotol was right, of course. People, as well as events, remain inextricably connected, and it is only the names of the entities which have the power to constrain us that change with time.

Beresina and the others live on, indelibly stamped within those rocky depths in an unambiguous resonance between person and place. Knowing little and expecting nothing, I found in the hazards of their company a slow apprenticeship. Like grammar, it repaid me later. Over the years since I've often had reason to recollect them, for the memories have had the power to convey benediction, release from the tedium of petty things, and the freedoms that abide in the authorship of choice—along of course with a messy imprecision of sentiment about peril and pain and friends forever failed.

Beresina was right, too, and his cheerful fatalism echoes still, through events both great and small: you ain't, after all, dead yet.

ABOUT THE AUTHOR

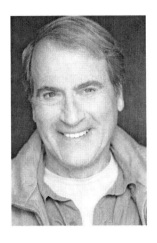

John Rixey Moore is an actor and writer. He has been a contract player on several TV soap operas and the on-camera announcer in over 460 network commercials, competed internationally for several years on the U.S. Bobsled team in the 1980s, served as boat tune-up crew and sail advisor for the America's Cup, and sailed a 73' trimaran across the Atlantic from Plymouth, England to Newport, Rhode Island in 1976. He has flown his Beech Bonanza across the United States some twenty-three times and built a home-made car out of parts scrounged from wrecks and yard sales (with a bit of reluctant professional help) which he has driven across the US twice so far.

He can be seen from time to time on The History Channel being interviewed on the crop circle phenomenon and on the subject of UFOs. An amateur historian, he enjoys walking ancient sites in Europe and maintains an extensive collection of antique books and household displays of medieval weapons. He lives in the Los Padres National Forest of Southern California, where he paints and enjoys firing his collection of antique cannons.

To contact: www.johnrixeymoore.com

Other Books by Bettie Youngs Book Publishers

Hostage of Paradox

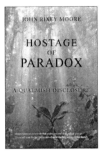

A Qualmish Disclosure

John Rixey Moore

Few people then or now know about the clandestine war that the CIA ran in Vietnam, using the Green Berets for secret operations throughout Southeast Asia.

This was not the Vietnam War of the newsreels, the body counts, rice paddy footage, and men smoking cigarettes on the sandbag bunkers. This was a shadow directive of deep-penetration interdiction, reconnaissance, and assassination missions conducted by a selected few Special Forces teams, usually consisting of only two Americans and a handful of Chinese mercenaries, called Nungs.

These specialized units deployed quietly from forward operations bases to prowl through agendas that, for security reasons, were seldom completely understood by the men themselves.

Hostage of Paradox is the first-hand account by one of these elite team leaders.

"A compelling story told with extraordinary insight, disconcerting reality, and engaging humor." **—David Hadley, actor, *China Beach***

ISBN: 978-1-936332-37-3 • ePub: 978-1-936332-33-5 • $29.95

On Toby's Terms

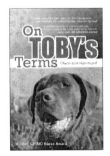

Charmaine Hammond

On Toby's Terms is an endearing story of a beguiling creature who teaches his owners that, despite their trying to teach him how to be the dog they want, he is the one to lay out the terms of being the dog he needs to be. This insight would change their lives forever.

"Simply a beautiful book about life, love, and purpose."
—Jack Canfield, compiler, *Chicken Soup for the Soul* series

"In a perfect world, every dog would have a home and every home would have a dog like Toby!" **—Nina Siemaszko, actress, *The West Wing***

"This is a captivating, heartwarming story and we are very excited about bringing it to film." **—Steve Hudis, Producer**

ISBN: 978-0-9843081-4-9 • ePub: 978-1-936332-15-1 • $15.95

The Maybelline Story

And the Spirited Family Dynasty Behind It

Sharrie Williams

Throughout the twentieth century, Maybelline inflated, collapsed, endured, and thrived in tandem with the nation's upheavals. Williams, to avoid unwanted scrutiny of his private life, cloistered himself behind the gates of his Rudolph Valentino Villa and ran his empire from a distance. This never before told story celebrates the life of a man whose vision rocketed him to success along with the woman held in his orbit: his brother's wife, Evelyn Boecher—who became his lifelong fascination and muse. A fascinating and inspiring story, a tale both epic and intimate, alive with the clash, the hustle, the music, and dance of American enterprise.

"A richly told story of a forty-year, white-hot love triangle that fans the flames of a major worldwide conglomerate."

—Neil Shulman, Associate Producer, *Doc Hollywood*

"Salacious! Engrossing! There are certain stories, so dramatic, so sordid, that they seem positively destined for film; this is one of them." **—New York Post**

ISBN: 978-0-9843081-1-8 • ePub: 978-1-936332-17-15 • $18.95

It Started with Dracula

The Count, My Mother, and Me

Jane Congdon

The terrifying legend of Count Dracula silently skulking through the Transylvania night may have terrified generations of filmgoers, but the tall, elegant vampire captivated and electrified a young Jane Congdon, igniting a dream to one day see his mysterious land of ancient castles and misty hollows. Four decades later she finally takes her long-awaited trip—never dreaming that it would unearth decades-buried memories, and trigger a life-changing inner journey.

A memoir full of surprises, Jane's story is one of hope, love—and second chances.

"Unfinished business can surface when we least expect it. *It Started with Dracula* is the inspiring story of two parallel journeys: one carefully planned vacation and the other an astonishing and unexpected detour in healing a wounded heart."
—Charles Whitfield, MD, bestselling author of *Healing the Child Within*

"An elegantly written and cleverly told story. An electrifying read."
—Diane Bruno, CISION Media

ISBN: 978-1-936332-10-6 • ePub: 978-1-936332-11-3 • $15.95

The Rebirth of Suzzan Blac

Suzzan Blac

A horrific upbringing and then abduction into the sex slave industry would all but kill Suzzan's spirit to live. But a happy marriage and two children brought love—and forty-two stunning paintings, art so raw that it initially frightened even the artist. "I hid the pieces for 15 years," says Suzzan, "but just as with the secrets in this book, I am slowing sneaking them out, one by one by one." Now a renowned artist, her work is exhibited world-wide.

A story of inspiration, truth and victory.

"A solid memoir about a life reconstructed. Chilling, thrilling, and thought provoking."
—Pearry Teo, Producer, *The Gene Generation*

ISBN: 978-1-936332-22-9 • ePub: 978-1-936332-23-6 • $16.95

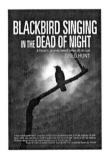

Blackbird Singing in the Dead of Night

What to Do When God Won't Answer

Gregory L. Hunt

Pastor Greg Hunt had devoted nearly thirty years to congregational ministry, helping people experience God and find their way in life. Then came his own crisis of faith and calling. While turning to God for guidance, he finds nothing. Neither his education nor his religious involvements could prepare him for the disorienting impact of the experience.

Alarmed, he tries an experiment. The result is startling—and changes his life entirely.

"In this most beautiful memoir, Greg Hunt invites us into an unsettling time in his life, exposes the fault lines of his faith, and describes the path he walked into and out of the dark. Thanks to the trail markers he leaves along the way, he makes it easier for us to find our way, too."
—Susan M. Heim, co-author, *Chicken Soup for the Soul,*
Devotional Stories for Women

"Compelling. If you have ever longed to hear God whispering a love song into your life, read this book."
—Gary Chapman, NY *Times* bestselling author, *The Love Languages of God*

ISBN: 978-1-936332-07-6 • ePub: 978-1-936332-18-2 • $15.95

DON CARINA

WWII Mafia Heroine

Ron Russell

A father's death in Southern Italy in the 1930s—a place where women who can read are considered unfit for marriage—thrusts seventeen-year-old Carina into servitude as a "black widow," a legal head of the household who cares for her twelve siblings. A scandal forces her into a marriage to Russo, the "Prince of Naples."

By cunning force, Carina seizes control of Russo's organization and disguising herself as a man, controls the most powerful of Mafia groups for nearly a decade. Discovery is inevitable: Interpol has been watching. Nevertheless, Carina survives to tell her children her stunning story of strength and survival.

"A woman as the head of the Mafia, who shows her family her resourcefulness, strength and survival techniques. Unique, creative and powerful! This exciting book blends history, intrigue and power into one delicious epic adventure that you will not want to put down!"
—**Linda Gray, Actress,** *Dallas*

ISBN: 978-0-9843081-9-4 • ePub: 978-1-936332-49-6 • $15.95

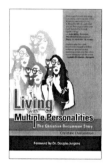

Living with Multiple Personalities

The Christine Ducommun Story

Christine Ducommun

Christine Ducommun was a happily married wife and mother of two, when—after moving back into her childhood home—she began to experience panic attacks and a series of bizarre flashbacks. Eventually diagnosed with Dissociative Identity Disorder (DID), Christine's story details an extraordinary twelve-year ordeal unraveling the buried trauma of her past and the daunting path she must take to heal from it.

Therapy helps to identify Christine's personalities and understand how each helped her cope with her childhood, but she'll need to understand their influence on her adult life. Fully reawakened and present, the personalities compete for control of Christine's mind as she bravely struggles to maintain a stable home for her growing children. In the shadows, her life tailspins into unimaginable chaos—bouts of drinking and drug abuse, sexual escapades, theft and fraud—leaving her to believe she may very well be losing the battle for her sanity. Nearing the point of surrender, a breakthrough brings integration.

A brave story of identity, hope, healing and love.

"Reminiscent of the Academy Award-winning *A Beautiful Mind,* this true story will have you on the edge of your seat. Spellbinding!" —**Josh Miller, Producer**

ISBN: 978-0-9843081-5-6 • ePub: 978-1-936332-06-9 • $15.95

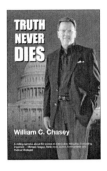

William C. Chasey

Truth Never Dies

William C. Chasey

A lobbyist for some 40 years, William C. Chasey represented some of the world's most prestigious business clients and twenty-three foreign governments before the US Congress. His integrity never questioned.

All that changed when Chasey was hired to forge communications between Libya and the US Congress. A trip he took with a US Congressman for discussions with then Libyan leader Muammar Qadhafi forever changed Chasey's life. Upon his return, his bank accounts were frozen, clients and friends had been advised not to take his calls.

Things got worse: the CIA, FBI, IRS, and the Federal Judiciary attempted to coerce him into using his unique Libyan access to participate in a CIA-sponsored assassination plot of the two Libyans indicted for the bombing of Pan Am flight 103. Chasey's refusal to cooperate resulted in the destruction of his reputation, a six-year FBI investigation and sting operation, financial ruin, criminal charges, and incarceration in federal prison.

"A somber tale, a thrilling read." —**Gary Chafetz, author, *The Perfect Villain***

ISBN: 978-1-936332-46-5 • ePub: 978-1-936332-47-2 • $24.95

Out of the
TRANSYLVANIA NIGHT

Aura Imbarus

Out of the Transylvania Night

Aura Imbarus

A Pulitzer-Prize entry

"I'd grown up in the land of Transylvania, homeland to Dracula, Vlad the Impaler, and worse, dictator Nicolae Ceausescu," writes the author. "Under his rule, like vampires, we came to life after sundown, hiding our heirloom jewels and documents deep in the earth." Fleeing to the US to rebuild her life, she discovers a startling truth about straddling two cultures and striking a balance between one's dreams and the sacrifices that allow a sense of "home."

"Aura's courage shows the degree to which we are all willing to live lives centered on freedom, hope, and an authentic sense of self. Truly a love story!"
—**Nadia Comaneci, Olympic Champion**

"A stunning account of erasing a past, but not an identity."
—**Todd Greenfield, 20th Century Fox**

ISBN: 978-0-9843081-2-5 • ePub:978-1-936332-20-5 • $14.95

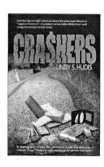

Crashers

A Tale of "Cappers" and "Hammers"

Lindy S. Hudis

The illegal business of fraudulent car accidents is a multi-million dol-lar racket, involving unscrupulous medical providers, personal injury at-torneys, and the cooperating passengers involved in the accidents. Innocent people are often swept into it. Newly engaged Nathan and Shari, who are swimming in mounting debt, were easy prey: seduced by an offer from a stranger to move from hard times to good times in no time, Shari finds herself the "victim" in a staged auto accident. Shari gets her payday, but breaking free of this dark underworld will take nothing short of a miracle.

"A riveting story of love, life—and limits. A non-stop thrill ride."
—**Dennis "Danger" Madalone, stunt coordinator,** *Castle*

ISBN: 978-1-936332-27-4 • Epub: 978-1-936332-28-1 • $16.95

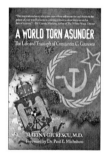

A World Torn Asunder

The Life and Triumph of Constantin C. Giurescu

Marina Giurescu, M.D.

Constantin C. Giurescu was Romania's leading historian and author of the seminal *The History of the Romanian People*. His granddaughter's fas-cinating story of this remarkable man and his family follows their struggles in war-torn Romania from 1900 to the fall of the Soviet Union. An "en-lightened" society is dismantled with the 1946 Communist takeover of Romania, and Constantin is confined to the notorious Sighet penitentiary.

Drawing on her grandfather's prison diary (which was put in a glass jar, buried in a yard, then smuggled out of the country by Dr. Paul E. Michelson—who does the FOREWORD for this book), private letters and her own research, Dr. Giurescu writes of the legacy from the turn of the century to the fall of Communism.

We see the rise of modern Romania, the misery of World War I, the blossoming of its culture between the wars, and then the sellout of Eastern Europe to Russia after World War II. In this sweeping account, we see not only its effects socially and culturally, but the triumph in its wake: a man and his people who reclaim better lives for themselves, and in the process, teach us a lesson in endurance, patience, and will—not only to survive, but to thrive.

"The inspirational story of a quiet man and his silent defiance in the face of tyranny."
—**Dr. Connie Mariano, author of** *The White House Doctor*

ISBN: 978-1-936332-76-2 • Epub: 978-1-936332-77-9 • $21.95

Diary of a Beverly Hills Matchmaker

Marla Martenson

Quick-witted Marla takes her readers for a hilarious romp through her days as an LA matchmaker where looks are everything and money talks. The Cupid of Beverly Hills has introduced countless couples who lived happily ever-after, but for every success story there are hysterically funny dating disasters with high-maintenance, out of touch clients. Marla writes with charm and self-effacement about the universal struggle to love and be loved.

"Martenson's irresistible quick wit will have you rolling on the floor."
—Megan Castran, international YouTube queen

ISBN 978-0-9843081-0-1 • Epub: 978-1-936332-03-8 • $14.95

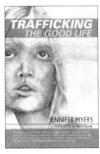

Trafficking the Good Life

Jennifer Myers

Jennifer Myers had worked long and hard toward a successful career as a dancer in Chicago, but just as her star was rising, she fell in love with the kingpin of a drug trafficking operation. Drawn to his life of luxury, she soon became a vital partner in driving marijuana across the country, making unbelievable sums of easy money that she stacked in shoeboxes and spent like an heiress.

Steeped in moral ambiguity, she sought to cleanse her soul with the guidance of spiritual gurus and New Age prophets—to no avail. Only time in a federal prison made her face up to and understand her choices. It was there, at rock bottom, that she discovered that her real prison was the one she had unwittingly made inside herself and where she could start rebuilding a life of purpose and ethical pursuit.

"A gripping memoir. When the DEA finally knocks on Myers's door, she and the reader both see the moment for what it truly is—not so much an arrest as a rescue."
—Tony D'Souza, author of *Whiteman and Mule*

"A stunningly honest exploration of a woman finding her way through a very masculine world . . . and finding her voice by facing the choices she has made."
—Dr. Linda Savage, author of *Reclaiming Goddess Sexuality*

ISBN: 978-1-936332-67-0 • Epub: 978-1-936332-68-7 • $18.95

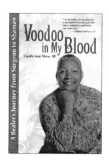

Voodoo in My Blood

A Healer's Journey from Surgeon to Shaman

Carolle Jean-Murat, M.D.

Born and raised in Haiti to a family of healers, US trained physician Carolle Jean-Murat came to be regarded as a world-class surgeon. But her success harbored a secret: in the operating room, she could quickly intuit the root cause of her patient's illness, often times knowing she could help the patient without surgery. Carolle knew that to fellow surgeons, her intuition was best left unmentioned. But when the devastating earthquake hit Haiti and Carolle returned to help, she had to acknowledge the shaman she had become.

"This fascinating memoir sheds light on the importance of asking yourself, 'Have I created for myself the life I've meant to live?'"
—**Christiane Northrup, M.D., author of the New York Times bestsellers:** *Women's Bodies, Women's Wisdom* **and** *The Wisdom of Menopause*

ISBN: 978-1-936332-05-2 • ePub: 978-1-936332-04-5 • $21.95

Fastest Man in the World

The Tony Volpentest Story

Tony Volpentest

Foreword by Ross Perot

Tony Volpentest, a four-time Paralympic gold medalist and five-time world champion sprinter, is a 2012 nominee for the Olympic Hall of Fame

"This inspiring story is about the thrill of victory to be sure—winning gold—but it is also a reminder about human potential: the willingness to push ourselves beyond the ledge of our own imagination. A powerfully inspirational story."
—**Charlie Huebner, United States Olympic Committee**

"This is a moving, motivating and inspiring book."
—**Dan O'Brien, world and Olympic champion decathlete**

"Tony's story shows us that no matter where we start the race, no matter what the obstacles, we all have it within us to reach powerful goals."
—**Oscar Pistorius, "Blade Runner," double amputee, world record holder in the 100, 200 and 400 meters**

ISBN: 978-1-936332-00-7 • ePub: 978-1-936332-01-4 • $16.95

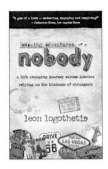

Amazing Adventures of a Nobody

Leon Logothetis

From the Hit Television Series Aired in 100 Countries!

Tired of his disconnected life and uninspiring job, Leon Logothetis leaves it all behind—job, money, home, even his cell phone—and hits the road with nothing but the clothes on his back and five dollars in his pocket, relying on the kindness of strangers and the serendipity of the open road for his daily keep. Masterful storytelling!

"A gem of a book; endearing, engaging and inspiring."
—Catharine Hamm, Los Angeles Times Travel Editor

"Warm, funny, and entertaining. If you're looking to find meaning in this disconnected world of ours, this book contains many clues." **—Psychology Today**

ISBN: 978-0-9843081-3-2 • ePub: 978-1-936332-51-9 • $14.95

MR. JOE

Tales from a Haunted Life

Joseph Barnett and Jane Congdon

Do you believe in ghosts? Joseph Barnett didn't, until the winter he was fired from his career job and became a school custodian to make ends meet. The fact that the eighty-five-year-old school where he now worked was built near a cemetery had barely registered with Joe when he was assigned the graveyard shift. But soon, walking the dim halls alone at night, listening to the wind howl outside, Joe was confronted with a series of bizarre and terrifying occurrences.

It wasn't just the ghosts of the graveyard shift that haunted him. Once the child of a distant father and an alcoholic mother, now a man devastated by a failed marriage, fearful of succeeding as a single dad, and challenged by an overwhelming illness, Joe is haunted by his own personal ghosts.

The story of Joseph's challenges and triumphs emerges as an eloquent metaphor of ghosts, past and present, real and emotional, and how a man puts his beliefs about self—and ghosts—to the test.

"Thrilling, thoughtful, elegantly told. So much more than a ghost story."
—Cyrus Webb, CEO, Conversation Book Club

"This is truly inspirational work, a very special book—a gift to any reader."
—Diane Bruno, CISION Media

ISBN: 978-1-936332-78-6 • ePub: 978-1-936332-79-3 • $18.95

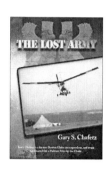

The Search For
The Lost Army

The National Geographic and Harvard University Expedition

Gary S. Chafetz

In one of history's greatest ancient disasters, a Persian army of 50,000 soldiers was suffocated by a hurricane-force sandstorm in 525 BC in Egypt's Western Desert. No trace of this conquering army, hauling huge quantities of looted gold and silver, has ever surfaced.

Nearly 25 centuries later on October 6, 1981, Egyptian Military Intelligence, the CIA, and Israel's Mossad secretly orchestrated the assassination of President Anwar Sadat, hoping to prevent Egypt's descent—as had befallen Iran two years before—into the hands of Islamic zealots. Because he had made peace with Israel and therefore had become a marked man in Egypt and the Middle East, Sadat had to be sacrificed to preserve the status quo.

These two distant events become intimately interwoven in the story of Alex Goodman, who defeats impossible obstacles as he leads a Harvard University/ National Geographic Society archaeological expedition into Egypt's Great Sand Sea in search of the Lost Army of Cambyses, the demons that haunt him, and the woman he loves. Based on a true story.

Gary Chafetz, referred to as "one of the ten best journalists of the past twenty-five years," is a former Boston Globe correspondent and was twice nominated for a Pulitzer Prize by the Globe.

ISBN: 978-1-936332-98-4 • Epub: 978-1-936332-99-1 • $19.95

The Tortoise Shell Code

V Frank Asaro

Off the coast of Southern California, the Sea Diva, a tuna boat, sinks. Members of the crew are missing and what happened remains a mystery. Anthony Darren, a renowned and wealthy lawyer at the top of his game, knows the boat's owner and soon becomes involved in the case. As the case goes to trial, a missing crew member is believed to be at fault, but new evidence comes to light and the finger of guilt points in a completely unanticipated direction.

Now Anthony must pull together all his resources to find the truth in what has happened and free a wrongly accused man—as well as untangle himself. Fighting despair, he finds that the recent events have called much larger issues into question. As he struggles to right this terrible wrong, Anthony makes new and enlightening discoveries in his own life-long battle for personal and global justice.

V Frank Asaro is a lawyer, musician, composer, inventor and philosopher. He is also the author of Universal Co-opetition.

ISBN: 978-1-936332-60-1 • Epub: 978-1-936332-61-8 • $24.95 US

The Morphine Dream

Don Brown with Boston Globe
Pulitzer nominated Gary S. Chafetz

*An amazing story of one man's loss and gain,
hope, and the revealing of an unexpected calling.*

At 36, high-school dropout and a failed semi-professional ballplayer Donald Brown hit bottom when an industrial accident left him immobilized. But Brown had a dream while on a morphine drip after surgery: he imagined himself graduating from Harvard Law School (he was a classmate of Barack Obama) and walking across America. Brown realizes both seemingly unreachable goals, and achieves national recognition as a legal crusader for minority homeowners. An intriguing tale of his long walk—both physical and metaphorical.

A story of perseverance and second chances.

"An incredibly inspirational memoir." —**Alan M. Dershowitz, professor, Harvard Law School**

ISBN: 978-1-936332-25-0 • ePub: 978-1-936332-26-7 • $16.95 US

The Girl Who Gave Her Wish Away

Sharon Babineau

Foreword by Graig Kielburger,
Co-Founder, FREE THE CHILDREN

The Children's Wish Foundation approached lovely thirteen-year-old Maddison Babineau just after she received her cancer diagnosis. "You can have anything," they told her, "a Disney cruise? The chance to meet your favorite movie star? A five thousand dollar shopping spree?"

Maddie knew exactly what she wanted. She had recently been moved to tears after watching a television program about the plight of orphaned children in an African village. Maddie's wish? To ease the suffering of these children half-way across the world. Despite the ravishing cancer, she became an indefatigable fundraiser for "her children."

In The Girl Who Gave Wish Away, her mother reveals Maddie's remarkable journey of providing hope and future to the village children who had filled her heart.

A special story, heartwarming and reassuring.

ISBN: 978-1-936332-96-0 • ePub: 978-1-936332-97-7 • $18.95

Bettie Youngs Books

We specialize in MEMOIRS

. . . books that celebrate

fascinating people and

remarkable journeys

In bookstores everywhere, online, Espresso,
or from the publisher, Bettie Youngs Books
VISIT OUR WEBSITE AT
www.BettieYoungsBooks.com
To contact:
info@BettieYoungsBooks.com

CPSIA information can be obtained
at www.ICGtesting.com
Printed in the USA
FFOW02n2003171114
8798FF

9 781936 332441